D1122441

ACTIVEX AND THE INTERNET

Forest Lin
Tulsa Community College

Scott/Jones, Inc., Publishers
P. O. Box 696
El Granada, CA 94018

Voice: (650) 726-2436
Fax: (650) 726-4693
E-mail: scotjones2@aol.com
Web: http://www.scottjonespub.com

ActiveX and the Internet

Forest Lin

Copyright © 1998 by Scott/Jones, Inc.
All rights reserved. No part of the contents of this book may be reproduced or transmitted in any form or by any means without the permission of the publisher.

ISBN 1-57676-016-2

Book Manufacturing: Malloy Lithographing, Ann Arbor, MI
Cover Design: Kristin Bernhisel-Osborn

0 9 8   X Y Z

ADDITIONAL TITLES OF INTEREST FROM SCOTT/JONES

by Forest Lin

> The DOS 6 Coursebook
> Visual Basic Programming
> Visual Basic 5 Coursebook

> Forthcoming . . .

> HTML Authoring
> JavaScript Programming
> VBScript Programming

ActiveX and the Internet
Table of Contents

3. ActiveX Documents   167

4. The Internet, HTML, and VBScript   253

Preface

This book is a logical extension of *The Visual Basic 5 Coursebook*. It covers some of the most popular advanced features available in Visual Basic 5 Professional Edition.

Here you learn to create three types of components Visual Basic has to offer: **ActiveX code components** (formerly known as OLE servers), **ActiveX controls** (formerly OLE controls), and **ActiveX documents**. (This book is not devoted to the additional ActiveX custom controls that come with the Professional Edition.)

Since ActiveX is the old OLE technology with additional Internet capabilities, it's logical to go beyond components to reach out to the Internet. So the second half of Chapter 3 and the entire Chapter 4 are devoted to the Internet. The coverage of Internet-related items, including HTML and VBScript, are less than thorough. A few books are planned to provide more in-depth coverage. See the backside of the cover page for a list of these forthcoming books.

Each chapter starts by explaining how to do things and ends with some lengthy examples. A companion disk contains the source files for all the lengthier programs. The text provides the file name at the beginning of each lengthy code listing. These files are located in the following five directories:

    1Code
    2Controls
    3Doc
    4Script
    Tutorials

These directories are closely tied to the book's chapter numbers and titles. So if you want to access a file in Chapter 2, for example, go to the specified file name in the 2Controls directory.

Each chapter contains 20 Practice questions. All the answers are supplied at the end of the questions. The complex and lengthy source files are also available on disk, in the directories shown above.

Each chapter includes 20 Drill questions. The answers are provided at the end of the questions. You can also play with their corresponding interactive tutorials stored in the Tutorials directory. These tutorials are written in JavaScript and VBScript. They can be run by Internet Explorer or Netscape Navigator. Read the Readme.txt file in the root directory for details. These tutorials and various script files are also available on the following Web site:

http://www.geocities/SiliconValley/Lab/7590/

-1-

ActiveX Code Components

TOPIC

ActiveX is a new name for **OLE** (Object Linking and Embedding). ActiveX is the old OLE, plus new Internet capabilities. Both come out of Microsoft's attempts to tie software components, sometimes from remote locations, and make them work together.

This chapter gives a brief introduction to ActiveX but concentrates mostly on one part of ActiveX, namely code components.

Component Programming

Code reuse has been a big issue in the programming world. Writing code is often tedious and time-consuming for programmers. It is also expensive for employers who have to pay their programmers, who are in short supply. So there are lots of incentives to reuse existing (and working) code.

Tool developers have responded by supplying new or more useful development tools. The first innovative device is known as structured programming. Programmers can divide lengthy code into procedures (subprograms) which can be repeatedly called from other procedures. This arrangement reduces code length, and makes the program structure more understandable. Revising such code becomes less laborious.

The next innovation comes in the form of putting code in multiple files. Related routines are stored separately. A file can be incorporated into other programs with little or no revision. This modular approach is implemented in Visual Basic. So a Visual Basic programmer can reuse his/her forms in multiple projects, or incorporate other programmers' forms.

Still, modules like forms are raw source files. They are useful to programmers, but useless to nonprogrammers. What if an office worker wants to use some functions in your program? She has neither Visual Basic (the development tool) nor any programming knowledge. The answer lies in compiling your program into an executable file (which doesn't depend on the development tool) and making your functions available to her.

That leads us to objects and classes. An **object** is a unit of code that contains (encapsulates) both code and data. The code is used to manipulate the data. The object is derived from a class—it is an instance of the class. A **class** is a formal blueprint or definition where you embed code and data.

In Visual Basic, you use a class module to create a class. In the class module, you add properties (public variables and property procedures), methods (sub and function procedures), and events. Users of your class can create an object from it and then access these services (properties, functions, and events) with little or no programming.

NOTE   Visual Basic manuals want you to be known as an **author** if you create components. If you use components to develop an application, you become a **developer**. What if you do both? Just call yourself a Visual Basic master, or whatever you fancy.

Component programming basically mimics the way modern society make things. Think of a recent story about a hotel builder using components to construct a high-rise hotel. He used uniform prefab rooms that included everything a typical hotel room has—electrical wiring, plumbing pipes, insulation, etc. The rooms were built in a factory. All the builder needed to do was to stack up the rooms on the desired site and connect them together. A large hotel was thus completed in a few days.

Another example is the way a PC is built. Numerous vendors produce standardized and interchangeable parts. An integrator vendor can put those parts together to quickly build a ready-to-run PC. This arrangement benefits users in many ways. Such PCs are cheap because they can be built quickly and economically. If parts malfunction, just buy new parts and plug them in. Since these parts are produced by many vendors, competition keeps their prices low and their quality high.

As computer programs become larger and do more complex jobs, programmers are forced to follow the component approach. Different programmers can concentrate on writing smaller components. Different components can then be integrated to become a large application. Some components can be reused in other applications. If something goes wrong in a large application, bugs can be identified more quickly by zeroing in on a component. If an update is needed, just change the affected components.

For the components to work together, somebody has to build an underlying infrastructure. Microsoft, the preeminent player in the software industry, has created the **COM** (**Component Object Model**) standard, which is adhered to by Microsoft's products and by most other vendors as well. Visual Basic 5 follows the COM standard. So the objects (classes) you create will work with other components following the same standard.

The components you create with Visual Basic can be **ActiveX code components** (formerly called OLE servers), **ActiveX controls** (formerly known as OLE controls), and **ActiveX documents** (this is a new item). As you can see from these terms, ActiveX is just a new name for OLE with some new capabilities. This chapter covers code components; the others will be covered in later chapters.

Code Component Overview

ActiveX code components used to be called OLE servers before VB5. With an expanded role, they've gained a new name as well. One can still call them ActiveX servers. But the word server is now mostly used in a network environment to designate a hardware-software system providing services to connected clients. So we often hear about Web servers, FTP servers, etc. To avoid confusion, Visual Basic manuals now mostly use "code components." Below we use the two terms interchangeably. "Server" is used when we want to contrast with "client."

Visual Basic provides two types of code components: **ActiveX DLL** (DLL comes from Dynamic-Link Library) and **ActiveX EXE** (executable). The former is an **in-process server** because it runs in the client's process (memory space). The latter is an **out-of-process server** because it runs in its own process. The former is speedier, but the latter can run on its own and provide services to multiple clients.

A **server** is a component that provides services to clients. **Clients** are programs that use a server's services. A server can have units as described below:

- A server is a file with either the **.dll** (in-process) or **.exe** (out-of-process) file name extension.

- A server has a project name, which may or may not be the same as the file name. The project name serves as the **type library** name and appears in the Object Browser's Project/Library combo box.

- A project/library has one or more class modules. Each is transformed into a class from which objects (instances) can be created.

- An author uses a class module to create a class. The source code is saved to an ASCII file with the **.cls** extension. Each class module contains one or more events, methods, and/or properties (they become Members when the class is shown in the Object Browser). A client can use an object (derived from a class) to access these members to get their services.

Windows applications are mostly based on code components. Windows itself consists of a series of these components. Win.com, the program that starts Windows operating system, is a small file. It's just a startup program that obviously can't do much. To provide numerous services that users demand, several large components are made available and called as needed. Visual Basic programmers can also access these components using API calls.

A Server Example

Before we discuss further, let's create a concrete server. From the Standard EXE project with Form1 already in place, add Class1 (choose Project | Add Class Module) to the current new project. Change Class1's Name property to **Wage**. Add the following public variable and Initialize procedure in its Code window:

```
'-----from Wage class module-----
Public MinWage As Single

Private Sub Class_Initialize()
    MinWage = 5.75
End Sub
```

Go to Form1 and add the following Click procedure:

```
'-----from Form1-----
Private Sub Form_Click()
    Dim wgNewWage As Wage
    Set wgNewWage = New Wage
        'create a new object from the Wage class
    Print wgNewWage.MinWage
        'read the MinWage property of wgNewAge object
End Sub
```

Run the project by pressing F5. Click the form and 5.75 will appear. You are now accessing the property of an object. You may want to use F8 to step through the code to see how Visual Basic connects the two modules together.

You can combine the first two lines in Form1, like the following:

```
    Dim wgNewWage As New Wage
```

In this case, the **Set** statement is not needed. The class's Initialize event is not triggered until the object is referenced for the first time.

You can maneuver this property as you do any other property—just remember to follow the syntax of using a dot to connect a property name to an object name, like the following:

```
    ObjectName.PropertyName
```

This is the same syntax as in using a variable in a user-defined type.

The following will print 6.9, 1.2 times of the original value:

```
    Print wgNewWage.MinWage * 1.2
```

The following code will assign the property, plus 20%, to a variable. The variable's value is then printed to the screen.

```
    Dim NewMinWage As Single
    NewMinWage = wgNewWage.MinWage * 1.2
    Print NewMinWage
```

You can add methods (sub and function procedures) and property procedures to a class. These can then be invoked by an application. Using this approach, you can quickly develop an application, which can use the services in the class.

As a demonstration, add the following procedure to the Wage (Class1) module:

```
Public Function CalcWage(Hours As Single, _
Rate As Single) As Single
    Dim TotPay As Single

    If Hours <= 40 Then
        TotPay = Hours * Rate
    Else
        TotPay = Rate * (40 + (Hours - 40) * 1.5)
    End If
    CalcWage = Format(TotPay, "#.00")
End Function
```

This function procedure will take two Single arguments and return a Single value. It will use the two passed values and return a wage which will take overtime into consideration

You can now quickly calculate a weekly wage by calling the function with two arguments. For example, the following code placed in Form1 will print 380.25.

```
    Dim WeekPay As Single
    WeekPay = wgNewWage.CalcWage(Hours:=41.5, Rate:=9)
    Print WeekPay
```

Here we use **named arguments** to pass values. In this situation, the order of the arguments no longer matters. You can place Rate before Hours, and the result will not change.

Object Scope and Lifetime

An object, like a variable, has its scope and lifetime. You need to be aware of how accessible it is and how long it is alive. To reduce resource consumption and potential side effects, you should keep an object to the narrowest possible scope and destroy it when it's no longer needed.

An object can be compared to a form. Several events are triggered at the beginning and at the end of the form's lifetime. Different events may happen at the end, depending on what is done to the form. An object you create from a class behaves in a similar but simpler manner.

A class module has only two events, namely **Initialize** and **Terminate**. The first is triggered when an object is created from the class. The second happens when that object is destroyed. If you wish, you can write code to respond to these events.

The following modified code serves as an example:

```
'-----from Wage class module-----//Listing 1//
Public MinWage As Single

Private Sub Class_Initialize()
    MsgBox "Beginning. . ."
    MinWage = 5.75
End Sub

Private Sub Class_Terminate()
    MsgBox "Terminating. . ."
End Sub

'-----from Form1-----
Private Sub Form_Click()
    Dim wgNewWage As Wage
    Set wgNewWage = New Wage
        'create a new object from the Wage class
    Print wgNewWage.MinWage
        'read the MinWage property of wgNewAge object
End Sub
```

NOTE　A code component normally doesn't have a user interface. It merely provides services in the background. So message boxes as well as other visible marks should not be used.

Run this program and click the form. The first message box appears when the Initialize event is triggered. Then a number is printed to the form. Then the second message box appears as the Terminate event procedure is executed.

If you use F8 to step through the Form_Click procedure, you'll find that when the Set statement is executed, the class's Initialize event procedure is called. At the end of the Form_Click procedure, the Terminate event is triggered. As the wgNewWage object goes out of scope, it's automatically destroyed. So a local object mimics the behavior of a local variable.

Now, move the Dim line in the Form_Click procedure to the form level. Run the program again and see what happens. The following observations apply:

- When you click the form the first time, the first message box appears first. A number (5.75) is then printed to the form. The second message box does not appear. The object is not destroyed.

- When you click the form the second time, the first message box appears first as a new object is being created. Then, surprise, the second message box appears. The old object has to be destroyed before a new one can be created using the same name. Finally, the number appears.

- Clicking the form's X button to close the form triggers the Terminate event and shows the second message box.

- Clicking the End button in the toolbar or executing the End statement (if any) ends the program without triggering the object's Terminate event.

Another behavior pattern you need to be aware of is when an object is actually created. When you use New with Dim, you are not creating an object. The object will be created only when its method or property is called for the first time. On the other hand, using Set with New immediately creates a new object. The following examples illustrate this point:

```
Private Sub Command1_Click()
    Dim wgNewWage As New Wage
    Print wgNewWage.MinWage      'call Initialize
End Sub

Private Sub Command2_Click()
    Dim wgNewWage As Wage
    Set wgNewWage = New Wage      'call Initialize
    Print wgNewWage.MinWage
End Sub
```

Here we've added two command buttons to Form1. When Command1 is clicked, the object is not created (only a reference to the object is created) until its property is first called. When Command2 is clicked, the Set line creates an object and thus triggers the Initialize event.

Here is a new twist:

```
Dim wgNewWage As Wage     'no New here

Private Sub Command1_Click()
    Set wgNewWage = New Wage      'creates object
    Print wgNewWage.MinWage
End Sub

Private Sub Command2_Click()
```

```
      Print wgNewWage.MinWage
End Sub
```

The object variable is now moved to the module level. Clicking Command1 will trigger the class's Initialize event but not the Terminate event. Clicking Command2 after clicking Command1 will simply print a number. The module-level object variable persists and is not destroyed after Command1_Click is exited. If you click Command2 first, an error will appear because you are calling a nonexisting object.

Here is another twist:

```
Dim wgNewWage As New Wage      'New here

Private Sub Command1_Click()
    Print wgNewWage.MinWage
End Sub

Private Sub Command2_Click()
    Print wgNewWage.MinWage
End Sub
```

Here a reference is created at the module level. A new object will be created by clicking either Command1 or Command2. Clicking either button after that will simply print a number without creating a new object. Clicking the form's X button after clicking either command button will trigger the Terminate event.

If you want to destroy this module-level object without closing the form, you can set it to **Nothing** to release the reference. Here is an example:

```
Private Sub Command2_Click()
    Print wgNewWage.MinWage
    Set wgNewWage =  Nothing
End Sub
```

The second line will trigger the Terminate event and destroy the object.

Methods and Properties

The main purpose of creating a class is to provide services. The common services are methods and properties. These are discussed in this section.

Methods are sub and function procedures. Function procedures return values, but sub procedures do not. They can be implemented easily, just as you do in a standalone executable.

Properties can be public variables (including enumerations, collections, or user-defined types) or property procedures.

A public variable becomes a property of a module. It is added to the intrinsic properties. To prove this point, try the following code in Form1:

```
Public Note As String

Private Sub Form_Load()
    Note = "This becomes a property of the form."
End Sub

Private Sub Form_Click()
    Print Form1.Note
End Sub
```

As you type Form1 followed by a dot, the Note property appears among the items in the popup list, together with the built-in properties of Form1.

This user-added property is also inherited by the form's clones. Consider the following example:

```
Private Sub Command1_Click()
    Dim frmX As New Form1
    frmX.Show
    frmX.Caption = frmX.Note
End Sub
```

When Command1 is clicked, a new form will be created. This form inherits the original copy's properties, including its public variables. So, our Note string will appear in the new form's caption.

A class module's public variable is also visible in the Visual Basic IDE. Suppose you have added Class1 to the current project and then created a reference to it like the following:

```
Dim clsX As New Class1
```

After that, typing clsX followed by a dot will pop up the public variables you have added to Class1.

Earlier we used the following example. We have a public variable in the class module. A client can access this property.

```
'-----from Wage class module-----
Public MinWage As Single

Private Sub Class_Initialize()
    MinWage = 5.75
End Sub
```

In this arrangement, the public variable's value can be altered by a client. The following procedure will change it to 6.25:

```
Private Sub Form_Click()
    Dim wgNewWage As New Wage
    wgNewWage.MinWage = 6.25
    Print wgNewWage.MinWage
End Sub
```

We can use a pair of **property procedures** to do the same thing. In the following arrangement, we use mMinWage as a module-level public variable and MinWage for property procedures.

```
'-----from Wage class module-----
Public mMinWage As Single

Private Sub Class_Initialize()
    mMinWage = 5.75
End Sub

Public Property Get MinWage() As Single
    MinWage = mMinWage
End Property

Public Property Let MinWage(ByVal vNewValue As Single)
    mMinWage = vNewValue
End Property

'-----from Form1-----
Private Sub Form_Click()
    Dim wgNewWage As Wage
    Set wgNewWage = New Wage
        'create new object, call Initialize
        'set initial mMinWage to 5.75
    wgNewWage.MinWage = 6.25
        'call Property Let to change mMinWage value
    Print wgNewWage.MinWage
        'call Property Get to read mMinWage's value
End Sub
```

In this arrangement, every time Form1 is clicked, a new object will be created and the old one destroyed. The server's Initialize event is also triggered.

If you use a module-level variable and the Form_Load procedure to create a new object, the Initialize event will be triggered only once, as shown below:

```
Dim wgNewWage As Wage

Private Sub Form_Load()
    Set wgNewWage = New Wage
End Sub
```

Our entire arrangement allows a client to directly manipulate the server's public variable. For example, the following statements will change the original value and then show its new value:

```
    wgNewWage.mMinWage = 6.25
    Print wgNewWage.mMinWage
```

The above statements will not execute the property procedures because we are accessing the public variable (mMinWage, not MinWage).

To prevent a client from directly manipulating a variable in a class, change its scope from Public to Private, like the following:

```
    Private mMinWage As Single
```

After this change, the mMinWage variable can no longer be directly accessed by the client. Doing so will lead to the *Method or data member not found* error. To maneuver the variable, the client has to go through the property procedures, which can serve to protect the property.

Property procedures usually come in a Get/Let pair. When you retrieve a property, such as printing it to the screen or assigning it to a variable, **Property Get** will be called. When you assign a value to the property, **Property Let** will be executed. When you want to manipulate an object, the corresponding property should be named **Property Set** (rather than Property Let). In that case, when you use the Set statement to assign a value to the property, the Property Set procedure will be called.

To prevent a client from altering a property, implement only the Property Get procedure—in addition to making the corresponding variable private. Without the corresponding Property Let procedure, the value assigned to the property cannot be changed by the client. This technique of shielding data from clients is commonly known as **data hiding**.

In the following arrangement, we assume that the MinWage value is scheduled to go up by 15% and then 25% from the original. Since we don't have a Property Let procedure, a client can only read this property whose value depends on what year it is read.

```
'-----from Wage class module-----
Private mMinWage As Single

Public Property Get MinWage() As Single
    Dim Yr As Date
    Yr = Year(Now)
    Select Case Yr
    Case 1997
        MinWage = mMinWage
    Case 1998
        MinWage = mMinWage * 1.15
    Case 1999
        MinWage = mMinWage * 1.25
    End Select
End Property
```

Property procedures can also be used for **data validation**. When unacceptable values are encountered, the procedures can reject them, alter them, or alert the user. This will be covered in another section below.

NOTE   Visual Basic manuals say that a public variable is actually treated and handled by Visual Basic as a pair of Get/Let public property procedures. So using public variables doesn't reduce overhead as compared to property procedures.

A method or property in a class can be public or private. A client can call a server's public methods/properties, but not private ones. A procedure in your component can also call another public procedure in a different class within the same component, but not a private one. What if a procedure in one class wants to call another procedure in another class in the same component? Make the second procedure a Public or Friend procedure. A **Friend** procedure can be called from inside the same component, but not by a client. Its scope lies between Public and Private. Another section below will demonstrate a Friend procedure.

Handling Events

Methods and properties are **incoming interfaces**. They can be invoked from outside. On the other hand, **events** are **outgoing interfaces**. They can reach outside. A server can **raise events**. Clients can then use code to respond to events raised by the server.

A server object that raises events is an **event source**. It communicates with clients by making events available. Only clients (not the server) can handle such events. Think of the CommandButton class in Visual Basic. When you add Command1, an instance of CommandButton, to your project, it makes the Click event available. Your project, which is a client, can have a Command1_Click event procedure to handle the event.

Handling object events requires two-way communications. First, you have to create a class that can raise events. Then, you'll have to create a client that can respond to the events.

Our demonstration project explored here requires a Standard EXE project with two modules, Form1 and Class1. The latter's name is changed to **EventDemo**. The procedures in the two modules are listed below.

```
'-----from EventDemo class module-----
Event TestEvent(ByVal Msg As String)
    'declare an event

Public Sub DemoEvent(EventMsg As String)
    MsgBox "Message from caller: " & EventMsg, , _
    "From Class Module"
    EventMsg = InputBox("Return message:", _
    "From Class Module")
    RaiseEvent TestEvent(ByVal EventMsg)
        'raise the TestEvent event to caller
End Sub

'-----from Form1-----
Private WithEvents medEventDemo As EventDemo
    'declare an event already in EventDemo class

Private Sub Form_Click()
    Dim Msg As String
    Dim edNew As New EventDemo
        'create a new object
    Msg = InputBox("Enter a message to pass to server", _
    "From Form1")
    Call edNew.DemoEvent(Msg)
        'call a method in class, pass msg
    medEventDemo_TestEvent (Msg)
        'invoke an event, pass msg
End Sub

Private Sub medEventDemo_TestEvent(ByVal Msg As String)
    'event procedure
    MsgBox "Return message: " & Msg, , "From Form1"
End Sub
```

NOTE   It's a good idea to create the server first. After the methods, properties, and events are in place, they will pop up at the right place at the right time in the client's Code window.

Handling object events requires you to be familiar with two keywords: **Event** and **WithEvents**. The former is used at the module-level of the server to declare an event. An event has a public scope by default. You can also precede it by the Public keyword without changing the outcome. The Private keyword is not allowed here.

An **event procedure** is comparable to a sub procedure in some respects. It returns no value. It can include optional arguments. However, these items are not permitted: named arguments, optional arguments, or ParamArray arguments.

The **WithEvents** keyword is used by a client to create an object that is an instance of the server class. This special object can then respond to the events raised by the server. We use Private in Form1's Declarations section to declare the variable. Dim will also work the same way. You can also use Public to broaden its scope.

To raise an event, you need to use the **RaiseEvent** keyword in a procedure in the server. When the procedure is called by the client, RaiseEvent communicates with the client by making the specified event available. The client can then invoke the event procedure.

After you use WithEvents to declare an object variable (assuming the server has been created), the variable (medEventDemo in our case) becomes a recognized object that is a part of the current project. It also enters the Object box in Form1's Code window. After you've selected it, the Procedure box shows only one event, namely TestEvent. When you click that, the medEventDemo_TestEvent procedure template appears. It is ready for you to add code. This event has to be handled on the client side, not the server side.

Our project basically lets the user click Form1 to trigger the Form_Click procedure. This procedure calls the server's DemoEvent sub procedure, which in turn raises the TestEvent event. The Form_Click procedure then calls this event procedure embedded in Form1.

Running and clicking the form will lead to four messages. They demonstrate how the form (client) and the server communicate. The first thing you encounter is the input box shown in Figure 1.1.

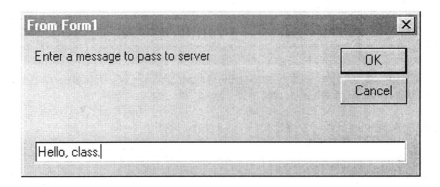

Figure 1.1   A message from the client

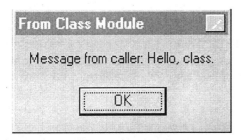

Figure 1.2   A message passed to the server

Figure 1.2 shows the server's response by displaying the message sent by the client.

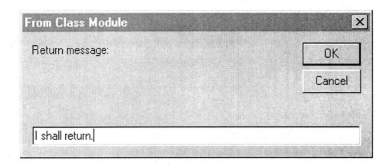

Figure 1.3   A message from the server

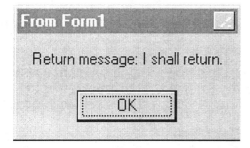

Figure 1.4   A message passed to the client

Figure 1.3 is from the server. It lets you enter a message to return to the client. Figure 1.4 shows the message received by the client.

Raising events is useful for an ActiveX control. Developers using your control can write code to handle those events, thus making your control more versatile. This will be covered in the next chapter.

Class Builder

You might want to take advantage of an add-in called **Class Builder utility**. It allows you to add classes and members for each new or existing class. It will also generate skeleton code for you.

Follow these steps to use this utility:

1.   Choose Add-In | Class Builder Utility. (If this option is not available, use the Add-In Manager to add it to this menu.)

2.   If there are existing class modules, they appear in the Classes list (see Figure 1.5). Click one to show its members. In the right tabbed dialog box, select a type to display its members.

3.   Use one of the buttons (or File | New) to add a new class module or add a new method, property, or event to the current module.

4. A dialog box appears to let you add a new name and a variety of attributes (description, arguments, return data type, etc.). After you finish filling in the required items, click OK.

5. Repeat steps 3 and 4 to add new members. To display an existing item, right-click it to pop up the shortcut menu and then choose Properties. The items you've entered will appear. You can't edit the contents here. To make a change, you can delete an old one and create a new one to replace it.

6. To include code for debugging and error raising (see the next section), choose View | Options and select one or both options.

7. When you're through, choose File | Update Project. This generates skeleton code for various members. You can now close this add-in and examine the Code window.

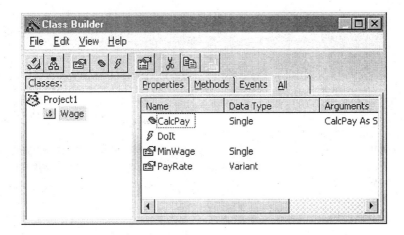

Figure 1.5   Class Builder Utility

Your Code window should resemble the following. In the case of a method, the utility doesn't do anything worthwhile. In the case of an event, it declares an event and provides an explanation. It provides most useful code fragment for property procedures. The required Get/Set pair are both added, together with the required parameters. So in the future, when you need to write properties for a class, you might want to use Class Builder to do the preliminary work for you.

```
Private mvarPayRate As Variant 'local copy
'To fire this event, use RaiseEvent with the following syntax:
```

```
'RaiseEvent DoIt[(arg1, arg2, ... , argn)]
Public Event DoIt()
Public Function CalcPay(CalcPay As Single) As Single
End Function

Public Property Let PayRate(ByVal vData As Variant)
'used when assigning a value to the property, on the left side
of an assignment.
'Syntax: X.PayRate = 5
    mvarPayRate = vData
End Property

Public Property Set PayRate(ByVal vData As Object)
'used when assigning an Object to the property, on the left
side of a Set statement.
'Syntax: Set x.PayRate = Form1
    Set mvarPayRate = vData
End Property

Public Property Get PayRate() As Variant
'used when retrieving value of a property, on the right side of
an assignment.
'Syntax: Debug.Print X.PayRate
    If IsObject(mvarPayRate) Then
        Set PayRate = mvarPayRate
    Else
        PayRate = mvarPayRate
    End If
End Property
```

Handling Errors

Your component can handle run-time errors just like any standalone executable. If an error is unhandled, it will be returned to the caller. If the caller has no error handler, an in-process server's error will be fatal to the client because they both run in the same process; this won't happen in the case of an out-of-process server.

In the Visual Basic IDE, where break occurs depends on the default error-trapping options. To change the default setting, use the Tools | Options | General tab. Then select an option in the Error Trapping frame (Figure 1.6). Here are the options:

Break on All Errors   Visual Basic enters break mode and highlights the error wherever that may be.

Break in Class Module   Visual Basic enters break mode and highlights the error in the class module. If you click Break (instead of End) when the error message is shown, break mode is entered. You can then press Alt+F5 or Alt+F8 to step past the error.

Break on Unhandled Errors   Error traps are enabled and break mode is not entered. When an unhandled error is encountered, execution stops on the calling statement.

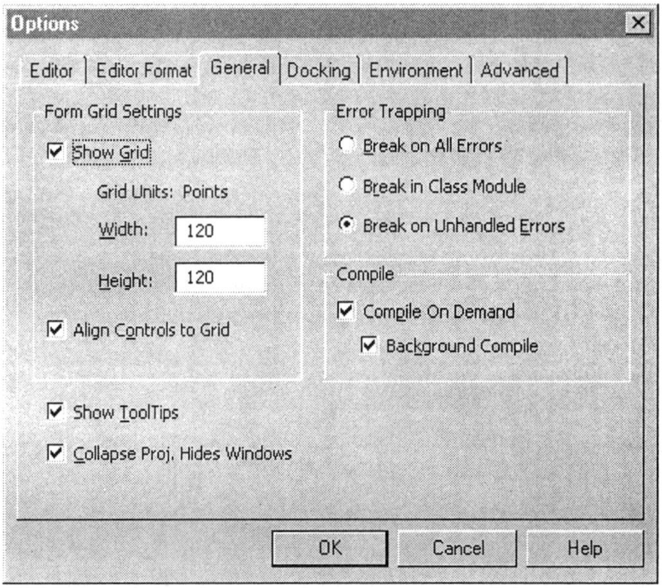

Figure 1.6   Error-trapping options

The following code demonstrates how Visual Basic handles a run-time error (division by zero). This project requires a Standard EXE with Form1 and an additional Class1 module. After you write the following code, right-click a Code window and choose Toggle. The options discussed above will pop up. Choose **Break in Class Module**. Choosing a option from the popup menu sets the value for the current session only (choosing an option from the Options dialog box sets the default—and future—value).

```
'-----from Class1-----
Public Property Get Division(Op1 As Single, _
Op2 As Single) As Single
    Division = Op1 / Op2
End Property
```

```
'-----from Form1-----
Private Sub Form_Click()
    Dim clsX As Class1

    Set clsX = New Project1.Class1
    On Error GoTo ErrTrap
    Print clsX.Division(10, 0)
    Exit Sub

ErrTrap:
    MsgBox "Error #: " & Err.Number & "---" _
    & Err.Description
End Sub
```

After you've done the above preparation, press F5 and click the form. The result is the error message shown in Figure 1.7.

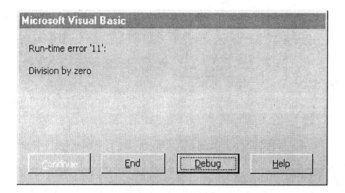

Figure 1.7   A standard Visual Basic error

Now, click Break to see the offending line in Class1 highlighted. Also notice "break" in the IDE's caption. If you press F8 at this time, you'll trigger the same error message again. If you press Alt+F8, execution leaves Class1 and goes to the error trap in Form1; break mode also continues. Pressing F5 or F8 at this time displays Figure 1.8. If you press Alt+F5 rather than Alt+F8, Visual Basic leaves break mode and resumes run mode, which will immediately trigger the same error.

Next, use the popup menu to choose Toggle and then **Break on Unhandled Errors**. Press F5 to run the program again. This time, as soon as you click the form, the handled error message shows up immediately. Our error trap is activated, and break mode is not entered.

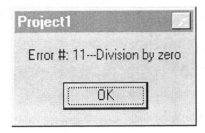

Figure 1.8   A handled error message

On some occasions, it may be desirable to make an object raise an error. Like raising an event discussed earlier, this technique enables a client to handle an error sent by the server.

You use the **Raise** event of the **Err** object to raise an error. Include at least two arguments, **Number** and **Description**, so that the client can use them to handle the raised error.

In the following rearrangement, we set up an error trap in Class1. When an error occurs, the trap is activated. If the divisor is 0, an error is raised, together with a number and a descriptive string. If another error occurs, the intrinsic error number and description are sent to the client. In our case, the result is shown in Figure 1.9.

Figure 1.9   An error raised by an object

```
'-----from Class1-----
Public Property Get Division(Op1 As Single, _
Op2 As Single) As Single
    On Error GoTo ErrTrap
    Division = Op1 / Op2
    Exit Property
```

```
ErrTrap:
    If Op2 = 0 Then
        Err.Raise Number:=vbObjectError + 512, _
        Description:="You've supplied 0 as a divisor"
    Else
        Err.Raise Err.Number, , Err.Description
    End If
End Property
```

The **Err.Raise** event can include up to five arguments. They will pop up after you type the expression and a space in the Code window. In our example, we use two **named arguments** of Number and Description to communicate with a client. The client then uses these values to handle the raised error.

The number we use is **vbObjectError**, plus 512. The former has the intrinsic value of -2147221504. Visual Basic manuals recommend this number, plus another number in the 512 (&H200) to 65535 (&HHFFF) range. This elaborate system is intended to prevent conflict with Visual Basic's own error numbers.

The other arguments can involve source and help files which can be loaded from disk with the **LoadResString** function. This arrangement is useful if you distribute your components internationally. A different resource file can be used for each separate language version. That way, people speaking different languages can all use your localized components.

We are going to provide a useful custom error message. This project lets you maintain an account that can prevent overdraft (this is an example of **data validation** mentioned earlier). At the outset, the account has a balance of 5000. This account lets you deposit and withdraw. It also has the Balance property to let you read its amount.

```
'-----from Account class-----
'class name is changed to Account
Private mBalance As Single

Private Sub Class_Initialize()
    mBalance = 5000
End Sub

Public Property Get Balance() As Single
    Balance = mBalance
End Property

Public Sub Withdraw(ByVal Amount As Single)
    If Amount > mBalance Then
        Err.Raise Number:=vbObjectError + 513, _
        Description:="Overdraft"
    End If
```

```
        mBalance = mBalance - Amount
End Sub

Public Sub Deposit(ByVal Amount As Single)
        mBalance = mBalance + Amount
End Sub

'-----from Form1-----
Dim maccNewAccount As New Account
        'module-level variable
        'to avoid triggering Initialize event
        'after the first call

Private Sub Form_Click()
        On Error GoTo ErrTrap
        maccNewAccount.Withdraw 6000
        Print maccNewAccount.Balance
        Exit Sub

ErrTrap:
        MsgBox "Error #: " & Err.Number & "---" _
        & Err.Description
End Sub
```

In the Form_Click procedure, we try to withdraw 6000, exceeding the 5000 balance. The Withdraw method raises an error by returning a number and a description to the client, which in turn displays Figure 1.10.

Figure 1.10   A custom error message

You can call the Deposit method to add to the balance, like this:

```
        maccNewAccount.Deposit 100
```

If you replace this statement with the original Withdraw statement in the Form_Click procedure, the form will continue to print a new number that is 100 greater than the previous. If we did not declare the object variable (maccNewAccount) at the form level, clicking the form each time would trigger the server's Initialize event and set the Balance back to 5000. That in turn would produce the same value, not an increased one.

Instancing, Testing, and Compiling

So far, we have added class modules to a Standard EXE project. This arrangement is convenient for testing how your components behave. In a Standard EXE project, Form1 is the startup object. At run time, Form1 immediately appears, and you can interact with it to test your components.

This arrangement, however, won't let you compile your code into independent servers—you can create only standalone executables. To create independent servers, you have to use a different project before you compile.

If you intend to create an independent component, there are two things you can do:

- Start a project other than Standard EXE.

- Convert a Standard EXE to another type of project.

In either case, you'll also need a Standard EXE project to test your component. We'll address each approach below.

To convert a Standard EXE project to another type, go to the **Project Properties** dialog box (Figure 1.11) and change a few things. This dialog box can be accessed by choosing Project | Project Properties. You can also right-click a project name in the Project window and choose Project Properties.

In the General tab, pull down the Project Type list and select one to change to another project type. Notice that as you change from Standard EXE to another type, the Startup Object box will automatically change to Sub Main. If you pull down the list, you'll find (None) as the only other option. Where is Form1? It's gone—you can't use it to start up any project other than Standard EXE. If you now switch back to Standard EXE in the Project Type list, Sub Main will remain as the startup object, but Form1 will reappear in the list box for you to select.

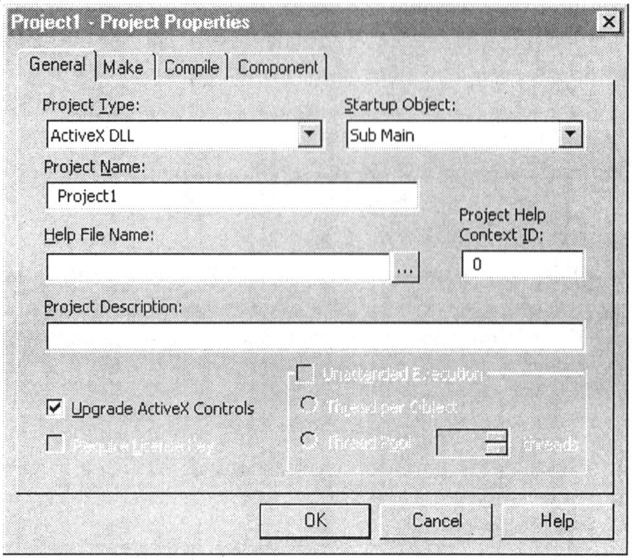

Figure 1.11   The Project Properties dialog's General tab

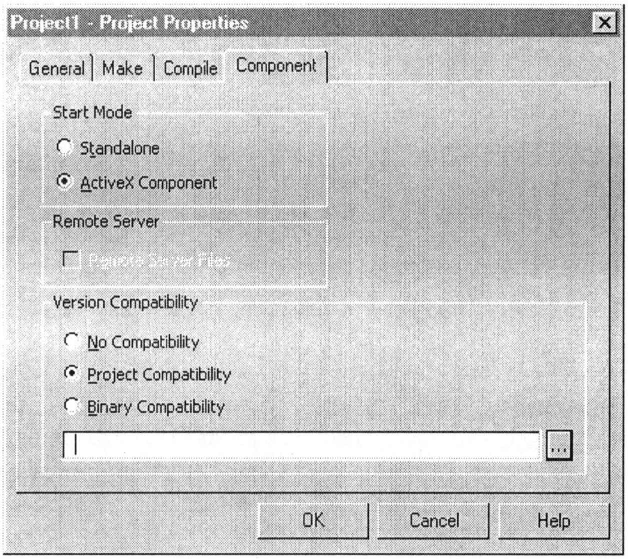

Figure 1.12   The Project Properties dialog's Component tab

Now, open the Component tab (Figure 1.12) to see what's there. You may or may not trigger the dialog shown in Figure 1.13. This message alerts you of a significant change. The Startup Mode frame in the General tab is dimmed (disabled) except in an ActiveX EXE project. This frame lets you decide whether you want this project to be a standalone executable or a component.

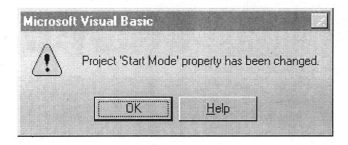

Figure 1.13   Alerting project change

In the Component tab's Version Compatibility frame, keep the Project Compatibility option checked (default) under most circumstances. If you wish, you can type a compiled component's file name or use the ellipsis to search for one. In this setting, Visual Basic will continue to use the same type library ID number (see Chapter 3 for an explanation) when you compile each time. If you are authoring a new version of your component, select Binary Compatibility to ensure that users can easily upgrade to the new version.

Normally a component should have no startup object, so the (None) option is the logical choice. But if you want it to perform some initializing tasks, select **Sub Main** as the startup object. Then you'll need to add a standard module and create a Sub Main procedure. If you put in a class module a sub procedure named Main, it can be called but it won't automatically run at startup.

Have you paid any attention to the Properties window of a class module added to a Standard EXE project? Like its counterpart in a standard (code) module, it has only the Name property and nothing else. Do you know what will happen to this Properties window after you convert the project to another type? Another property, **Instancing**, will be added, and the default setting is 1 - Private. You need to change this to something else if you intend to create instances from this class. Otherwise, Figure 1.14 will show up.

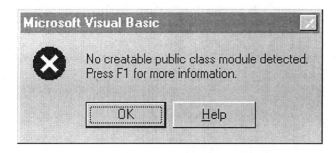

Figure 1.14   Error due to Private Instancing property

When you add an ActiveX EXE or ActiveX DLL project, Class1 is automatically added. Examine this module's Properties window, and you'll find the default setting of MultiUse in its Instancing property.

Instancing Options	ActiveX EXE	ActiveX DLL
1 - Private	Yes	Yes
2 - PublicNotCreatable	Yes	Yes
3 - SingleUse	Yes	No
4 - GlobalSingleUse	Yes	No
5 - MultiUse	Yes	Yes
6 - GlobalMultiUse	Yes	Yes

The **Instancing** property has six possible options, as shown above. Their effects are described below.

Private   For use only within the component, but not by clients.

PublicNotCreatable   Clients can use but not create objects. **Dependent objects** can be created only by the component itself.

SingleUse   Allows a client to create multiple objects each of which is a new instance; allowed only in ActiveX EXE.

GlobalSingleUse   Same as above, except there is no need to create an instance to access the class's services.

MultiUse   Default option for both ActiveX EXE and DLL. Allows clients to create instances each of which can provide multiple objects.

GlobalMultiUse   Same as above, except allowing clients to access methods and properties like global functions—without explicitly creating an object.

To test an ActiveX DLL component project, you need to do the following—after the project is in place:

1. Add a Standard EXE project with a form. This test project will access your component and test its methods, properties, and events.

2. Designate the above as the startup project. This can be done by right-clicking the project name in the Project window and then choose **Set as Start Up** from the popup menu. The startup project appears bolded in the Project window, so you can tell it apart from the others.

3. Set a reference to the component name. To do that, choose Project | References to show the **References** dialog box (Figure 1.15). Check the component project's name ("Check" in our example) and click OK. (A descriptive string for your component will appear in this dialog box if you have used the Project | Project Properties | General tab to add a description to the project.)

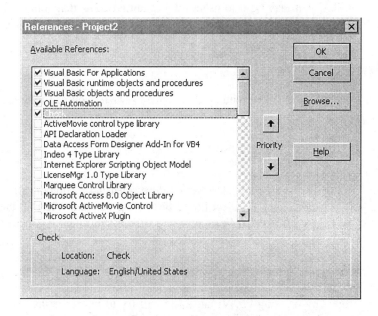

Figure 1.15   Setting a reference to a component

4. Press Ctrl+F5 (or choose Run | Start With Full Compile) to run the projects. F5 (Run | Start) will also work in this situation. But Start With Full Compile will resolve compile problems before going into run mode.

If you did not set a reference as described in step 3, you would get the error shown in Figure 1.16. When you see this error in the future, you should remind yourself to check the References dialog box.

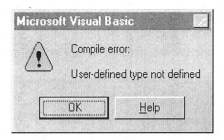

Figure 1.16   Failing to set a component reference

To avoid confusion or conflict, you may want to use a **fully qualified name** that combines the component name and the class name (ProjectName.ClassName), such as the following:

```
Dim accNewAccount As New Check.Account
Print accNewAccount.Balance
```

Suppose the Check component (project) has another class named Owner, you can reference it this way:

```
Dim ownNewOwner As New Check.Owner
Print ownNewOwner.Name
```

You may also want to thoroughly test a compiled version before releasing a component. Before you compile, go to the component's Project Properties dialog box and select all the desired settings. Then choose File | Make *FileName*.dll. You'll be asked to enter a name to save the compiled file.

To test the compiled version, remove the existing component project from the IDE. A warning message says that the project is referenced from another project. Click OK to remove it. Run the test project by pressing F5. Visual Basic will try to reference the compiled .dll file. If you reload the removed project file, Visual Basic will switch references to the one in the IDE.

An ActiveX EXE component runs in a separate process. So testing and debugging it requires you to run two instances of Visual Basic. First, work on the component and, if necessary, set breakpoints and watch variables. Press Ctrl+F5 to put it in run mode. Then start another copy of Visual Basic from Windows. Work on the test project, and press F5 to run the test project. To test the compiled version, compile it and run this compiled version. Switch to the test project and run it. In this situation, Visual Basic will switch references to the compiled copy.

Friends and Implements

This section demonstrates the use of a Friend method and the Implements statement. **Friend** is used to designate a procedure in a class that can be called by another class in the same component, but is not accessible to others from outside. It is half way between a Public and a Private procedure.

Implements is used to implement **polymorphism**. Polymorphism is an arrangement in which multiple classes can use one interface. This is Visual Basic's way of substituting for **inheritance** that is used by C++ to implement polymorphism.

To implement polymorphism, you need to follow these general steps:

1.. Add an **abstract class**. It contains procedure templates for other classes.

2. Use the Implements statement in other classes to implement the templates.

3. In a client's calling statements, assign a class to the abstract class and call the latter's methods or properties.

These steps are illustrated in the code below. It's a round-about way of calculating a worker's weekly wage based on the number of hours and the pay rate per hour, taking overtime into consideration. It consists of three class modules, plus Form1 to serve as a client. The Worker class is the abstract class. It has a public variable and two procedure templates. The Wage class provides a Friend procedure to be called by the Doe class. The Doe class encapsulates data and two property procedures.

```
'-----from Worker class-----//Listing 2//
Public GrossPay As Single

Private Property Let Worker_GrossPay(ByVal RHS As Single)

End Property
```

```
Private Property Get Worker_GrossPay() As Single

End Property

'-----from Wage class-----
Friend Function CalcWage(Rate As Single, _
Hours As Single) As Single
    If Hours <= 40 Then
        CalcWage = Hours * Rate
    Else
        CalcWage = Rate * (40 + (Hours - 40) * 1.5)
    End If
End Function

'-----from Doe class-----
Private mGrossPay As Single
Private mHours As Single
Private mRate As Single
Implements Worker

Private Sub Class_Initialize()
    mHours = 45
    mRate = 10
    Dim wgNew As New Wage
    mGrossPay = wgNew.CalcWage(mRate, mHours)
    'call a Friend procedure in another class
End Sub

Private Property Let Worker_GrossPay(ByVal RHS As Single)
    mGrossPay = RHS
End Property

Private Property Get Worker_GrossPay() As Single
    Worker_GrossPay = mGrossPay
End Property

'-----from Form1-----
Private Sub Form_Click()
    Dim doNew As Doe
    Dim wkNew As Worker
    Set doNew = New Doe
    Set wkNew = New Worker
    Set wkNew = doNew
    Print wkNew.GrossPay
End Sub
```

After you've entered the public variable (GrossPay) in the Worker class and added the Implements statement in the Doe class, the templates in the former now become available in the latter. Go to the Doe class's Object box and you'll see Worker in the list of objects. If you comment out the Implements line, Worker will disappear from this list.

After you select Worker in the Object box, pull down the Procedure box to see what's there. You'll see the following:

GrossPay [PropertyGet]
GrossPay [PropertyLet]

If you select one after the other, you'll create two procedure templates like below:

```
Private Property Let Worker_GrossPay(ByVal RHS As Single)

End Property

Private Property Get Worker_GrossPay() As Single

End Property
```

Notice that these templates are identical to those shown in the Worker class. Those in the Worker class are not automatically entered, so you've to type those yourself. To save you the trouble, you can copy those from the Doe class to the Worker class's Code window. The absence of these may sometimes trigger an error.

Handling Complex Data Types

When you have a small number of data to manipulate, using scalar (single-value) variables are satisfactory. With more complex and numerous data, you should take advantage of other ways to handle them. Here we explore enumerations, arrays, user-defined types, and collections. Control arrays will be illustrated in the last project in this chapter and in different projects in later chapters.

Enumerations

An **enumeration** is a set of **constants** you create with the **Enum-End Enum** statement. You can also define a single constant with the Const command. With Enum, however, you can define an entire list of them at a time. Multiple lists are permitted. In that case, a member can be referenced with a dotted name like EnumName.MemberName.

You can use **Const** inside a procedure to define a local variable or in the General Declarations section to define a module-level variable. It defaults to Private in scope. The word Public or Global is allowed only at the module level of a standard (code) module, not in a form or class module.

Enum can be placed only at the module level of any module, but not inside a procedure. It also defaults to Public in scope, so the word Public is redundant. Public enumerations placed in any module are global in scope. They share the same status as the public (global) constants defined with Const in a standard module. On the other hand, Private enumerations are module-level in scope.

As an example, enter the following in the Code window (of any module):

```
Option Explicit
Enum Groups
     Alpha
     Beta
     Gamma
     Delta
     Epsilon
End Enum
```

Here Groups is an enumeration. It contains five members. Each member is a constant that holds a fixed value.

Open the **Object Browser** (F2) to see how these variables are handled. If your display shows < All Libraries > in the top combo box, change it to Project1. The result is shown in Figure 17.

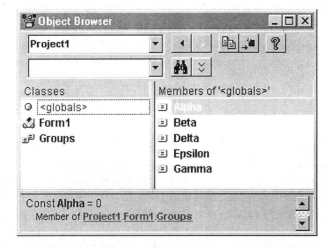

Figure 1.17   An enumeration shown in the Object Browser

Notice that Groups, our enumeration's name, appears in the Classes list, together with Form1 and < globals >; so a public enumeration is treated like a module. If you click Groups, all the members will appear in the Members list (right panel). The same thing also happens if you click < globals >; so the members in a public enumeration are treated as global constants.

If you now click Alpha, the bottom panel will show how this member is related to other items. Its value (0) is also shown. This exposure is useful to anybody using your code components. Users of your compiled components can get useful information by using the Object Browser, OLEViewer (bundled with Visual C++), and other tools. (In addition to public constants, the Object Browser can also expose many other things which a component's author wishes to expose.)

Where does this 0 value come from? If you assign no value, the first member defaults to 0, the second to 1, and so on. Of course, you are free to assign another value just as you do with Const. If you assign a value to a member but not the subsequent members, then the next member will have 1 higher value.

Suppose you assign 1 to Alpha and do nothing else. What happens to the rest? Beta will have the value of 2, and so on.

You can use a previous member to maneuver a subsequent member in the list. Here is an example:

```
Enum Groups
    Alpha = 10
    Beta = Alpha - 1
    Gamma = Beta - 1
    Delta = Gamma - 1
    Epsilon = Delta - 1
End Enum
```

The result of this is that Epsilon will have the value of 6.

You can use each constant alone or as a member of the enumeration. So you can use Alpha or Groups.Alpha. They will both have the value of 10. Notice that as you type the enumeration name followed by a dot, a list of its members will pop up for you to choose one.

You may have one constant name appearing in two enumerations. In that case, you cannot use that constant's name alone in code. So you must use a dot to connect the enumeration name and the constant name. Otherwise, an error will appear.

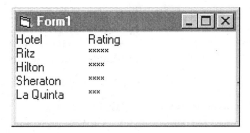

Figure 1.18   Using constant values

After an enumeration has been defined, you can use its members just as you use other constants. Instead of specifying a numeric literal, you can use a constant, whose value cannot be changed like a variable's. Below is an example. It produces the display shown in Figure 1.18.

```
Enum Stars
    One = 1
    Two
    Three
    Four
    Five
End Enum

Private Sub Form_Click()
    Dim I As Integer, J As Integer
    Dim Hotels
    Dim Ratings
    On Error Resume Next
    Hotels = Array("Ritz", "Hilton", _
    "Sheraton", "La Quinta")
    Ratings = Array(Five, Four, Four, Three)

    Print "Hotel", "Rating"
    For I = 0 To UBound(Hotels)
        Print Hotels(I),
        For J = 1 To Ratings(I)
            Print "*";
        Next J
        Print
    Next I
End Sub
```

Here we use two Variant variables and the **Array** function to make each store multiple items. These variables behave like arrays. Another section below provides more details about this topic.

In the J loop, we use the Ratings(I) array to determine the upperbound value in order to print the number of stars. When I has the value of 0, Ratings(0) has the value of Five, which is a constant with the value of 5. As I changes to 1, Ratings(1) becomes 4, and so on.

After an enumeration is in place, you can treat it as a data type. Suppose the Stars enumeration has been created as shown above. After you type As in declaring a variable, the popup list will include Stars. However, this new variable is just a Long type and does not contain the members in the original list. In the following statements, the first is legal, but the second will lead to an error:

```
Dim X As Stars
Print X.Two
```

So once in place, an enumeration's name, its members' names, or the members' values cannot change, just like a variable defined with Const. An enumeration thus cannot be maneuvered like a collection or user-defined type.

Another severe limitation is that an enumeration can contain only Long values and nothing else. If you assign a decimal value, it will be rounded to a whole number. Assigning a string will lead to an error.

Collections

A **collection** is a user-defined container that can store multiple items of different data types (Variants). It's like a garbage can into which you can stuff anything you want. A collection behaves like a Variant variable, but it is handled like an object with its own methods and properties.

To create a collection object, you need to invoke the built-in **Collection** class, such as the following:

```
Dim colNew as New Collection
```

After that, colNew becomes a collection object. Don't forget the **New** keyword. If you omit it, you merely declare a variable but not create an object. In that case, you can still create an object with Set and New.

The collection object has the following three methods and one property:

Add	Adds a new member to the collection.
Remove	Removes an existing member from the collection.

Item   A method to access an existing member in the collection.
Count   A property that returns the count of all the existing members.

A collection maintains an internal index to keep track of the members being added or deleted. It's a **1-based** indexing system. So the first member has the index value of 1, not 0. The last index value is the same as the value of **Count**. So if you have five members, they are numbered from 1 to 5, and the count is 5.

A member's index position can change. If you remove the first member, the second will become first, and the rest will move up to fill the void. The count will also reduce by one.

To add a member, you can follow this syntax:

```
colNew.Add(Item, Key, before | after)
```

In its simplest form, you need only to have one item to add a member, like this:

```
colNew.Add("one")
```

This will add "one" to the end of the existing members, if any. You can remove the parentheses and just use a space as a separator.

You can use the **Key** parameter to track a particular member, such as the following:

```
colNew.Add Item:=10, Key:="Alpha", before:=1
```

Notice that we are using **named arguments**. In such a case, we can place the three arguments in any order.

Here we add 10 as a member and place it before the first existing member. (If the collection has no existing member, the *before* argument will cause an error). We also assign Alpha as the key to this member. We can now reference this member by using the key, but not the reverse.

After the above statement of adding a member, we can reference it with any of the following statements:

```
Print colNew(1)
Print colNew.Item(1)
Print colNew("Alpha")
Print colNew!Alpha
```

Since **Item** is the default method (yes, it's called a method in Visual Basic manuals), it can be omitted as in our first example. Or you can spell it out as in the second example.

The last two examples use the Key value to reference a member. In this case, you don't need to know its index position. In the third example, you can add Item to before the parentheses as in the second example. But you cannot do the same to the fourth example.

You can add one or more collections to another collection. The second collection will then become the container of the other collections. This is like putting smaller cans in a larger can. It's also like assigning one or more arrays to a Variant variable.

Figure 1.19   Manipulating collections

How can you reference a member in such an arrangement? The same way you handle a Variant variable to which you have assigned multiple arrays. Below is an example. It produces the result shown in Figure 1.19.

```
Private Sub Form_Click()
    Dim I As Integer, J As Integer
    Dim colAll As New Collection
    Dim colLetters As New Collection
    Dim colNumbers As New Collection

    For I = 1 To 10
        colLetters.Add Chr(I + 64)
        'add A, B, C ...
        colNumbers.Add I
        'add 1, 2, 3 ...
    Next I

    colAll.Add colLetters
    colAll.Add colNumbers

    For I = 1 To colAll.Count
        For J = 1 To colLetters.Count
            Print colAll(I)(J);
        Next J
        Print
    Next I
End Sub
```

Here we use this syntax to reference each member:

```
Print colAll(I)(J);
```

So colAll(1) contains all the letters and colAll(2) all the numbers. colAll(1)(1) contains A, and colAll(2)(1) stores 1. The following statements will prove this:

```
Dim Temp As Variant
Set Temp = colAll(1)
Print Temp(1)           'A
Set Temp = colAll(2)
Print Temp(1);          '1
```

Here the Temp variable must be a Variant, Object, or Collection. Since a collection is an object, you must also use the **Set** statement to assign a value. On the contrary, assigning an array to a Variant doesn't require the use of Set.

You can use **For Each-Next** to loop through all the members in a collection, the same way you do with a one-dimensional array. The following statements will print all the members in the colLetters collection:

```
Dim Item
For Each Item In colLetters
     Print Item;
Next Item
```

Visual Basic maintains three internal collections to manage objects. These are known as **forms collection**, **controls collection**, and **printers collection**. So you can use Forms(0) to reference the first loaded form, and FormName(0) or FormName.Controls(0) (here FormName is the name of a form such as Form1) to reference the first loaded control. This is a 0-based system. So the last object has the index of Count minus 1.

User-Defined Types

You can create a **user-defined data type** in which you can specify multiple variables (including arrays) to hold different data types. This type then becomes a template from which you can declare individual variables, each holding the type you've defined. You can use this mechanism to tie together disparate data types into one unit.

You can create a user-defined type only at the module level. It defaults to public in scope. In a standard module, you can use Private to limit its cope to that module. If this word is not used, the scope is public by default, and it can be accessed by all the modules in the same project.

When a user-defined type is created in a form or class module, you must add Private to limit its scope to the current module. The absence of this word will trigger an error.

After a user-defined type has been created as described above, you can declare a variable to be that type. Such a variable can be private or public in a standard module. It must be private in the module level of a form or class module. It can be local if declared inside a procedure.

After a user-defined type has been created, you can view it in the Object Browser. The type appears in the Classes list, together with other class modules in the current project. The bottom panel shows whether it's public or private. Its members also appear in the Members list in the right panel.

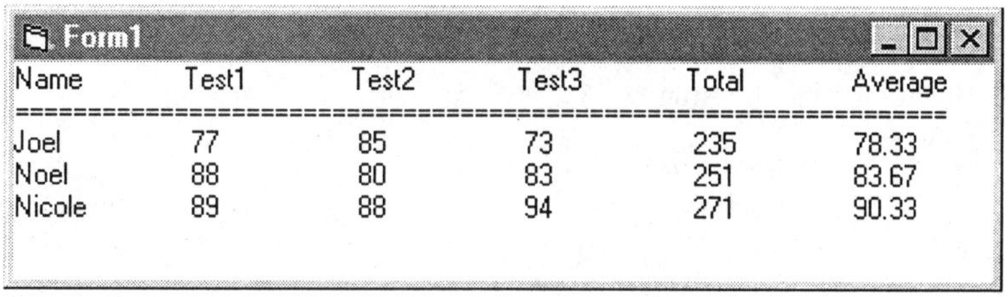

Name	Test1	Test2	Test3	Total	Average
Joel	77	85	73	235	78.33
Noel	88	80	83	251	83.67
Nicole	89	88	94	271	90.33

Figure 1.20   Manipulating a user-defined type

The following code provides an example of using a user-defined type. It produces the display shown in Figure 1.20.

```
'----- Listing 3 -----
Private Type Student
    Name As String
    Test1 As Integer
    Test2 As Integer
    Test3 As Integer
End Type

Private Sub Form_Click()
    Dim I As Integer
    Dim Sum As Single
    Dim Grades(2) As Student

    Grades(0).Name = "Joel"
    Grades(0).Test1 = 77
    Grades(0).Test2 = 85
    Grades(0).Test3 = 73
    Grades(1).Name = "Noel"
```

```
Grades(1).Test1 = 88
Grades(1).Test2 = 80
Grades(1).Test3 = 83
Grades(2).Name = "Nicole"
Grades(2).Test1 = 89
Grades(2).Test2 = 88
Grades(2).Test3 = 94

Print "Name", "Test1", "Test2", _
"Test3", "Total", "Average"
Print String(65, "=")
For I = 0 To UBound(Grades)
    With Grades(I)
        Print .Name,
        Print .Test1,
        Print .Test2,
        Print .Test3,
        Sum = .Test1 + .Test2 + .Test3
        Print Sum,
        Print Format(Sum / 3, "0.##")
    End With
Next I
End Sub
```

We create a module-level user-defined type in a form module. The **Private** keyword is required here. Then we declare a local array to be this type. This array is then used to store data.

Notice the use of **With-End Width** to maneuver the members inside each variable. Here a variable is handled like an object.

You might be tempted to use For Each-Next to loop through the array, each of whose members contains a user-defined type. The following change looks perfectly reasonable. But it will produce the error shown in Figure 1.21.

```
Dim Item
For Each Item In Grades
    With Item
        Print .Name,
        Print .Test1,
        Print .Test2,
        Print .Test3,
        Sum = .Test1 + .Test2 + .Test3
        Print Sum,
        Print Format(Sum / 3, "0.##")
    End With
Next Item
```

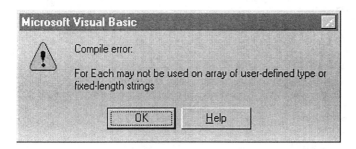

Figure 1.21   **Error caused by using For Each on a user-defined type**

So remember these rules: 1) use With-End With to loop through the members in an object or a user-defined type and 2) use For Each-Next to loop through the members in an array or a collection (even though a collection is an object).

Variants and Multidimensional Arrays

When you have a large number of organized data of various types, multidimensional arrays can be used to handle them. On many occasions, Variant variables can be even more versatile. This section demonstrates both of them.

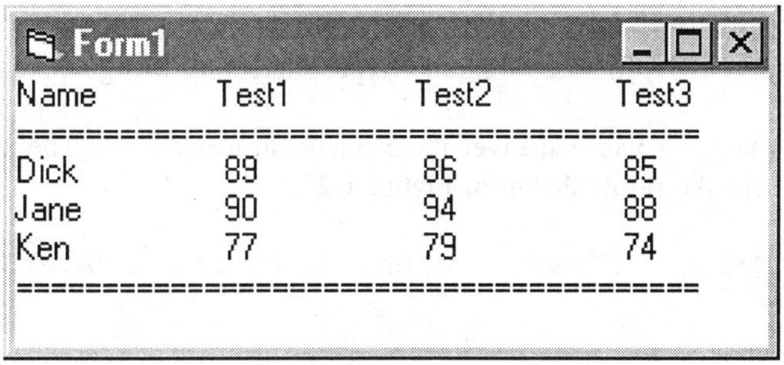

```
Form1
Name        Test1        Test2        Test3
==========================================
Dick         89           86           85
Jane         90           94           88
Ken          77           79           74

==========================================
```

Figure 1.22   **A two-dimensional array**

Suppose you have the kind of data shown in Figure 1.22. You can maneuver them with a two-dimensional array shown below.

```
Private Sub Form_Click()
    Dim I As Integer, J As Integer
    Dim Grades(2, 3) As Variant
    Dim Sum As Integer
    Dim Avg As Single

    Grades(0, 0) = "Dick"
    Grades(0, 1) = 89
    Grades(0, 2) = 86
    Grades(0, 3) = 85
    Grades(1, 0) = "Jane"
    Grades(1, 1) = 90
    Grades(1, 2) = 94
    Grades(1, 3) = 88
    Grades(2, 0) = "Ken"
    Grades(2, 1) = 77
    Grades(2, 2) = 79
    Grades(2, 3) = 74

    Print "Name", "Test1", "Test2", "Test3"
    Print String(40, "=")
    For I = 0 To 2
        For J = 0 To 3
            Print Grades(I, J),
        Next J
        Print
    Next I
    Print String(40, "=")
End Sub
```

Here we use a two-dimensional array. Each element in the array is assigned separately. Here the Grades array has be the Variant type or unspecified because we want it to contain both strings and integers. If you specify another type, something will go wrong.

Once we have the array in place, we can maneuver the elements in many ways. The following changes will produce the result shown in Figure 1.23.

```
Print "Name", "Test1", "Test2", "Test3", "Total", "Average"
Print String(65, "=")
For I = 0 To 2
    For J = 0 To 3
        Print Grades(I, J),
        If VarType(Grades(I, J)) <> vbString _
        Then Sum = Sum + Grades(I, J)
    Next J
    Avg = Format(Sum / 3, "#.00")
    Print Sum, Avg
    Sum = 0        'clear for reuse
Next I
Print String(65, "=")
```

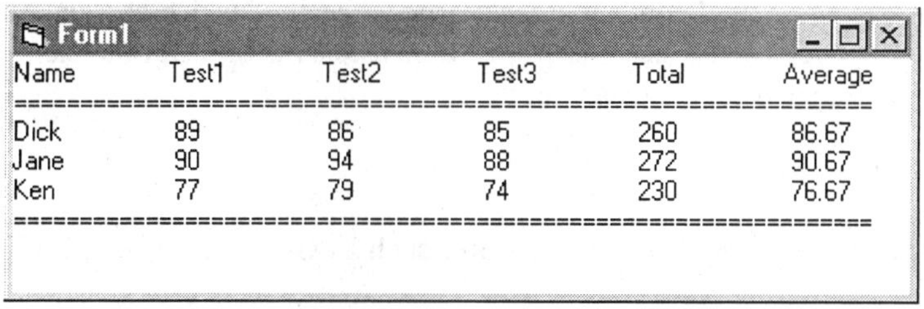

Figure 1.23   Manipulating a two-dimensional array

We use the **VarType** function to tell us whether a particular element is a string. If it is, it's ignored. If not, it's added to the others to get the sum.

Assigning a value to each element in such a multidimensional array is cumbersome. We can simplify the job by using the **Array** function to assign multiple values to a single Variant variable. This variable can then be manipulated like an array. The following changes will produce the same result as before. The code is now much shorter.

```
Private Sub Form_Click()
    Dim I As Integer, J As Integer
    Dim Grades, Dick, Jane, Ken
    Dim Sum As Integer
    Dim Avg As Single

    Dick = Array("Dick", 89, 86, 85)
    Jane = Array("Jane", 90, 94, 88)
    Ken = Array("Ken", 77, 79, 74)
    Grades = Array(Dick, Jane, Ken)

    Print "Name", "Test1", "Test2", "Test3", "Total", "Average"
    Print String(65, "=")
    For I = 0 To 2
        For J = 0 To 3
            Print Grades(I)(J),
            If VarType(Grades(I)(J)) <> vbString _
            Then Sum = Sum + Grades(I)(J)
        Next J
        Avg = Format(Sum / 3, "#.00")
        Print Sum, Avg
        Sum = 0        'clear for reuse
    Next I
    Print String(65, "=")
End Sub
```

The Grades variable is a Variant. It contains three Variants, each of which contains four Variant elements. In the end, Grades becomes a two-dimensional array. But the elements are referenced differently, such as this example:

```
Print Grades(I)(J),
```

In this arrangement, referencing an element as before, such as Grades(I, J), will lead to an error.

Each Variant variable can also be treated like a one-dimensional array. So we can use the **UBound** and **LBound** functions to specify the array's boundaries. The following modifications of the two beginning For lines will produce the same result as before:

```
For I = LBound(Grades) To UBound(Grades)
    For J = LBound(Dick) To UBound(Dick)
```

Since each Variant variable is holding a one-dimensional array, we can use the **For Each-Next** command to manipulate its elements. This can further shorten and simplify coding. Our two For-Next loops can be changed as follows, and the result won't change:

```
Dim Item, SubItem
For Each Item In Grades
    For Each SubItem In Item
        Print SubItem,
        If VarType(SubItem) <> vbString _
        Then Sum = Sum + SubItem
    Next SubItem
    Avg = Format(Sum / UBound(Item), "#.00")
    Print Sum, Avg
    Sum = 0        'clear for reuse
Next Item
```

We now use two Variant variables. Variable Item is used to represent each subsequent element in the Grades variable. Variable SubItem is then used to represent each subsequent element in variable Item.

This version has no numeric literals such as beginning or ending numbers for looping. Even the average is calculated by using the upperbound value of an array. This kind of generic code can be more flexible and handle more situations. This final versions is shown below:

```
Private Sub Form_Click()
    Dim Item, SubItem
    Dim Grades, Dick, Jane, Ken
    Dim Sum As Integer
    Dim Avg As Single
```

```
    Dick = Array("Dick", 89, 86, 85)
    Jane = Array("Jane", 90, 94, 88)
    Ken = Array("Ken", 77, 79, 74)
    Grades = Array(Dick, Jane, Ken)

    Print "Name", "Test1", "Test2", "Test3", "Total", "Average"
    Print String(65, "=")

    For Each Item In Grades
        For Each SubItem In Item
            Print SubItem,
            If VarType(SubItem) <> vbString _
            Then Sum = Sum + SubItem
        Next SubItem
        Avg = Format(Sum / UBound(Item), "#.00")
        Print Sum, Avg
        Sum = 0        'clear for reuse
    Next Item
    Print String(65, "=")
End Sub
```

As shown in the listing above, a Variant variable can be assigned an array by simply using the = sign with the Array keyword. The variable can then be maneuvered like an array.

Income Tax Project

This project lets you quickly figure out your federal income tax (Figure 1.24). Just type a taxable income in the text box and click a filing status in the list box. The result will appear in the label below the text box. As you click each different item in the list box, a different result will appear.

This is a complex manipulation requiring lots of what-if scenarios. We can put all the complex rules in a class module and use it again and again. Once that's done, it's simple to enlist the module's services. The front-end is controlled by the two simple procedures in Form1, as shown below.

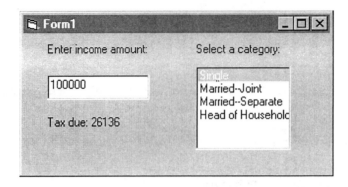

Figure 1.24   Calculating federal income tax

```
'-----FedTax.vbp-----
'-----from FedTax.frm-----
Dim ftTax As New FedTax

Private Sub Form_Load()
    lstCategory.AddItem "Single"
    lstCategory.AddItem "Married--Joint"
    lstCategory.AddItem "Married--Separate"
    lstCategory.AddItem "Head of Household"
End Sub

Private Sub lstCategory_Click()
    If txtIncome.Text = "" Then
        Beep      'if no entry
        Exit Sub
    End If

    Select Case lstCategory.ListIndex
    Case 0
        ftTax.SSingle = txtIncome.Text
        lblTax.Caption = ftTax.SSingle
    Case 1
        ftTax.Joint = txtIncome.Text
        lblTax.Caption = ftTax.Joint
    Case 2
        ftTax.Separate = txtIncome.Text
        lblTax.Caption = ftTax.Separate
    Case 3
        ftTax.Head = txtIncome.Text
        lblTax.Caption = ftTax.Head
    End Select

    lblTax.Caption = "Tax due: " & lblTax.Caption
```

```
      Set ftTax = Nothing
End Sub
```

The Form_Load procedure adds the four items in the list box. The list box's Click procedure then calls a proper **property procedure** in the FedTax class, where a lot work is done, as shown below.

```
'-----from FedTax.cls-----
Private TaxBracket(1 To 4) As Single
Private EarnAmount(1 To 4) As Long
Private Const TaxRate0 As Single = 0.15
Private Const TaxRate1 As Single = 0.28
Private Const TaxRate2 As Single = 0.31
Private Const TaxRate3 As Single = 0.36
Private Const TaxRate4 As Single = 0.396

    'module-level private properties
Private mSSingle As Long
Private mJoint As Long
Private mSeparate As Long
Private mHead As Long

Public Property Let SSingle(ByVal vData As Long)
    'can't use Single as proc name
    TaxBracket(1) = 3600
    TaxBracket(2) = 13162
    TaxBracket(3) = 32738.5
    TaxBracket(4) = 84020.5

    EarnAmount(1) = 24000
    EarnAmount(2) = 58150
    EarnAmount(3) = 121300
    EarnAmount(4) = 263750

    vData = CalcTax(vData)  'call func, pass amount

    mSSingle = vData     'assign value to property
End Property

Public Property Get SSingle() As Long
    SSingle = mSSingle   'read property
End Property

Public Property Let Head(ByVal vData As Long)
    TaxBracket(1) = 4822.5
    TaxBracket(2) = 19074.5
    TaxBracket(3) = 35024
    TaxBracket(4) = 81554
```

```
        EarnAmount(1)  =  32150
        EarnAmount(2)  =  83050
        EarnAmount(3)  =  134500
        EarnAmount(4)  =  263750

        vData = CalcTax(vData)

        mHead = vData
End Property

Public Property Get Head() As Long
        Head = mHead
End Property

Public Property Let Separate(ByVal vData As Long)
        TaxBracket(1)  =  3007.5
        TaxBracket(2)  =  10959.5
        TaxBracket(3)  =  18833.5
        TaxBracket(4)  =  39722.5

        EarnAmount(1)  =  20050
        EarnAmount(2)  =  48450
        EarnAmount(3)  =  73850
        EarnAmount(4)  =  131875

        vData = CalcTax(vData)

        mSeparate = vData
End Property

Public Property Get Separate() As Long
        Separate = mSeparate
End Property

Public Property Let Joint(ByVal vData As Long)
        TaxBracket(1)  =  6015
        TaxBracket(2)  =  21919
        TaxBracket(3)  =  37667
        TaxBracket(4)  =  79445

        EarnAmount(1)  =  40100
        EarnAmount(2)  =  96900
        EarnAmount(3)  =  147700
        EarnAmount(4)  =  263750

        vData = CalcTax(vData)

        mJoint = vData
End Property

Public Property Get Joint() As Long
```

```
        Joint = mJoint
End Property

Private Function CalcTax(vData) As Single
    Dim TaxDue As Single

    Select Case vData
    Case Is > EarnAmount(4)
        TaxDue = TaxBracket(4) + (vData - EarnAmount(4)) *
TaxRate4
    Case Is > EarnAmount(3)
        TaxDue = TaxBracket(3) + (vData - EarnAmount(3)) *
TaxRate3
    Case Is > EarnAmount(2)
        TaxDue = TaxBracket(2) + (vData - EarnAmount(2)) *
TaxRate2
    Case Is > EarnAmount(1)
        TaxDue = TaxBracket(1) + (vData - EarnAmount(1)) *
TaxRate1
    Case Else
        TaxDue = vData * TaxRate0
    End Select

    CalcTax = TaxDue       'return call
End Function
```

Suppose you click Single in the list box. Then these two lines are executed:

```
    ftTax.SSingle = txtIncome.Text
    lblTax.Caption = ftTax.SSingle
```

The first statement calls the Public Property Let SSingle procedure (a public property can be called from outside); the number entered in the text box is also passed to it. Here two module-level arrays' elements are assigned proper values. Then the Private Function CalcTax function is called (a private function can be called only from inside the same class) and the original number is passed to it. This function calculates and then returns the tax due.

The second statement simply calls Public Property Get SSingle( ) to read the property produced earlier by the corresponding Property Let procedure.

This arrangement provides lots of examples of maneuvering property procedures. However, it's not the most elegant solution. We can simplify the class module as follows.

```
'-----FedTax1.vbp-----
'-----from FedTax1.cls-----

Public Function CalcTax(Income As Single, Status)
```

```
    Dim TaxDue As Single
    Dim B0, B1, B2, B3, E0, E1, E2, E3
    Dim Bracket(3), Earn(3)
    Dim Rate(4) As Single
    Dim Brackets, Earns
    Dim I As Integer

    I = Status

'tax rates for all
    Rate(0) = 0.15
    Rate(1) = 0.28
    Rate(2) = 0.31
    Rate(3) = 0.36
    Rate(4) = 0.396

'Single
    B0 = 3600
    B1 = 13162
    B2 = 32738.5
    B3 = 84020.5
    Bracket(0) = Array(B0, B1, B2, B3)
    E0 = 24000
    E1 = 58150
    E2 = 121300
    E3 = 263750
    Earn(0) = Array(E0, E1, E2, E3)

'Joint
    B0 = 6015
    B1 = 21919
    B2 = 37667
    B3 = 79445
    Bracket(1) = Array(B0, B1, B2, B3)
    E0 = 40100
    E1 = 96900
    E2 = 147700
    E3 = 263750
    Earn(1) = Array(E0, E1, E2, E3)

'Separate
    B0 = 3007.5
    B1 = 10959.5
    B2 = 18833.5
    B3 = 39722.5
    Bracket(2) = Array(B0, B1, B2, B3)
    E0 = 20050
    E1 = 48450
    E2 = 73850
    E3 = 131875
    Earn(2) = Array(E0, E1, E2, E3)
```

```
'Head
    B0 = 4822.5
    B1 = 19074.5
    B2 = 35024
    B3 = 81554
    Bracket(3) = Array(B0, B1, B2, B3)
    E0 = 32150
    E1 = 83050
    E2 = 134500
    E3 = 263750
    Earn(3) = Array(E0, E1, E2, E3)

    Brackets = Array(Bracket(0), Bracket(1), _
    Bracket(2), Bracket(3))
    'put all in 2-dimensional arrays
    Earns = Array(Earn(0), Earn(1), Earn(2), Earn(3))

    Select Case Income
    Case Is > Earns(I)(3)
        TaxDue = Brackets(I)(3) + (Income - _
        Earns(I)(3)) * Rate(4)
    Case Is > Earns(I)(2)
        TaxDue = Brackets(I)(2) + (Income - _
        Earns(I)(2)) * Rate(3)
    Case Is > Earns(I)(1)
        TaxDue = Brackets(I)(1) + (Income - _
        Earns(I)(1)) * Rate(2)
    Case Is > Earns(I)(0)
        TaxDue = Brackets(I)(0) + (Income - _
        Earns(I)(0)) * Rate(1)
    Case Else
        TaxDue = Income * Rate(0)
    End Select

    CalcTax = TaxDue  'return call
End Function
```

Here we use the **Array** function and a series of Variant variables to maneuver lots of data. In the end, two two-dimensional arrays store all the items. We then use a single **Select Case** structure to figure the tax due.

Notice the way we reference a Variant variable storing a two-dimensional array, as shown below. The two dimensions are separate and each enclosed in its own pair of parentheses.

```
Case Is > Earns(I)(3)
```

The calling procedure is also greatly simplified, as shown below.

```
'-----from FedTax1.frm-----
Option Explicit

Private Sub Form_Load()
    lstCategory.AddItem "Single"
    lstCategory.AddItem "Married--Joint"
    lstCategory.AddItem "Married--Separate"
    lstCategory.AddItem "Head of Household"
End Sub

Private Sub lstCategory_Click()
    Dim ftTax As New FedTax

    If txtIncome.Text = "" Then
        Beep      'if no entry
        Exit Sub
    End If

    lblTax.Caption = ftTax.CalcTax(txtIncome.Text, _
    lstCategory.ListIndex)
End Sub
```

The last line calls the CalcTax procedure in the FedTax class and passes two argument. That's all there's to it. This is a good example of reusing code to simplify your life.

Suppose at run time you click Single, the first item in the list box. That will pass the amount entered in the text box and the ListIndex value of 0. This 0 is passed to Status and then assigned to I. This value then determines which elements in the two arrays should be used in calculating the tax due. If you click another item in the list box, a different index value will be passed and another result will be returned.

Instead of using arrays, you can use enumerations, collections, or user-defined types. But they are not as versatile as Variant arrays in simplifying your code.

Calendar Project

The project discussed in this section lets you create a calendar shown in Figure 1.25. You click the current form at run time to show an input box prompting you to enter mm/yy to show that particular month/year. The current month/year is automatically shown as the default entry in the input box. So you can just click OK to show it.

To create a calendar, you need to know the weekday of the first day of the month. That's easily obtained with the **WeekDay** function. The last day of the month is more difficult.

You need to figure out whether a particular February has 28 or 29 days, depending on whether a leap year is involved.

Figure 1.25   A calendar

A simpler way is to trigger an error in order to identify the last day of each month. For example, 2/98 has 28 days. So WeekDay("2/28/98") returns 7, meaning Saturday or the 7th day starting from Sunday. On the other hand, WeekDay("2/29/98") triggers the *Type mismatch* error. So if you subtract the date number (29) by 1, you'll get the last day of the month. This system will work with any month, not just February.

```
'-----Calendar.vbp-----
'----- from Calendar.frm -----
Private Sub Form_Click()
    Dim UserDate As Date
    Static CurrDate As String
    Dim Month1, Year1
    Dim LastDay As Integer
    Dim clnCal As New Calendar

    On Error Resume Next

    If CurrDate = "" Then
        CurrDate = Month(Now) & "/" & Format(Now, "yy")
        'use current date for the first time
    End If
    UserDate = InputBox("Enter mm/yy", "Calendar", CurrDate)
    'prompt for entry, default is current mm/yy
    'becomes 9/1/98 because UserDate is a Date var

    If Err.Number = 13 Then 'Cancel clicked
        Exit Sub      'Type mismatch error
    Else
        CurrDate = UserDate
        'if not Cancel, retain previous user
```

```
                'entry stored in static var
        End If

        If Not IsDate(UserDate) Then
            Beep
            MsgBox "Your entry is not valid."
            Exit Sub
        End If

        Month1 = Month(UserDate)
        Year1 = Year(UserDate)
        LastDay = clnCal.GetLastDay(Month1, Year1)
        'call function, pass month and year
        Call PrintOut(UserDate, Month1, Year1, LastDay)
        'call sub & pass data to print output
End Sub

Sub PrintOut(UserDate, Month1, Year1, LastDay)
        Dim I As Integer
        Dim Arr       'variant to store array
        Dim Temp As String
        Dim Gap As Integer   'distance between items
        Dim CY  'get CurrentY
        Dim FirstDay As Integer

        On Error GoTo ErrTrap

        AutoRedraw = True
        BackColor = vbCyan
        Cls
        FontName = "arial"
        FontSize = 20

        FirstDay = WeekDay(UserDate)
        'get 1st weekday, 1=sunday

        Gap = 600        '600 twips apart
        Month1 = Format(UserDate, "mmmm")
        'get month text, spelled out
        Temp = Month1 & ", " & Year1     'month & year string
        CurrentX = (Gap * 6.5 - TextWidth(Temp)) / 2
        'get center position of string
        Print Temp   'print month/year

        FontSize = 10
     Arr = Array("Sun", "Mon", "Tue", "Wed", "Thu", "Fri", "Sat")

        CurrentY = CurrentY + Gap / 6    'move down print head
        For I = 0 To 6
            CurrentX = I * Gap
            Print Arr(I);    'print weekday names at top
```

```
    Next I

    Print
    CY = CurrentY
    Line (0, CY)-(Gap * 6.7, CY)
    'draw horizontal line

    CurrentX = (FirstDay - 1) * Gap
    'set beginning print position based on 1st day of month
    For I = 1 To LastDay
        Print I;
        CurrentX = ((FirstDay + I - 1) Mod 7) * Gap
        'set print position for each number
        If (FirstDay + I - 1) Mod 7 = 0 Then Print
        'new line after 7th day
    Next I
    Exit Sub

ErrTrap:
    MsgBox Err.Description
End Sub

'-----from Calendar.cls-----
Public Property Get GetLastDay(Month1, Year1)
    Dim Temp As Integer, Temp1 As Integer
    Dim Date1 As String

    On Error GoTo ErrTrap
    Temp = 28          'start with 28
    Do
        Temp = Temp + 1        'test each subsequent number
        Date1 = Month1 & "/" & Str(Temp) & "/" & Year1
        Temp1 = WeekDay(Date1)
        'trigger type mismatch error, exit loop
    Loop
    Exit Property

ErrTrap:
    If Err = 13 Then      'type mismatch error
        GetLastDay = Temp - 1
        'return the number before error was triggered
    Else
        MsgBox Err.Description
    End If
End Property
```

We could have put the GetLastDay property (it could also be implemented as a function) in the Form1 module. Instead, here we put it in a class module. In this arrangement, this

property can be called anytime. For example, in a new project, you might use the
following statements:

```
Dim clnCal As New Calendar
Print "The last day of " & Month1 _
& "/" & Year1 & ": " & LastDay
```

Then you can quickly get the result like this:

The last day of 2/98: 28

To make the class module more useful, we could move the PrintOut procedure to it. In
that case, Form1's Form_Click procedure needs only to call the GetLastDay property and
then call the PrintOut procedure to produce the result. You'll have a chance to sweat it out
in a practice question below.

Poker Game

The final project in this chapter lets you play a poker game (Figure 1.26). At the outset,
click the Deal button to display eight cards, four at the top and four at the bottom. Each
player is supposed to click zero or more displayed cards to discard them. So if the top
player wants to discard the four of club, he just clicks that card and it will disappear.
After both players have discarded their unwanted cards, if any, click the Redraw button to
fill in the blank spaces. After that, Redraw will be dimmed and Deal will become visible.
Clicking Deal will draw two new hands.

Figure 1.26   A poker game

Our user interface in Form1 consists of eight picture boxes on which characters are drawn at run time. These boxes are from two **control arrays** named picCard1 and picCard2. Each is indexed from 0 to 3.

Most of the work is done in the Poker.cls class module shown below:

```
'-----Poker.vbp-----
'-----from Poker.cls-----
Dim OldNum As Integer    'track num of cards drawn
Dim OldCard() As String
    'store all drawn cards to prevent repetition

Public Sub GetCard(ObjName As Object, Cards(), row, col)
    Dim TxtSize As String
    Dim Suit As Integer
    Dim Num As Variant
    Dim Color As Long
    Dim NewCard As String
    Dim I As Integer
    Dim J As Integer

    Randomize    'get new random seed

    OldNum = OldNum + 1
    ReDim Preserve OldCard(OldNum)
        'redim and add 1 more element

    Do        'check duplicates
        Suit = Int(Rnd * 4)
            'random number 0 - 3
        Num = Int(Rnd * 13) + 1
            'random number in range 1 - 13

        NewCard = Suit & "x" & Num

        For J = 1 To OldNum - 1
            If OldCard(J) = NewCard Then
                Exit For
            End If  'get out of For loop if matching
        Next J
    Loop While J < OldNum
        'loop back if For terminated prematurely

    OldCard(OldNum) = NewCard
        'put new card in array
        'controls all drawn cards
    Cards(row, col) = NewCard
        'put all shown cards in array

    Suit = Suit + 167
```

```
              '167 club, 168 diamond, 169 heart, 170 spade
     Select Case Suit      'get a color for a suit
         Case 167, 170
             Color = vbBlack        'club, spade
         Case 168, 169
             Color = vbRed          'diamond, heart
     End Select

     Select Case Num       'if num is 11 - 13, 1
         Case 11
             Num = "J"
         Case 12
             Num = "Q"
         Case 13
             Num = "K"
         Case 1
             Num = "A"
         Case Else
             Num = Trim(Num) 'trim leading space for a numeric
     End Select

     With ObjName
         .Cls
         .ForeColor = Color
         .FontName = "arial"       'font for num
         .FontSize = 20
         ObjName.Print Num
         .FontName = "symbol"       'font for suit
         .FontSize = 80
         TxtSize = Chr(Suit)
         .CurrentX = (.ScaleWidth - .TextWidth(TxtSize)) / 2
         .CurrentY = (.ScaleHeight - .TextHeight(TxtSize)) / 2
             'center display
         ObjName.Print Chr(Suit)
     End With
 End Sub
```

From Form1, we have two Click procedures to respond to the Deal and Redraw buttons being clicked. Each time the Deal button is clicked, the GetCard procedure in the class module is called to get eight new cards, each of which must be different from the rest. When the Redraw button is clicked, the deleted cards are passed to the same procedure to get replacements, which must also be different from those shown or discarded.

```
 '-----from Poker.frm-----
 Dim Cards(1 To 2, 3) 'store two rows of displayed cards
 Dim crdNew As New Card  'module-level new object

 Private Sub cmdDeal_Click()
     Dim I As Integer
```

```
    On Error GoTo ErrTrap

    For I = 0 To 3
        Call crdNew.GetCard(picCard1(I), Cards(), 1, I)
        'deal each side one card at a time
        'pass array, row, col position
        Call crdNew.GetCard(picCard2(I), Cards(), 2, I)
    Next

    cmdRedraw.Enabled = True
    cmdDeal.Enabled = False
    Exit Sub

ErrTrap:
    MsgBox Err.Description
End Sub

Private Sub cmdRedraw_Click()
    Dim I As Integer
    Dim J As Integer
    Dim PicName As Object

    Set PicName = picCard1    'top row box name
    For I = 1 To 2
        For J = 0 To 3
            If Cards(I, J) = "" Then
            Call crdNew.GetCard(PicName(J), Cards(), I, J)
            End If
        Next J
        Set PicName = picCard2    'bot row box name
    Next I

    Set crdNew = Nothing       'destroy object, start with new
values

    cmdRedraw.Enabled = False
    cmdDeal.Enabled = True
End Sub

Private Sub picCard1_Click(Index As Integer)
    picCard1(Index).Cls      'clear when clicked
    Cards(1, Index) = ""     'remove from array
End Sub

Private Sub picCard2_Click(Index As Integer)
    picCard2(Index).Cls
    Cards(2, Index) = ""
End Sub

Private Sub cmdQuit_Click()
```

```
      End
End Sub
```

The class module uses a **dynamic array** to prevent two identical cards on the same occasion. The **ReDim Preserve** statement redimensions the array while preserving the existing elements.

Drill

_____ 1. Assuming that Class1 exists as well as the following code in Form1. Pressing F5 and then closing the form by clicking the X button will trigger Class1's Initialize and Terminate events. True or false?

```
Option Explicit
Dim objX As Class1

Private Sub Form_Click()
    Set objX = New Class1
End Sub
```

_____ 2. In the following arrangement, objX is destroyed after Form_Click is executed. True or false?

```
Option Explicit
Dim objX As New Class1

Private Sub Form_Click()
    Call objX.Calc
    Set objX = Nothing
End Sub
```

_____ 3. This is used on the client side to declare an event.

a. Event
b. RaiseEvent
c. WithEvents
d. Click

_____ 4. You can use the _____._____ event in a class module to let a client handle an error that may occur in the class.

___ 5. When you have a component project and a Standard EXE project running in the Visual Basic IDE, you need to use the _____ dialog box to enable the latter project to access the objects in the former.

___ 6. If a class's Instancing property is set to GlobalSingleUse or GlobalMultiUse, a client can access it without creating an instance. True or false?

___ 7. This is used to create polymorphism:
a. instancing
b. Implements
c. Friend
d. Event
e. COM

___ 8. After the Enum declaration below, C has the value of:
a. 0
b. empty string
c. 2
d. 3

```
Enum Alphabet
    A
    B
    C
End Enum
```

___ 9. In the enumeration below, C will have the value of _____ .

```
Enum Alphabet
    A = 10
    B
    C
End Enum
```

___ 10. An enumeration can contain floating-point values. True or false?

___ 11. An enumeration declared inside a procedure is _____ in scope.
a. local
b. module level
c. global
d. illegal

___ 12. The following will add 10 to a collection named colX. True of false?

```
Dim colX As Collection
colX.Add "10"
```

_____ 13.   The last statement below will produce 10. True or false?

```
Dim colA As New Collection
Dim colB As New Collection
colA.Add "10"
colB.Add colA
Print colB(1)(1)
```

_____ 14.   The second statement below will produce
    a.   an error
    b.   nothing
    c.   Ten
    d.   Top

```
colA.Add "Ten", "Top"
Print colA!Ten
```

_____ 15.   After the following statements have been executed, colX(1) will have the value of _____ .

```
Dim colX As New Collection
colX.Add "Alpha"
colX.Add "Beta"
colX.Add "Gamma", , 1
```

_____ 16.   Assuming the previous statements, colX.Count will have the value of _____ .

_____ 17.   The following declaration can be placed at the module level of a form or class module. True or false?

```
Type Worker
    Name As String
    SSN As String * 9
    Salary As Single
End Type
```

_____ 18.   After the above declaration, the following statement will assign a string to a member. True or false?

```
Worker.Name = "Joe"
```

_____ 19.   You can loop through each member in a user-defined variable with:
    a.   For-Next

      b.   For Each-Next

      c.   With-End With

      d.   both a and b

_____ 20.   You can loop through each member in a collection with:

      a.   For-Next

      b.   For Each-Next

      c.   With-End With

      d.   both a and b

Answers

1.F; 2.T; 3.c; 4.Err.Raise; 5.References; 6.T; 7.b; 8.c; 9.12; 10.F; 11.d; 12.F; 13.T; 14.a; 15.Gamma; 16.3; 17.F; 18.F; 19.c; 20.d

Practice

1.   Suppose the Wage class has been created as discussed in the text and that Form1 contains the code shown below. Explain what happens in the following run-time scenarios:

      a.   Clicking Command1 and then clicking Command2.

      b.   Clicking the X button on the form after the above.

      c.   Clicking Command2 without clicking Command1.

```
Dim wgNewWage As Wage    'form-level object variable, no New

Private Sub Command1_Click()
    Set wgNewWage = New Wage
    Print wgNewWage.MinWage
End Sub

Private Sub Command2_Click()
    Print wgNewWage.MinWage
End Sub
```

◙   2.   Assuming the Wage class exists as shown in Listing 1 and assuming the following
         procedures are written in Form1, explain the behavior of Command1 and
         Command2.

```
Dim wgNewWage As Wage

Private Sub Command1_Click()
    Dim wgNewWage As Wage
    Set wgNewWage = New Wage
    Print wgNewWage.MinWage
End Sub

Private Sub Command2_Click()
    Print wgNewWage.MinWage
End Sub
```

◙   3.   Assuming that the following procedures exit. What will happen when you run the
         program and click the form?

```
Private Sub Form_Load()
    Dim Note As String
    Note = "This becomes a property of the form."
End Sub

Private Sub Form_Click()
    Print Form1.Note
End Sub
```

◙   4.   Construct a class named Joe. This class should have a public variable named
         HourlyPay. It should initialize to the value of 15. From Form1, enter a statement
         to print the total weekly pay based on 40 hours.

◙   5.   Add to the previous class a public method (function procedure) called
         CalcWeekPay. It should take two arguments, hourly rate and number of hours,
         and return a value based on the product of the two, taking overtime into
         consideration. From Form1, call this method with two arguments to print the
         outcome. What will be printed if the pay rate is 15.25 and the hours are 42?

◙   6.   Add to the previous class a pair of Property Let/Get procedures named
         WeeklyPay. There should be two calling statements from Form1. The first
         statement should pass the number of hours to Property Let. This procedure should
         use this number and the HourlyPay value (initialized to 15, used in an earlier
         question) to calculate the total pay. The second calling statement should invoke
         the Property Get procedure to return the total pay.

◙   7.   Do the following:

1. Create a Numbers class with the following two functions. It should take an array of numerics and return a value as specified below:

   a. AddNumbers—returns the sum of the passed numbers.
   b. HiNumber—returns the highest value.

2. From Form1, write a Form_Click procedure that passes an array to the above class and prints the results.

8. Convert the above function procedures to property procedures. Then make calls to these procedures to produce the same results as before.

9. Add a Smith class to Listing 2 and change the code in Form1's Form_Click to calculate Smith's weekly gross pay. Assuming that he works 43 hours at $9.50 an hour, what is his gross pay?

10. Create a class named Die. The class's Initialize event should raise an event named Roll. From Form1, call this event to generate a random number in the 1 - 6 range. The number should then be printed to the form.

11. In the above Die class, raise another event named Guess. From Form1, use Form1's Form_Click to trigger the event. When this event occurs, an input box prompts the user to enter a number in the 1 - 6 range. This number is then compared to the one produced by the Roll event. A final message box from Form1 tells the user whether the numbers match.

12. What can you do if you want a project to start with the Sub Main procedure? How can you attach a descriptive string to a project? What's the significance of doing so?

13. Explain what the following procedure does.

```
Private Sub Form_Click()
    Dim I As Integer
    Dim Item
    Dim colX As New Collection

    For I = 1 To 10
        colX.Add I
    Next I

    For Each Item In colX
        Print Item;
    Next Item
End Sub
```

◎ 14. Modify the above to create a multiplication table as shown in Figure 1.27. The display output should be controlled by two For Each-Next loops and CurrentX.

```
 Form1                                    _ □ ✕
1    2    3    4    5    6    7    8    9
2    4    6    8   10   12   14   16   18
3    6    9   12   15   18   21   24   27
4    8   12   16   20   24   28   32   36
5   10   15   20   25   30   35   40   45
6   12   18   24   30   36   42   48   54
7   14   21   28   35   42   49   56   63
8   16   24   32   40   48   56   64   72
9   18   27   36   45   54   63   72   81
```

Figure 1.27   A multiplication table

◎ 15. Explain what the following loop does.

```
Do While colX.Count > 0
    colX.Remove 1
Loop
```

◎ 16. Create a class module named Wage. It should contain a public enumeration containing a list of worker names and their hourly pay rates as constants. There should be one function that calculates and returns a total weekly wage amount based on the enumeration and the number of hours passed to it from the calling module. For example, the following calling statement passes the hour number and the worker's name, which matches a corresponding constant in the enumeration. The calculated return is assigned to the WeekWage variable.

```
WeekPay = wgWage.CalcWage(Hours:=41.5, _
WorkerName:=Jim)
```

Also, raise an error that may occur in the class module and set up a routine in the calling module to handle the raised error.

◎ 17. Modify Listing 3 as follows:

a. Create the type as a public user-defined type.
b. Transfer the code in the Form_Click procedure to a sub procedure named ShowRecords in a class module named Record.

    c. From Form1, call the above procedure to show the same result as before.

◙ 18. Use collections to handle the data in Listing 3 and produce the result shown in Figure 1.28. The items related to each person should be displayed in a column. (Use CurrentX and CurrentY to control the display.) The code should be placed in a sub procedure named ShowRecords in a class module named Record as in the previous question. The calling should also be done the same way.

Name	Joel	Noel	Nicole
Test1	77	88	89
Test2	85	80	88
Test3	73	83	94
Total	235	251	271
Average	78.33	83.67	90.33

Figure 1.28   Tabular data manipulated with collections

◙ 19. In the Calendar project shown in the text, move the PrintOut procedure to the Calendar class module and modify the rest to produce the same result as before.

◙ 20. The two methods in the above Calendar class contains error traps. Modify them so that when a error occurs here, it will be raised and the number and description will be passed to the caller. In the Visual Basic IDE, how can you make a class module raise an error so that it can be trapped by the calling module?

Answers

1.
    a. Clicking Command1 triggers the Initialize event and print the number. The form-level object is created by the Set-New combination. Clicking Command2 simply prints the number and doesn't trigger Initialize.

    b. It will trigger the Terminate event and destroy the object.

    c. An error will result because no object has been created.

2. Command1 creates a local object variable and calls a property of the object. The object is destroyed at the end. Using the same name for both local and module levels lets the local variable shadow the module-level variable. In this situation, no module-level object is created by Command1_Click. So when you click Command2 after Command1, an error will appear because you're calling a property of a nonexisting object. If you take away the Dim line in Command1_Click, Command1_Click will create a module-level object, which Command2 can access.

3. You'll get the "Method or data member not found" error. A local variable is not a property of the form. The "Print Form1.Note" statement calls a property of Form1. Unless you've a public variable named Note, Visual Basic can't see this member.

4.
```
'-----from Joe (Class1)-----
Public HourlyPay As Single

Private Sub Class_Initialize()
    HourlyPay = 15
End Sub

'-----from Form1-----
Private Sub Form_Click()
    Dim jNewJoe As New Joe
    Print jNewJoe.HourlyPay * 40
End Sub
```

This will print 600.

5.
```
'-----from Joe (Class1)-----
Public Function CalcWeekPay(Hours As Single, _
Rate As Single) As Single
    Dim TotPay As Single

    If Hours <= 40 Then
        TotPay = Hours * Rate
    Else
        TotPay = Rate * (40 + (Hours - 40) * 1.5)
    End If
    CalcWeekPay = Format(TotPay, "#.00")
End Function
```

```
'-----from Form1-----
Private Sub Form_Click()
    Dim jNewJoe As New Joe
    Print jNewJoe.CalcWeekPay _
    (Rate:=15.25, Hours:=42)
End Sub
```

Print output: 655.75.

6.
```
'-----from Joe (Class1)-----
Private mWeeklyPay As Single
    'module-level private variable

Public Property Get WeeklyPay() As Single
    WeeklyPay = mWeeklyPay
End Property

Public Property Let WeeklyPay(ByVal Hours As Single)
    Dim TotPay As Single

    If Hours <= 40 Then
        TotPay = Hours * HourlyPay
    Else
        TotPay = HourlyPay * (40 + (Hours - 40) * 1.5)
    End If
    mWeeklyPay = Format(TotPay, "#.00")
End Property

'-----from Form1-----
Private Sub Form_Click()
    Dim jNewJoe As New Joe
    jNewJoe.WeeklyPay = 42      'call Property Let
    Print jNewJoe.WeeklyPay     'call Property Get
End Sub
```


7.
```
'-----from Numbers class module-----
Public Function AddNumbers(Nums) As Single
    Dim Item
    Dim Sum As Single
```

```
      For Each Item In Nums
         Sum = Sum + Item
      Next Item
      AddNumbers = Sum
   End Function

   Public Function HiNumber(Nums) As Single
      Dim I As Integer
      Dim HiNum As Single

      HiNum = Nums(0)
      For I = 1 To UBound(Nums)
         If HiNum < Nums(I) Then HiNum = Nums(I)
      Next I
      HiNumber = HiNum
   End Function

   '-----from Form1-----
   Private Sub Form_Click()
      Dim Nums
      Dim numNew As New Numbers
      Nums = Array(34.55, 65, 87, 12, 33)
      Print numNew.AddNumbers(Nums)
      Print numNew.HiNumber(Nums)
   End Sub


8.
   '-----from Numbers class module-----
   Private mAddNumbers As Single
   Private mHiNumber As Single

   Public Property Let AddNumbers(Nums)
      Dim Item
      Dim Sum As Single

      For Each Item In Nums
         Sum = Sum + Item
      Next Item
      mAddNumbers = Sum
   End Property
```

```
Public Property Get AddNumbers()
    AddNumbers = mAddNumbers
End Property

Public Property Let HiNumber(Nums)
    Dim I As Integer
    Dim HiNum As Single
    HiNum = Nums(0)
    For I = 1 To UBound(Nums)
        If HiNum < Nums(I) Then HiNum = Nums(I)
    Next I
    mHiNumber = HiNum
End Property

Public Property Get HiNumber()
    HiNumber = mHiNumber
End Property

'-----from Form1-----
Private Sub Form_Click()
    Dim Nums
    Dim numNew As New Numbers
    Nums = Array(34.55, 65, 87, 12, 33)
    numNew.AddNumbers = Nums
    Print numNew.AddNumbers
    numNew.HiNumber = Nums
    Print numNew.HiNumber
End Sub
```

9.
```
'-----from Smith class-----
Private mGrossPay As Single
Private mHours As Single
Private mRate As Single
Implements Worker

Private Sub Class_Initialize()
    mHours = 43
    mRate = 9.5
    Dim wgNew As New Wage
    mGrossPay = wgNew.CalcWage(mRate, mHours)
End Sub
```

```
Private Property Let Worker_GrossPay(ByVal RHS As Single)
    mGrossPay = RHS
End Property

Private Property Get Worker_GrossPay() As Single
    Worker_GrossPay = mGrossPay
End Property

'-----from Form1-----
Private Sub Form_Click()
    Dim doNew As Smith
    Dim wkNew As Worker
    Set doNew = New Smith
    Set wkNew = New Worker
    Set wkNew = doNew
    Print wkNew.GrossPay
End Sub
```

Print output: 422.75

10.
```
'-----from Die class-----
Event Roll()

Private Sub Class_Initialize()
    RaiseEvent Roll
End Sub

'-----from Form1-----
Private WithEvents mDie As Die

Private Sub Form_Click()
    mDie_Roll    'trigger Roll event
End Sub

Private Sub mDie_Roll()
    Dim Num As Integer
    Randomize
    Num = Fix(Rnd * 6) + 1
        '1 - 6
    Print "You've rolled " & Num
End Sub
```

11.
```
'-----from Die class-----
Event Guess()

Private Sub Class_Initialize()
    RaiseEvent Guess
End Sub


'-----from Form1-----
Dim Num2 As Integer

Private Sub Form_Click()
    mDie_Roll    'triggers an event
    mDie_Guess
    If Num = Num2 Then
        MsgBox "You're right."
    Else
        MsgBox Num2 & " is wrong."
    End If
End Sub


Private Sub mDie_Guess()
    Num2 = InputBox("Enter 1 - 6")
    If Num2 > 6 Or Num2 < 1 Then
        MsgBox "Your number must be in the 1 - 6 range."
        Exit Sub
    End If
End Sub
```

12. Add a standard module to the project. Add a procedure named Sub Main in this module. Put startup code in this procedure. Go to the Project Properties dialog box (Project | Project Properties). The General tab has the Startup Object combo box. Open it and select Sub Main. Click OK to exit. If you now press F5 to run the project, the code in Sub Main will be executed first. If this procedure cannot be found in a standard module, an error will occur. The Project Properties will also open up to let you choose a startup object.

    Use Project | Project Properties. The Project Properties dialog appears. The General tab has the Project Description field. Enter a description here. This description appears in the References dialog box as well as the Object Browser. Users of your components can get a general idea as to what you're up to.

13. It creates a new collection named colX. A For-Next loop adds 10 numbers to the collection. A For Each-Next loop prints the numbers.

14.
```
Private Sub Form_Click()
    Dim I As Integer
    Dim Item1, Item2
    Dim colX As New Collection

    For I = 1 To 9
      colX.Add I
    Next I
    I = 0
    For Each Item1 In colX
        For Each Item2 In colX
        CurrentX = I * 400
            Print Item1 * Item2;
        I = I + 1
        Next Item2
        Print
        I = 0
    Next Item1
End Sub
```

15. It will remove all the existing members in the colX collection. The removal will start from the first until there is nothing left.

16.
```
'----- from Form1 -----
Private Sub Form_Click()
    Dim WeekPay As Single
    Dim wgWage As New Wage

    On Error GoTo ErrTrap
    WeekPay = wgWage.CalcWage(Hours:=41.5, WorkerName:=Jim)
    Print WeekPay / 100
    Exit Sub

ErrTrap:
    MsgBox Err.Description
End Sub
```

```
'----- from Wage class module -----
Enum WorkerNames
    Joe = 1150              '11.50 multiplied by 100
    Jim = 920
    Jill = 1030
End Enum

Public Function CalcWage(Hours As Single, _
WorkerName As Long) As Single
    On Error GoTo ErrTrap

    Dim TotPay As Single

    If Hours < = 40 Then
        TotPay = Hours * WorkerName
    Else
        TotPay = WorkerName * (40 + (Hours - 40) * 1.5)
    End If
    CalcWage = Format(TotPay, "#.00")
    Exit Function

ErrTrap:
    Err.Raise Err.Number, , Err.Description
End Function
```

17.
```
'----- from Module1 -----
Public Type Student
    Name As String
    Test1 As Integer
    Test2 As Integer
    Test3 As Integer
End Type

'----- from Record class module -----
Public Sub ShowRecords(FormX As Form)
    Dim I As Integer
    Dim Sum As Single
    Dim Grades(2) As Student

    Grades(0).Name = "Joel"
    Grades(0).Test1 = 77
```

```
      Grades(0).Test2 = 85
      Grades(0).Test3 = 73
      Grades(1).Name = "Noel"
      Grades(1).Test1 = 88
      Grades(1).Test2 = 80
      Grades(1).Test3 = 83
      Grades(2).Name = "Nicole"
      Grades(2).Test1 = 89
      Grades(2).Test2 = 88
      Grades(2).Test3 = 94

      FormX.Print "Name", "Test1", "Test2", _
      "Test3", "Total", "Average"
      FormX.Print String(65, "=")
      For I = 0 To UBound(Grades)
         With Grades(I)
            FormX.Print .Name,
            FormX.Print .Test1,
            FormX.Print .Test2,
            FormX.Print .Test3,
            Sum = .Test1 + .Test2 + .Test3
            FormX.Print Sum,
            FormX.Print Format(Sum / 3, "0.##")
         End With
      Next I
   End Sub


   '----- from Form1 -----
   Private Sub Form_Click()
      Dim recNew As New Record
      Call recNew.ShowRecords(Form1)
   End Sub



18.
   '----- from Record class module -----
   Sub ShowRecords(FormX)
      Dim I As Integer
      Dim J As Integer
      Dim Sum(1 To 3) As Integer

      Dim colN As New Collection
      Dim colT1 As New Collection
```

```
Dim colT2 As New Collection
Dim colT3 As New Collection
Dim colGrades As New Collection

colN.Add "Joel"
colN.Add "Noel"
colN.Add "Nicole"

colT1.Add 77
colT2.Add 85
colT3.Add 73

colT1.Add 88
colT2.Add 80
colT3.Add 83

colT1.Add 89
colT2.Add 88
colT3.Add 94


colGrades.Add colN
colGrades.Add colT1
colGrades.Add colT2
colGrades.Add colT3

'print 6 lines at left column
FormX.Print "Name"
FormX.Print "Test1"
FormX.Print "Test2"
FormX.Print "Test3"
FormX.Print "Total"
FormX.Print "Average"
FormX.CurrentY = 0
'move print head to top

For I = 1 To colGrades.Count
    FormX.CurrentX = 1200
    'position print head 1200 twips from left
    For J = 1 To colN.Count
        FormX.Print colGrades(I)(J),
        If VarType(colGrades(I)(J)) _
            < > vbString Then
            Sum(J) = Sum(J) + colGrades(I)(J)
```

```
        End If  'add test scores
     Next J
     FormX.Print
  Next I

  FormX.CurrentX = 1200

  For I = 1 To 3
     FormX.Print Sum(I),
  Next I
  FormX.Print

  FormX.CurrentX = 1200
  For I = 1 To 3
     FormX.Print Format(Sum(I) / 3, "#.##"),
  Next I
End Sub

'----- from Form1 -----
Private Sub Form_Click()
  Dim recNew As New Record
  Call recNew.ShowRecords(Form1)
End Sub
```

19.
The calling statement in Form1 can be changed to this:

```
  Call clnCal.PrintOut(Form1, UserDate, Month1, Year1, LastDay)
```

Here you pass a form (Form1 in our example), plus the original arguments.

The sub procedure's header is modified to include the passed form (FormPassed in our example). Inside the procedure, you need to reference this form whenever it is involved.

```
'-----from Calendar1.cls-----
Sub PrintOut(FormPassed, UserDate, Month1, Year1, LastDay)
  Dim I As Integer
  Dim Arr     'variant to store array
  Dim Temp As String
  Dim Gap As Integer  'distance between items
  Dim CY  'get CurrentY
  Dim FirstDay As Integer
```

```
On Error GoTo ErrTrap

FormPassed.AutoRedraw = True
FormPassed.BackColor = vbWhite
FormPassed.Cls
FormPassed.FontName = "arial"
FormPassed.FontSize = 20

FirstDay = WeekDay(UserDate)
'get 1st weekday, 1=sunday


Gap = 600      '600 twips apart
Month1 = Format(UserDate, "mmmm")
'get month text, spelled out
Temp = Month1 & ", " & Year1    'month & year string
FormPassed.CurrentX = (Gap * 6.5 - FormPassed.TextWidth(Temp)) / 2
'get center position of string
FormPassed.Print Temp  'print month/year

FormPassed.FontSize = 10
Arr = Array("Sun", "Mon", "Tue", "Wed", "Thu", "Fri", "Sat")

FormPassed.CurrentY = FormPassed.CurrentY + _
Gap / 6   'move down print head
For I = 0 To 6
   FormPassed.CurrentX = I * Gap
   FormPassed.Print Arr(I);   'print weekday names at top
Next I

FormPassed.Print
CY = FormPassed.CurrentY
FormPassed.Line (0, CY)-(Gap * 6.7, CY)
'draw horizontal line

FormPassed.CurrentX = (FirstDay - 1) * Gap
'set beginning print position based on 1st day of month
For I = 1 To LastDay
   FormPassed.Print I;
   FormPassed.CurrentX = ((FirstDay + I - 1) Mod 7) * Gap
   'set print position for each number
   If (FirstDay + I - 1) Mod 7 = 0 Then FormPassed.Print
   'new line after 7th day
```

```
    Next I
    Exit Sub

ErrTrap:
    MsgBox Err.Description
End Sub
```

20. Change the error trap in each procedure in the class module to the following:

```
    ErrTrap:
     Err.Raise Err.Number, , Err.Description
```

In Form1's Form_Click procedure, you need to change Resume Next to something like the following:

```
    On Error GoTo ErrTrap
```

Then in the ErrTrap area, you need to display the number and description passed by the Err.Raise event.

Normally, when an error occurs in a class module, Visual Basic goes into break mode and highlights the offending line. If you want to trap an error occurring in a class module, you need to right-click the Code window and choose Toggle | Break on Unhandled Errors. After that, an error raised from a class module can be handled from the calling module.

TOPIC

A. Overview
B. A Timer Control
C. UserControl Events and Life Cycles
D. UserControl Methods and Properties
E. Control Interface Wizard
F. A Dice Control
G. Supplying a Bitmap for a Control
H. Coding the Dice Control
I. Handling Events
J. Property Issues
K. Life Cycles Revisited
L. Property Pages
M. Magic Square
N. Bridge Game
O. Clock Control
P. Calendar Control and Control Array

You can use Visual Basic 5 Professional Edition to create ActiveX controls and add them to the Toolbox. These user-created controls can then be added to applications just like any custom control that comes with Visual Basic.

Overview

At the outset, it may be useful to clarify a few terms and connect them together to provide you a bird's-eye view.

Here are the major considerations:

- A **control component** is a compiled file with the **.ocx** extension. It contains one or more **control classes.** Visual Basic users can load a control component by using the **Components** dialog box (Project | Components). After a component file is loaded, one or more controls will become available and their bitmaps will all appear in the Toolbox.

- At authoring time, an author (the one who creates controls) develops an ActiveX Control project. When compiled, this project becomes an **.ocx** file. The project name becomes a **type library** and appears in the Project/Library box of the Object Browser.

- An ActiveX Control project consists of one or more **UserControl** modules. These modules behave like forms. They are saved to ASCII files with the **.ctl** extension. Binary data supplied at design time, such as pictures, are saved to a companion file with the **.ctx** extension—just as their counterparts in a form are saved to a binary file with the **.frx** extension. A .ctl module can be added to any project. Just right-click the Project window and choose Add | Add Files to load it. Its bitmap will appear in the Toolbox. You can then add this control to a form.

- Existing controls can be added to a UserControl module and integrated into a new control. These are known as **constituent controls.** They are **encapsulated** in the UserControl.

- A UserControl module becomes a **control class** like the way a class module becomes a class (see Chapter 1). **Control instances** are derived from this class, similar to the way an object is an instance of a class in an ActiveX code component.

- By default, each control instance is sequentially numbered, just like Command1, Command2, etc. If an author doesn't change the module's default name of UserControl1, it becomes the default base name for each control instance. So the first instance is named UserControl11, second UserControl12, third UserControl13, and so on. This can be confusing. So it's not a good idea to use the default name.

- A control instance cannot have a separate existence. It must be **sited** in (hooked to) a container like a Visual Basic form (or a UserControl). So an author has to be aware of the issues related **siting**.

- A control has three major parts: appearance, interface (methods, properties, and events), and implementation (code). The first two are public, but the last is private.

- In the Visual Basic IDE, a control has two separate life cycles: design time and run time. Only one can exist at any given time. Before the run-time instance is created, the design-time instance is destroyed first. After the run-time instance is destroyed, the design-time instance may come back to life.

If you want to test a control of your own, you can start with a Standard EXE with a typical form and add a UserControl module. The UserControl becomes a control and can be added to the form like any other control. You can run and close the form to see how the control behaves. Such a control can be included in an application you develop and distribute. But it cannot be accessed by other applications.

If you intend to compile the control as a separate unit and thus accessible by other applications, you need to put the UserControl in an ActiveX Control project. To test this control, you need to open a Standard EXE project as a second project in the IDE. The test project can then run and debug the control project.

If you already have another type of project, you can use the Project | Project Properties | General tab to convert it to a control project. Some project and module properties may change—a message will inform you of that.

A Timer Control

We're going to create a timer control to illustrate the concrete steps of control creation. When finished, this control will display the current date/time, updating the time very second.

Follow these steps to create and use this control:

1. Start a Standard EXE project with a default form.

2. Add a UserControl (Project | Add UserControl). A new UserControl designer, like a form designer, is added to the screen. Notice that a new module with the name of UserControl1 is added to the Project window. It's also marked by a distinct icon.

3. Observe the Toolbox. The OLE control is dimmed (that means this control cannot be added to this module). A new icon, also dimmed at this time, is also added. If you point to this new icon, you'll pop up the UserControl1 tooltip.

4. Click the control designer's X button to close it. The two dimmed icons appear normal and are thus enabled.

5. Use the Project window to reopen the control designer window. Notice that two icons in the Toolbox are dimmed again.

6. Use the Properties window to change UserControl1 to CurrentTime. Notice that the new name appears in the Project window and in the designer window's caption. (This change has the same effect as changing a form's name.) Point to the new icon in the Toolbox, and the CurrentTime (the new module name) tooltip will pop up.

7. With the CurrentTime designer having the focus, double-click the Timer control and then the Label control in the Toolbox. This adds two **constituent controls** to the CurrentTime module. This is comparable to adding controls to a form.

8. Place the Label1 control at the top left corner of CurrentTime and stretch it horizontally to about five inches.

9. Adjust CurrentTime's size to slightly larger than Label1. (Timer1 can be placed anywhere because it's invisible at run time.) The result is shown in Figure 2.1.

Figure 2.1   UserControl designer window

10. Add the following code in CurrentTime's Code window:

```
Private Sub UserControl_Initialize()
    Timer1.Interval = 1000
        'set timer interval at 1 sec
    With Label1
        .FontName = "arial"
        .FontSize = 15
        .ForeColor = vbRed
        .BackColor = vbCyan
    End With
End Sub

Private Sub Timer1_Timer()
    Label1.Caption = "Current time: " & Now
```

```
End Sub
```

11. Close CurrentTime's designer window by clicking its X button. The CurrentTime icon in the Toolbox is now enabled and can be used like any other control.

12. Open Form1 and make it visible. Select CurrentTime in the Toolbox by clicking it. Draw the control on Form1. The timer begins to work, as shown in Figure 2.2. The design -time instance, with the default name of CurrentTime1, now begins its life cycle.

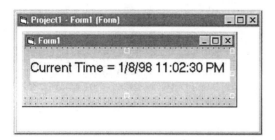

Figure 2.2   The UserControl working at design time

13. Use the Project window to open CurrentTime's designer window. Its icon in the Toolbox is now dimmed. It's control instance on Form1 is also disabled. Hatch lines now cover up the control, and it stops working, as shown in Figure 2.3. So when the UserControl class is activated at design time, its design -time instances are destroyed.

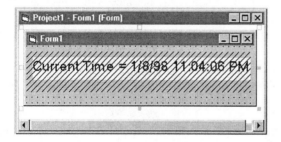

Figure 2.3   UserControl disabled at design time

14. Close the CurrentTime designer window. The instance on Form1 comes alive again. So when the class is disabled at design time, its design -time instances come to life.

15. Press F5 to shift to run mode. The control's run-time cycle begins, as shown in Figure 2.4. Its design -time counterpart is also destroyed.

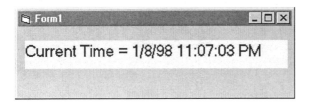

Figure 2.4   UserControl working at run time

16. End run mode by clicking the form's X button or the End icon in the Standard toolbar. The run -time instance is destroyed. The previous state returns. Whether or not the timer comes to life depends on whether the class is active, as demonstrated before.

NOTE   Changing the code in the UserControl's Code window may sometimes destroy the design-time life of the control. In that case, right-click the form (any empty area) hosting the control and choose **Update UserControls** to make the control come to life. This option can always be used to revive a control instance at design time. If the control's designer window is open, this action will also close it.

You can now do a number of things to play with your new control. If you close CurrentTime's designer window, its icon in the Toolbox becomes active and its instance on the form begins a new life. If you open this window, the instance is destroyed and the icon is dimmed. Closing the form's designer window destroys a control instance on that form. Reopening the form makes the instance begin its new life cycle and closes CurrentTime's designer window—if it was open.

If you wish, you can draw multiple control instances on Form1. They will all behave the same way.

Now that you have created a new control, you might want to explore it as you explore any standard or custom control. Select the new control on Form1 and open its Properties window. There are 15 properties here. (In contrast, the CurrentTime module has many more properties.) Notice the default name CurrentTime1. If you add more instances to Form1, the number will change, just like Command1, Command2, and so on.

Double-click CurrentTime1 to open its Code window. Pull down the Procedure list and you'll find four default events here.

If you open the Object Browser, you'll find CurrentTime1 becoming a property member of Form1, just like Text1 or Command1 which you might add to a form.

What if you press F1 after selecting CurrentTime1? Nothing. For the control to respond to F1, you'll need to write a help file and connect it to this control. To provide user help for the control, you need to use the General tab of the **Project Properties** dialog box (Project | Project Properties) to add a description and connect the control to an existing help file.

Examine the Properties window of the CurrentTime UserControl module. You'll find that the **Public** property is set to False. This is the case when you add a UserControl to a Standard EXE project. That makes the UserControl a private member of the project and is thus not accessible to other applications.

What if you change the Public property's value to True? No good. Visual Basic won't let you. Figure 2.5 will appear instead.

Figure 2.5   Changing Public from False to True

What if you want to make a UserControl public? You'll have to open an ActiveX Control project. Doing so will add a new project to the Project window and a UserControl (with its own designer window) to the IDE. Examine this UserControl's Properties window, and you'll find the Public property set to True. What if you change it to False. No problem. This UserControl will simply become a private member of the project and thus not accessible to other applications. So an ActiveX Control project may have multiple UserControls, some of them may be public (accessible to another application) and some private (accessible only from inside the project).

If you started out with a Standard EXE project, you can use the Project | Project Properties | General tab to change to a control project. In that case, the startup object will be changed to Sub Main, and a UserControl module's Public property can be changed to True or False.

NOTE   Creating a control requires an extra stage. Normally we talk about design time and run time. Now we need to add **authoring time**. That's when you create a control. When you test a control which you are authoring, you put it in design mode and run mode to observe its behavior. So creating a control can involve you in all the three stages..

UserControl Events and Life Cycles

The previous section amply demonstrates that a UserControl object has two life cycles, one at design time and the other at run time. The two don't coexist. Before one begins, the other has to end. As one replaces the other, a number of events are triggered.

To see the two life cycles of a UserControl, try the following demonstration. Basically we want to see what events are triggered on what occasions.

1. Start a Standard EXE project. Add UserControl1 to the project. Change its BorderStyle from None to Fixed Single (this is to distinguish the control from the hosting form).

2. Add the following code to UserControl1. The event procedure templates can be pulled down from the Procedure box. The last one is a general procedure to be called by all the others to show a counter number and the event triggered.

```
Dim mintNum As Integer

Private Sub UserControl_Initialize()
    GetNum "Initialize"
End Sub

Private Sub UserControl_InitProperties()
    GetNum "InitProperties"
End Sub

Private Sub UserControl_ReadProperties(PropBag As _
PropertyBag)
    GetNum "ReadProperties"
End Sub

Private Sub UserControl_Terminate()
```

```
    GetNum "Terminate"
End Sub

Private Sub UserControl_WriteProperties(PropBag As _
PropertyBag)
    GetNum "WriteProperties"
End Sub

Private Sub GetNum(Msg As String)
    mintNum = mintNum + 1
    Debug.Print mintNum, Msg
End Sub
```

3. Close the UserControl's designer window by clicking the X button. The control's icon is now available in the Toolbox.

4. Draw the control on Form1. Two lines are written to the Immediate window. (Open the Immediate window if it's closed.)

5. Close Form1 by clicking its X button. Two more lines are written. The Terminate event is triggered.

6. Use the Project window to reopen the form. This triggers two events.

7. Press F5 to run Form1. This triggers three events.

Figure 2.6   A control's life cycles

8. Unload the form by clicking the X button. The same events are triggered. The results are shown in Figure 2.6. (The lines without numbers are comments added to clarify the lines produced by the code.)

Each time the control begins its life, number 1 begins to appear and the event that occurs is always **Initialize**. The highest number in each cycle indicates the total number of events triggered, and the last event is always **Terminate**.

Notice that the control is terminated before it begins a new cycle. Properties are read on several occasions, but are written only when the form is closed at design time (when the design-time instance is about to be destroyed). We'll cover the property-related issues later in this chapter.

A UserControl has **Paint**, **Show**, and **Resize** events as a form does. They behave in similar ways and so may be triggered on different occasions. When the container is shown or repainted, the control's corresponding events are triggered. When the container is resized, the control's Resize event is also triggered.

The UserControl module sports 32 events. these can be pulled down from the Procedure combo box in its Code window. Many of them are shared with the form module, including some of those discussed above. These are unique:

AccessKeyPress
AmbientChanged
InitProperties
Hide
ReadProperties
WriteProperties

The Hide event occurs when the control's Visible property is set to False. The others are more significant and will be discussed in later sections.

UserControl Methods and Properties

A UserControl greatly resembles a form. A UserControl is a container for constituent controls just as a form is a container for Visual Basic controls. Both also serve as output devices, allowing you to output text lines and graphical drawings. So most of the Form methods, such as Print, Line, Circle, etc., are also available for a UserControl. A UserControl has no border, so Width and ScaleWidth have the same value, just as Height and ScaleHeight. These property values don't change even if you change the **BorderStyle**'s property value from None to Fixed Single. Also, the Show, Hide, and Move methods are not available.

A form has some unique properties which a UserControl doesn't have. A UserControl has quite a few properties which a form doesn't have. These and their default values are listed below:

AccessKeys	(blank)
Alignable	False
CanGetFocus	True
ControlContainer	False
DefaultCancel	False
EditAtDesignTime	False
ForwardFocus	False
InvisibleAtRuntime	False
PropertyPages	(None)
Public	False
ToolboxBitmap	(None)

A UserControl instance you add to a form has a **TabIndex** value just like other controls added to the same form. If the UserControl contains constituent controls, their TabIndex values also play a role at run time. These values determine which object will get the focus when you press the Tab key repeatedly.

If you don't want your control to get the focus, set the **CanGetFocus** to False. This is not allowed if you already added to it a constituent control capable of receiving the focus. After CanGetFocus is set to False, all the controls in the Toolbox that are capable of receiving the focus will be dimmed, thus not allowing you to add them to the UserControl.

You can use one or more access keys to let the user set the focus on your control at run time. To set access keys, go to the **AccessKeys** field in the UserControl's Properties window and type the letters. Suppose you type CT (uppercase or lowercase) in our previous CurrentTime control. In that case, we want to press Alt+C or Alt+T to access our control. In addition, CanGetFocus has to remain True and **ForwardFocus** remain False. When all these conditions exist, pressing an access key moves the focus to the UserControl at run time (or to the first constituent control capable of receiving the focus); this also triggers the **AccessKeyPress** event of the UserControl. Pressing Tab after that shifts the focus to each control of the next tab order.

If the value of ForwardFocus is True or if CanGetFocus is set to False in the above scenarios, pressing an access key moves the focus instead to the control having the next tab order after the UserControl. This pattern mimics the way you can use a label control to access the control having the next tab order. In this scenario, pressing Tab can't access the UserControl. But you can still click the UserControl to set the focus on it.

You can use the **DefaultCancel** property to give your control Default and Cancel properties. If it's set to True at authoring time, a control instance will have these properties appearing in its Properties window at design time. Users can then designate your control or another control to have the Default or Cancel property.

You are probably familiar with the concept of **Default** and **Cancel** properties. A command button has these properties. Normally when a command button has the focus, pressing Enter will execute its Click procedure. If the focus is on another object that is not a command button, a text box for example, pressing Enter will not affect the button. But if you set its Default property to True, pressing Enter in this situation will execute its Click procedure. If its Cancel property is set to True, pressing Esc will do the same thing. If both are set to True, an unlikely scenario, the same procedure will be executed by pressing Esc or Enter. On the other hand, only one button in a container can have its Cancel or Default set to True.

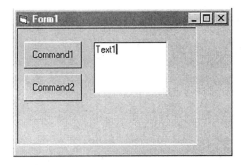

Figure 2.7   Testing the DefaultCancel property

This is a confusing issue because so many factors are involved. It calls for a concrete example. Suppose UserControl1 has three constituent controls: Command1, Command2, and Text1 (whose MultiLine is set to True); and the following procedures are in place:

```
Private Sub Command1_Click()
    MsgBox "Command1"
End Sub

Private Sub Command2_Click()
    MsgBox "Command2"
End Sub
```

```
Private Sub UserControl_AccessKeyPress(KeyAscii As Integer)
    MsgBox KeyAscii     'show code of pressed key
End Sub
```

Figure 2.7 shows an instance of this control at run time. If the focus is in Text1, pressing Enter inserts a carriage return in the text box.

Suppose you now set the UserControl's **DefaultCancel** to True. Doing the same thing as before will execute the **AccessKeyPress** procedure.

Suppose you now change Command1's Default to True and Command2's Cancel to True at authoring time. Pressing Enter at run time will now execute Command1_Click and pressing Esc will execute Command2_Click. To insert a carriage return in the text box, you'll need to press Ctrl+Enter (instead of Enter alone).

To execute UserControl_AccessKeyPress in this last scenario, you'll need to add an access key to the UserControl, as described earlier. After that, pressing the access key will execute this procedure. If this procedure doesn't exist, the constituent control with the first TabIndex property gets the focus. This will also trigger the **EnterFocus** event. (When the focus moves away from your control, the **ExitFocus** or **LostFocus** event may be triggered depending on whether there are constituent members.)

If a control's Default or Cancel property is set to True, another control in the same container cannot have the same True property. Suppose you now add Command3 to Form1, in addition to the previous UserControl instance. You have now two objects on Form1. Changing one's Default/Cancel to True will change the other's Default/Cancel to False (if it was True). If your control has the True value, no other control can have the same thing.

Suppose you now add Text2 to Form1, thus having three objects. What happens if you press Enter when the focus is inside Text2? If Command3 has its Default set to True, then its Click procedure will be executed. If your control has the Default instead, then its Default member's Click will be executed instead.

The **EditAtDesignTime** property, when set to True, adds the **Edit** option to the popup menu. This option appears when the control is active at design time and you right-click the control. Choosing Edit makes the control simulate its run-time identity. For example, if the control contains a UserControl_Click procedure, clicking the control at this time will execute that procedure.

The other properties are obvious. **Public** determines the scope of the control, as explained in a previous section. If you set **Alignable** to True, the control will have the Align property to let the user set its alignment. **ControlContainer**, if set to True, allows your control to contain other controls, like a form or UserControl. **InvisibleAtRuntime** makes the control invisible like the timer control. **ToolboxBitmap** lets you load a picture to represent this control, thus replacing the default bitmap. **PropertyPage** will be explained in another section below.

Control Interface Wizard

A control has an **interface** consisting of events, methods, and properties. We can add these manually, as we'll demonstrate later. You can also use the **Control Interface Wizard** to do some preliminary work for you. This is demonstrated here.

After the CurrentTime control is in place as explained before, follow these steps to use the ActiveX Control Interface Wizard:

1. Choose Add-In | ActiveX Control Interface Wizard. (If the wizard does not appear, choose Add-In | Add-In Manager, check the wizard in the list, and click OK.)

2. The initial dialog box appears. Read it and click Next. The initial dialog box (Introduction) has this to say:

    The ActiveX Control Interface Wizard helps you perform the following steps in creating an ActiveX control in Visual Basic:

    - Defining the interface (properties, methods, events)

    - Creating the underlying code for the interface

    Note: Before you begin, you must have added all the interface elements that make up the control's appearance.

3. The Select Interface Members dialog box (Figure 2.8) appears. Here you can move members back and forth by selecting them and clicking one of the arrow buttons (> or < for selected ones; > > or < < for all). For this demonstration, click < < to move all to the left; that will make the right box empty. Then select BackColor and Click from the left box and click > to move them to the right. The right box now has only two items.

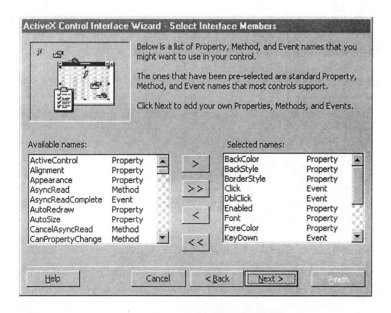

Figure 2.8   The Select Interface Members dialog box

4. Click Next. The Create Custom Interface Members dialog box appears. The middle list box named My Custom Members shows all the existing custom members (your own public events and procedures). To create a new one, click the New button. The Add Custom Member dialog box (Figure 2.9) appears. After clicking OK, your new entry is added to the existing list. After that, you can edit or delete your entries.

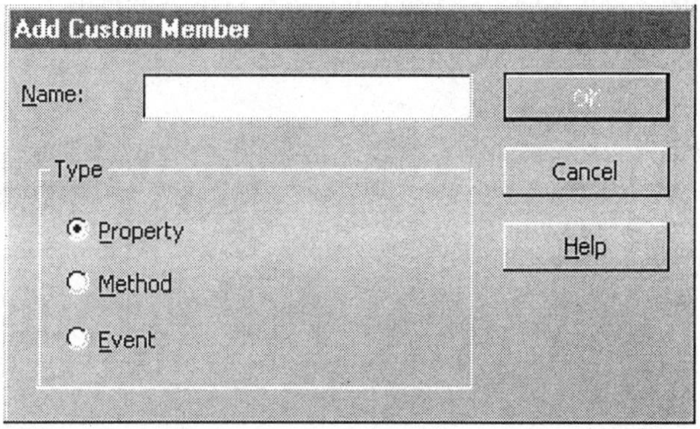

Figure 2.9   The Add Custom Member dialog box

5. The Set Mapping dialog box (Figure 2.10) appears. The two members we've selected appear in the left box. You are now asked to connect them to appropriate controls. Select BackColor in the left box. Then click the down arrow in the Control box and select Label1 from the list of available controls. This maps BackColor to Label1, one of the constituent controls we have added. Finally, map Click to UserControl. This will make the UserControl (any blank area) respond to clicking at run time. The area covered up by a constituent control will not respond to clicking in this arrangement.

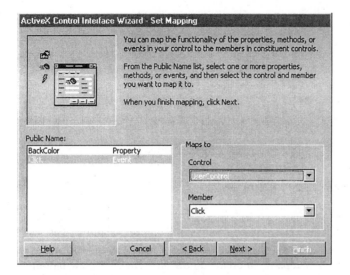

Figure 2.10   The Set Mapping dialog box

6. Click Next. The Finished dialog box appears. You can check View Summary Report if you want to view (and optionally save) a text report. For now, uncheck the check box and click Finish.

7. Go to the UserControl's Code window to see what the wizard has wrought. The added code is shown below. The original procedures are sandwiched by new declarations at the top and new procedures at the bottom.

```
'Event Declarations:
Event Click() 'MappingInfo=UserControl,UserControl,-1,Click

    'the original procedures
    'remain intact here
```

```
Private Sub UserControl_Click()
    RaiseEvent Click
End Sub

'WARNING! DO NOT REMOVE OR MODIFY THE FOLLOWING COMMENTED
LINES!
'MappingInfo=Label1,Label1,-1,BackColor
Public Property Get BackColor() As OLE_COLOR
    BackColor = Label1.BackColor
End Property

Public Property Let BackColor(ByVal New_BackColor As OLE_COLOR)
    Label1.BackColor() = New_BackColor
    PropertyChanged "BackColor"
End Property

'Load property values from storage
Private Sub UserControl_ReadProperties(PropBag As PropertyBag)
    Label1.BackColor = PropBag.ReadProperty("BackColor",
&H8000000F)
End Sub

'Write property values to storage
Private Sub UserControl_WriteProperties(PropBag As PropertyBag)
    Call PropBag.WriteProperty("BackColor", Label1.BackColor,
&H8000000F)
End Sub
```

The **Event** Click( ) declaration makes Click a new member of the CurrentTime1 instance. If you go to Form1's Code window and pull down CurrentTime1 from the Object box, you can pull down the events from the Procedure box. Click is now added to the original four. If you comment out this declaration, this event will be removed from Form1 where CurrentTime1 is sited.

If the Event Click ( ) declaration is commented out or if there is no **RaiseEvent** Click statement, then clicking CurrentTime1 at run time does nothing. And CurrentTime1_Click becomes a general procedure belonging to Form1.

After going through the above steps, the BackColor property now appears in CurrentTime1's Properties window. You can now change the default color (set in the UserControl module) to a new one, and it will persist at design time and run time.

You can also write code for the raised Click event, such as the following:

```
Private Sub CurrentTime1_Click()
    CurrentTime1.BackColor = vbWhite
End Sub
```

If you now click the CurrentTime1 control (in any area not covered up by a constituent control) at run time, its background color will be changed to white.

The property procedures require much more attention. We'll return to this issue in another section below.

Notice the warning message in the code listing. It tells you not to erase the MappingInfo line. It shows how objects and properties are connected. If you go back to the wizard to make changes, the information here is used to present the previous settings for you to make changes.

If you want the wizard to start from the beginning, erase all the additional items and start from step 1 above.

A Dice Control

Besides using the wizard as shown above, we can manually add interface elements. Before we do that, we intend to create a dice control first. And then we'll add events, methods, and properties. This arrangement lets us use concrete examples to illustrate how to add interface elements to a control.

The dice control we intend to create will show a visual object that has a number of dots ranging from one to six. Users of this control can add it to a project to simulate dice rolling.

The creation of the dice control follows these steps:

1. Add UserControl1 to a Standard EXE project. Change the name to **Dice**.

2. Add Picture1 to the Dice module. Make the box square. Change its Name to picDie and Index to 0. (We intend to create a control array of picture boxes; it is easier to maneuver than individual controls.)

3. Copy the picture box to the Clipboard and paste it into the Dice module five times. This creates a **design-time control array** of the picture box, each with an index ranging from 0 to 5. So their names become picDie(0) to picDie(5).

4. Move each box to a different location, such as shown in Figure 2.11.

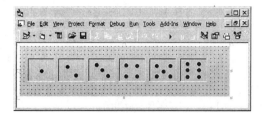

Figure 2.11   Six dice in the Dice UserControl module

5. Add Shape1 (Shape control) inside picDie(0). Change its Shape property to Circle. Adjust the size and move it to the center as shown. Change its Name to shpDot and its Index to 0. Its Name thus becomes shpDot(0).

6. Copy shpDot(0) to the Clipboard. Paste two copies to picDie(1), three copies to picDie(2), and so on. At the end, there are 21 copies ranging from shpDot(0) to shpDot(20).

7. Stack up the copies as shown in Figure 2.12. This will reduce the size of the UserControl. You can stack them in any order. The one you want the user to see should be on top.

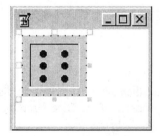

Figure 2.12   The six dice are stacked up

Supplying a Bitmap for a Control

We need a picture to visually represent our control. When a control is added to the Toolbox, this picture lets the user identify the control just by looking at it. Otherwise, the user will have to point to the control in order to pop up its name, which is the Name property of the UserControl module given by the author.

To supply a bitmap for the Toolbox, you can use a UserControl module's **ToolboxBitmap** property to load a bitmap (but not icon or metafile) file. You can also use Windows Paint to draw and save a bitmap, and then use the ToolboxBitmap property to enter it into the Properties window. But its file size tends to be huge (300KB and up).

Another solution is to use graphics methods such as Line and Circle statements to draw a picture and then use the **SavePicture** statement to save the resulting drawing to a bitmap file. The following procedure will do just that:

```
Private Sub Command1_Click()
    Dim PB As PictureBox

    Set PB = Picture1
    PB.AutoRedraw = True
        'needed to save picture
    PB.FillStyle = 0      'solid fill for circle

    PB.Circle (PB.ScaleWidth / 4, _
    PB.ScaleHeight / 4), 500      'top left dot

    PB.Circle (PB.ScaleWidth / 2, _
    PB.ScaleHeight / 2), 500      'middle dot

    PB.Circle (PB.ScaleWidth * 0.75, _
    PB.ScaleHeight * 0.75), 500 'bottom right dot

    SavePicture PB.Image, "Dice.bmp"
End Sub
```

This will draw three dots in a picture box (Figure 2.13) and then save the picture to disk a file named Dice.bmp. After that, use the ToolboxBitmap property of the Dice UserControl module to open the file. It will appear in the Toolbox (Figure 2.14).

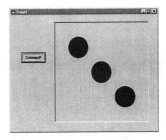

Figure 2.13   Drawing and saving a bitmap

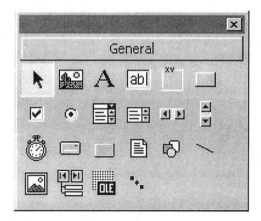

Figure 2.14   Using a custom bitmap for a control

Coding the Dice Control

We now need to add interface elements to the Dice control so that the events, methods, and properties will do something when the control is used at design time and run time. You could use the wizard as shown earlier. Here we intend to do it manually.

The Dice module needs to provide the mechanism of showing the die that is requested. The code is shown below:

```
'-----Dice.vbp-----
'-----from Dice module-----//Listing 3//
Private mintDieNum As Integer

Public Property Let DieNum(ByVal Num As Integer)
    Call Hide
    mintDieNum = Num + 1
        'show die number
    picDie(Num).Visible = True
        'make that die visible
End Property

Public Property Get DieNum() As Integer
    DieNum = mintDieNum
        'current die number
        '1 higher than index number
End Property

Private Sub Hide()
```

```
    Dim I As Integer

    For I = 0 To 5
        'make all dice invisible
        picDie(I).Visible = False
    Next I
End Sub
```

You can now use the control. After adding Dice1 to Form1, the #6 die will appear. The same thing happens when you add Dice2 or Dice3. At the beginning of run time, the same number will also appear. If you want the object to be invisible at run time, change the Dice module's **InvisibleAtRuntime** property from default False to True.

If you want the control to show no number at design time as well, you need to add code to the Initialize procedure, such as the following:

```
Private Sub UserControl_Initialize()
    Call Hide
End Sub
```

This will call the Hide procedure and make each member in the picDie control array invisible at both design time and run time.

To show two dice, add Dice1 and Dice2 to the form and write the following procedure:

```
'-----from Form1-----
Private Sub Form_Click()
    Dim Num1 As Integer
    Dim Num2 As Integer

    Randomize
    Num1 = Fix(Rnd * 6)
        '0 - 5 random number
    Dice1.DieNum = Num1
        'call Property Let DieNum to assign a new num
    Num2 = Fix(Rnd * 6)
    Dice2.DieNum = Num2
        '2nd die
    Caption = Dice1.DieNum & "+" & Dice2.DieNum
        'call Property Get DieNum to read nums
End Sub
```

In this arrangement, random numbers are generated in the Form1_Click procedure. These numbers are passed to the Property Let procedure to display the desired dice and hide the rest.

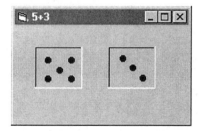

Figure 2.15   Two dice with random numbers

Form1's caption also shows the two random numbers (Figure 2.15). We could have used the random numbers generated in the Form_Click procedure; that would have speeded up execution. Instead, we are here demonstrating how to pass a value to the Property Get procedure to read a property value.

Handling Events

If you are confused as to how to add an interface element, use the wizard to provide the skeleton code. The wizard can be used again and again when you want to add a new element. New procedures may be added, and old ones may be commented out depending on your new selections in various dialog boxes. The wizard won't do much for a sub or function procedure. It's most helpful for events and property procedures.

To demonstrate how to raise events so that your control's users can trigger them, follow these steps (after you get the wizard going as explained earlier):

1. In the Select Interface Members dialog box, select only the Click event.

2. In the Create Custom Interface Members, click the New button. Enter Roll in the Name box and select Event (Figure 2.16). If you want to make changes after clicking OK, click the Edit button to bring back this dialog box.

3. In the Set Mapping dialog box, connect both the Click and Roll events to the UserControl object.

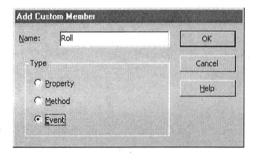

Figure 2.16   Adding a custom member

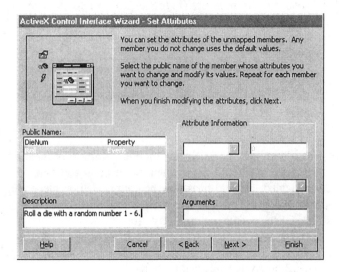

Figure 2.17   Setting member attributes

4. In the Set Attributes dialog box, enter a description for the Roll event (Figure 2.17). This description is visible in the Object Browser, so the user of you compiled control can see what you're up to. This string can also be entered and edited in the **Procedure Attributes** dialog box (Tools | Procedure Attributes; Figure 2.18). The wizard may enter additional strings here (check the Click procedure). Chapter 3 will provide more details about control attributes.

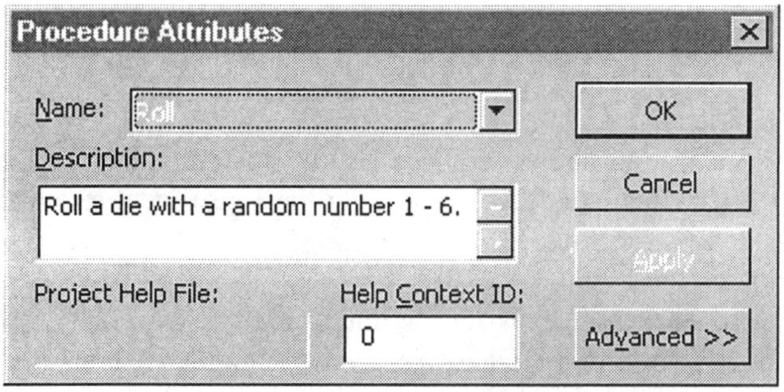

Figure 2.18   The Procedure Attributes dialog box

The above steps will add the following code to the UserControl module's Code window:

```
Event Click()  'MappingInfo=UserControl,UserControl,-1,Click
Event Roll()

Private Sub UserControl_Click()
    RaiseEvent Click
End Sub
```

If you decide not to go through the above steps, you can manually enter the above lines in the Code window. If you want to add descriptions, use the Procedure Attributes dialog box from the Tools menu.

The **Event** keyword has the Public scope. Adding Public is redundant but self-documenting. Adding Private will lead to an error. The Event keyword tells Visual Basic that this is an event, just as you use Sub, Function, or Property to declare another type of procedure.

The **RaiseEvent** statement is used to communicate with the user. It makes the specified event, Click in our example, available to an instance of the control class. When the user of an instance of this control, such as Dice1, clicks that object, then Dice1_Click event occurs. A developer using your control can put code in the Dice1_Click procedure to do something in response to the user clicking Dice1.

After adding the above code, either manually or through the wizard, go to Form1's Code window and see what has happened. If you select Dice1 in the Object box and then pull down the list from the Procedure box, you'll find two new events here. Our events, Click and Roll, are added to the original four events. If you now click the Click event, the following template will appear. A developer using the control can now add code to respond to the control being clicked.

```
Private Sub Dice1_Click()

End Sub
```

If you comment out an Event declaration line in the Dice UserControl module, the related event will disappear from Form1's Code window. If you omit the RaiseEvent statement, the specified event is not available at run time.

In our original Dice control, a random number is sent by the user from the Form_Click procedure. The following public method in the Dice UserControl module can replace the Form_Click procedure and the properties called by it:

```
Public Sub RollDie()
    Dim Num As Integer

    Randomize
    Call Hide    'hide all dice
    Num = Fix(Rnd * 6)
    picDie(Num).Visible = True
        'show new die
End Sub
```

We can now take advantage of the raised events. The following procedures, added to Form1, serve as examples:

```
Private Sub cmdRoll_Click()
    Dice1_Click
    Dice2_Click
End Sub

Private Sub Dice1_Click()
    Dice1.RollDie
End Sub

Private Sub Dice2_Click()
    Dice2.RollDie
End Sub
```

Figure 2.19   Rolling two dice

We have now added a command button (named cmdRoll and with &Roll as its caption). When the Roll button is clicked, it calls two event procedures, namely Dice1_Click and Dice2_Click. Each, in turn, calls a public method in the Dice UserControl module. The result is shown in Figure 2.19.

You can also click each control instance at run time to trigger the Click event to roll that particular die. There is a problem with this. If you click the control outside the large picture box, it will work just fine. But if you click the middle part occupied by the original picture box, the control instance's Click property is not triggered, so nothing will happen.

To remedy this situation, add the following code to the Dice module. The first line should be placed in the Declarations section. The procedure can be placed anywhere else. After you select the picDie object in the Object box, the Click procedure is available in the Procedure box.

```
Public Event picDie()

Private Sub picDie_Click(Index As Integer)
    RaiseEvent Click
End Sub
```

If you now run the program again, clicking each control, including inside a picture box, will work well. The only exception is when you aim the pointer at a tiny dot inside a picture box. That may not trigger the Click event of either the control or the picture box inside it.

Property Issues

Have you examined the Properties window of an instance of the control you have created? You may be surprised to find a list of properties which you have done nothing to add. These include Name, Left, Top, Visible, etc.

Each control instance is automatically endowed with an object known as the **Extender** object. This object is extended by and made available to the control by the container where the control is sited. So different containers may extend different numbers of available interface elements. As an object, the Extender comes with its own events, methods, and properties. Use the online help to find Extender, and you'll find more details.

After you add Dice1 (in our previous examples) to Form1, the Properties window shows Dice1's design time **Extender properties**, plus any public property procedures you may have added to the Dice UserControl module. These are design time properties that a developer can use the Properties window to change.

NOTE   Your custom properties are available only when the control instance is active at design time. They are unavailable when the instance is disabled (when the control designer is open). Extender properties, on the other hand, are available on both occasions.

There are also run-time-only Extender properties as well. These will pop up when you type the object name (Dice1 in our example), followed by a dot. The list here is slightly different from the design-time counterpart. The major run-time properties include Container, Parent, and Object.

Extender events are easy to identify—they appear in the Code window's Procedure box. After selecting the name of a control instance in the Procedure box, clicking the down arrow in the Procedure box pulls down a list of events. There are four Extender events automatically added without your doing anything. The events you have used the Event keyword to declare are also shown here.

The interface elements not included in the Extender object must be added by the author. We've added custom methods, events, and properties in previous sections. Custom properties, however, require more elaboration. Because users can change property values at design time, your control needs to respond by implementing the specified change and save the value for later use.

If a property is included in the Extender object, you need not do anything unusual. The changes made at design time will be available at run time and the next design time. For example, if you change a control instance's Name property from Dice1 to MyDice, this new name is available at run time. It will still be available when you return from run time to design time.

On the other hand, your custom properties need a lot more care. Suppose you have at authoring time implemented the BackColor property, which is not part of the Extender object. You can change this property at design time, and the change will take effect at design time. Suppose you then switch to run mode. The change is gone, and the default value returns. When you now return to design mode, your change doesn't return. To make your change persistent, you need some elaborate coding.

How do you implement the BackColor property? You can add the following code in a UserControl module:

```
Public Property Get BackColor() As OLE_COLOR
    BackColor = UserControl.BackColor
```

```
End Property

Public Property Let BackColor(ByVal NewColor As OLE_COLOR)
    UserControl.BackColor = NewColor
    PropertyChanged "BackColor"
End Property
```

Why **OLE_COLOR**? It's a data type. After you type As in the above procedures and press the spacebar, a list of options will pop up. The list includes OLE_COLOR. Using this data type will make your life easier. The resulting Properties window will provide the normal Visual Basic services. When your BackColor is selected, a down arrow will appear. Clicking it will display the default color palette where you can choose a new color.

In the above arrangement, when a control instance is active at design time (by adding a new instance or by closing the control designer window), the Property Get procedure is executed. Its Properties window shows the BackColor property reflecting the value read from the Property Get procedure.

When the user makes a change in the Properties window, the Property Let procedure is triggered. The selected value is assigned, thus actually changing the control instance's color. Then the **PropertyChanged** method is executed to save the change. This method is necessary if you want Visual Basic to coordinate other related changes and to use the WriteProperty method (see below) to save changes for later use.

NOTE   To defend your control, it's a good idea to set up an error trap in each property procedure. If the user supplies an unacceptable value at design time, the trap will deflect it and gracefully exit. The simplest way is to add this line at the beginning of the procedure:

```
On Error Resume Next
```

We can use this mechanism to alter the properties of constituent controls. Suppose we want to let the user change the picture box's BackColor property. Change the Property Let procedure as follows:

```
Public Property Let BackColor(ByVal NewColor As OLE_COLOR)
    Dim I As Integer
    For I = 0 To picDie.Count - 1
        picDie(I).BackColor = NewColor
    Next I
    PropertyChanged "BackColor"
End Property
```

After making the code change, changing the BackColor property of a control instance at design time will instead change the color of the picture boxes inside the control.

What if you want to let the user change the color of the dots in a die? Use the following code:

```
Public Property Get ForeColor() As OLE_COLOR
    ForeColor = UserControl.ForeColor
End Property

Public Property Let ForeColor(ByVal NewColor As OLE_COLOR)
    Dim I As Integer
    For I = 0 To shpDot.Count - 1
        shpDot(I).FillColor = NewColor
        shpDot(I).BorderStyle = 0
    Next I
    UserControl.ForeColor = NewColor
        'change color in ForeColor panel
        'in the Properties window
    PropertyChanged "ForeColor"
End Property
```

The code will add the ForeColor property to the Properties window. If you now change this property of a control instance, you will actually change each dot's FillColor and BorderStyle properties.

Do you know what will happen if you have only the above Property Get/Let procedures? The color changes made at design time will take effect immediately, but they will not stay. If you shift to run mode, they will disappear. They won't reappear when you return to design time. To make the changes persist, you need to do more.

To use code to maneuver custom properties, you need to use three items: **WriteProperty** method, **ReadProperty** method, and **PropertyBag** object. You use WriteProperty to write changes to the PropertyBag object. Then you need to use ReadProperty to read the values saved to PropertyBag.

The WriteProperty method follows this syntax:

```
ObjectName.WriteProperty(Name, Value[, DefaultValue])
```

The ReadProperty method follows this syntax:

```
VarName = ObjectName.ReadProperty(Name[, DefaultValue])
```

At the right moment, a popup tip in the Code window will show you the syntax.

We are going to implement the ForeColor property for the Dice control. The purpose is to let the user change the color of the dots inside a die. The procedures below will then save and apply the change at both design time and run time.

```
'-----from Dice module-----
Private mFColor As Long
    'module-level, default ForeColor

Private Sub UserControl_InitProperties()
    'triggered when each new control instance
    'is first sited in the container;
    'sets default color for each Dice instance
    Dim I As Integer
    For I = 0 To shpDot.Count - 1
        shpDot(I).FillColor = vbRed
        shpDot(I).BorderStyle = 0
    Next I
    mFColor = vbRed
    ForeColor = mFColor
        'call Property Let ForeColor
        'set red in Properties window
End Sub

Private Sub UserControl_WriteProperties(PropBag As PropertyBag)
    'called when design-time instance is about
    'to be destroyed
   PropBag.WriteProperty "ForeColor", ForeColor
End Sub

Private Sub UserControl_ReadProperties(PropBag As PropertyBag)
    On Error Resume Next
    ForeColor = PropBag.ReadProperty("ForeColor",mFColor)
    'call Property Let ForeColor and pass vbRed
End Sub
```

If you use the wizard to map the three property-related events to the UserControl, the following code will be added to the UserControl's Code window:

```
Event InitProperties()
'MappingInfo=UserControl,UserControl,-1,InitProperties
Event WriteProperties(PropBag As PropertyBag)
'MappingInfo=UserControl,UserControl,-1,WriteProperties
Event ReadProperties(PropBag As PropertyBag)
'MappingInfo=UserControl,UserControl,-1,ReadProperties

Private Sub UserControl_WriteProperties(PropBag As PropertyBag)
    RaiseEvent WriteProperties(PropBag)
End Sub

Private Sub UserControl_ReadProperties(PropBag As PropertyBag)
    RaiseEvent ReadProperties(PropBag)
End Sub
```

After the code is added, the three property events will become available from Form1's Code window. A developer can then write code to respond to these events.

With these new procedures added, color changes at design time will persist at both run time and design time.

NOTE   You can set a breakpoint in each procedure to see which event is triggered at various points of a control instance's lifetime.

Your control may want to take advantage of **ambient properties** provided by Visual Basic or by another container. By keeping your control's properties, such as BackColor, in sync with the container, your control may behave or appear more harmoniously with the container. Changing an ambient property triggers the **AmbientChanged** event. For example, changing the host form's BackColor property at design time will trigger the UserControl_AmbientChanged procedure. The code in this procedure can do something in response. The following procedure will change all the control instances on the form to have the same newly changed background color:

```
Private Sub UserControl_AmbientChanged(PropertyName As String)
    BackColor = Parent.BackColor
End Sub
```

These ambient properties belong to the **AmbientProperties** object. They are visible in the Object Browser. If you open the VBRUN library and select AmbientProperties, 16 members will appear, as shown in Figure 2.20.

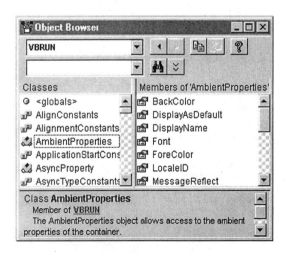

Figure 2.20   The ambient properties

The same list also pops up after you type the following in the UserControl module's Code window:

```
UserControl.Ambient.
```

The last item in the list is **UserMode**. This property has the Boolean value of True when the end user is using your control. That means UserMode has the True value in run mode. When the developer is using it at design time, UserMode has the False value.

Life Cycles Revisited

This section recaps the multiple life cycles of a control. When a control instance is placed on a form, the following events occur. Besides executing any existing pertinent procedures such as UserControl_Initialize, they also trigger a number of related events.

Placing an Instance on a Form:

Initialize   Constituent controls are created; the control is not yet sited.

InitProperties   Sets default property values; the control is sited on the form, so the Extender and AmbientProperties objects become available to the developer.

Resize, Show   Constituent controls are adjusted and displayed; writing and painting to the UserControl occur.

The control instance is now available for the developer to manipulate, such as resizing and setting properties. Then the developer presses F5 to put the control instance in run mode. It now begins its run-time cycle. The following events occur.

From Design Mode To Run Mode:

WriteProperties   Property values set at design time are saved in RAM (this is an in-memory copy of the form file, not a disk file).

Terminate   The control is unsited; constituent controls are destroyed; the control itself is then destroyed.

Initialize   The constituent controls are created; the control is not yet sited.

ReadProperties   The in-memory properties are read; the control's run-time instance is sited on the form; the Extender and AmbientProperties objects become available.

Resize, Show   Constituent controls are adjusted and displayed; writing and painting to the UserControl occur.

When the developer closes the form and returns to design time, the following events occur.

From Run Mode To Design Mode:

Terminate   The run-time instance is destroyed; the properties set by code at run time are discarded.

Initialize   The design-time instance is created but not sited.

ReadProperties   The in-memory properties are read and restored; the control is sited and the Extender and AmbientProperties objects are available.

Resize, Show   The same as described earlier.

Closing a form at design time will trigger the Terminate event to destroy the design-time instance. It also triggers the WriteProperties event if properties have been changed; this event doesn't happen if there is no property change. Reopening the form will trigger Initialize and ReadProperties.

Compiling an application containing your control will trigger ReadProperties and WriteProperties events in a pattern similar to the above scenarios. So does executing the compiled application.

Property Pages

You can endow your control with **property pages**. This will add a **Custom property** to the control's Properties window, together with a typical ellipsis. When this ellipsis is clicked, the Property Pages dialog box opens. Users can then click a tab to open a page to set properties. This provides an alternative to adding properties in the Properties window.

To add a property page, you need to add a **PropertyPage** module to the current project. If you want to supply multiple pages, you need to deploy multiple such modules. These pages will be automatically grouped into a tabbed dialog. Follow these steps:

1. Add a PropertyPage module by choosing Project | Add PropertyPage. PropertyPage1 is added to the current project. Change the Name and Caption properties. The caption will appear as the tab caption of the page.

2. Design the page by adding controls and writing code.

3. Repeat steps 1 and 2 if you want more pages.

4. Open the UserControl designer and select the UserControl (not a constituent control).

5. Open the UserControl's Properties window and click the ellipsis (...) in the **PropertyPages** property. The **Connect Property Pages** dialog box appears (Figure 2.21). The pages (PropertyPage modules) you've developed will appear here, plus three standard pages which you can incorporate into your control.

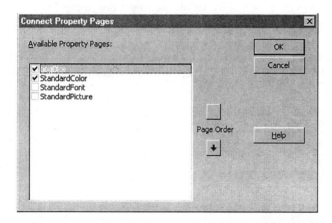

Figure 2.21   The Connect Property Pages dialog box

6. Check all the desired pages. If necessary, use the ↑ and ↓ buttons to rearrange the order of the pages. This order determines the order of the tabs in your custom page. After you're done, click OK to exit or Cancel to abort.

7. Select a control instance you've added to the form. If the control is activated, its Properties window shows a **Custom** property. Clicking it shows an ellipsis (...). Clicking this ellipsis opens the Property Pages dialog box.

8. Click a tab to bring it to the top. Set the desired properties. And click OK, Apply, or Cancel.

A **PropertyPage** module behaves like a form. They both possess similar properties and events. Like a form, a PropertyPage begins its life by executing the Initialize event and ends by triggering the Terminate event. However, if you pull down the list in the Code window's Procedure box, you'll find these three unique events:

ApplyChanges   Occurs when another page is selected or when OK or Apply is clicked. This event can be triggered only if the **Changed** property is set to True.

EditProperty   Occurs when a property page is opened.

SelectionChanged   Occurs when selection of controls in the container (form) has changed. The event procedure can tell the property page what to do to respond to the user's selecting different controls. You can use the **SelectedControls** collection (containing all selected controls) to handle the selected controls.

PropertyPage is an object. When you type this word followed by a dot in the Code window, a list of its members will pop up for you to make a selection.

It's time to do something after the above discussion. Our goal in this venture is to create two tabs: a custom tab named General (Figure 2.22) and a standard tab (StandardColor, Figure 2.23) that comes with Visual Basic.

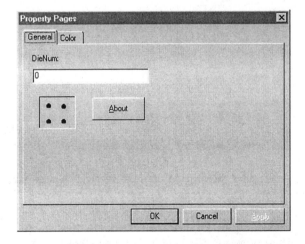

Figure 2.22   A custom tab named General

The first thing you need to do is to create the two tabs as demonstrated earlier. The General tab's module name is ppgDice, and its caption is General (you can use any name).

In this tab's designer, add a command button captioned About. Use a form or message box to respond to the clicking of this button. The die shown in the figure is simply added from the Toolbox. It serves as a decoration only.

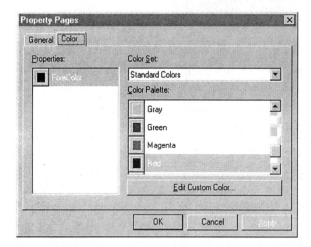

Figure 2.23   The Standard Color tab

The Color tab is intended to let the user change a die's ForeColor (dot color). This tab requires no work from you. You just connect it to the UserControl module, as demonstrated earlier.

The General tab has a label and a text box. We'll let the **Property Page Wizard** add these and the necessary code. After you've done the above preparation, follow these steps to use the wizard:

1. Choose Add-Ins | Property Page Wizard. (If the name doesn't appear, use Add-Ins | Add-In Manager to bring it to the menu first.)

2. The Introduction dialog box appears. Read the message and click Next.

3. The Select the Property Pages dialog box appears (Figure 2.24). Check/uncheck the available pages. Use the ↑ and ↓ arrows to rearrange their order. If you wish, use the Add button to add additional pages.

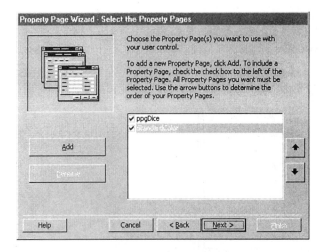

Figure 2.24   The Select the Property Pages dialog box

4. Click Next. The Add Properties dialog box appears. Go to each tab and use > or
    > > to move the desired properties to the right box. In our example, move the
    DieNum property in the ppgDice tab and the ForeColor property in the StandardColor
    tab.

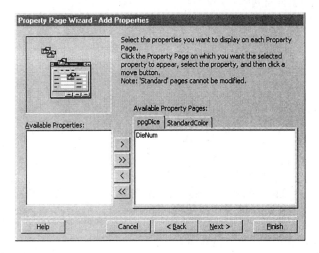

Figure 2.25   The Add Properties dialog box

5. Click Next. In the next dialog box, check No to see no summary report. Click Finish in the last dialog box. A message box tells you it's done.

The wizard has now added two controls to the General tab. If they are placed in undesirable locations, you can move them as you wish. In addition, the following code also enters the PropertyPage module's Code window:

```
Private Sub txtDieNum_Change()
    Changed = True
    'activates Apply button when
    'textbox content is changed
End Sub

Private Sub PropertyPage_ApplyChanges()
    SelectedControls(0).DieNum = txtDieNum.Text
End Sub

Private Sub PropertyPage_SelectionChanged()
    txtDieNum.Text = SelectedControls(0).DieNum
End Sub
```

The first procedure (with the comment added by this author) activates the General tab's Apply button when the user types something in the text box.

The second procedure will call the Property Let DieNum procedure and pass the value supplied by the user. Since we use a base 0 index system in our picDie control array, we need to subtract this number by 1. For example, if the user supplies 5, we need to pass 4 to the called procedure. So the following adjustment is necessary:

```
SelectedControls(0).DieNum = Val(txtDieNum.Text) - 1
```

Also, the user could enter a weird number that could cause an error. After the following modification, entering a number outside of the 1 - 6 range will show a message and cause no further harm.

```
Private Sub PropertyPage_ApplyChanges()
    If Val(txtDieNum.Text) <= 0 _
    Or Val(txtDieNum.Text) > 6 Then
        MsgBox "Number must be 1 - 6"
        Exit Sub
    End If

    SelectedControls(0).DieNum = Val(txtDieNum.Text) - 1
End Sub
```

If you want your code to respond to multiple selections, you need to loop through each object in the SelectedControls collection.

The About button can be coded like the following. When the General tab is open, the user can click the About button to show a message.

```
Private Sub cmdAbout_Click()
    Dim Msg As String
    Msg = "Authored by Forest Lin" & vbCr _
    & "as a demo in creating" & vbCr _
    & "ActiveX controls."
    MsgBox Msg, , "Property Page"
End Sub
```

There are three **standard property pages**: StandardColor (see Figure 2.23), StandardFont, and StandardPicture. These don't involve separate property pages. Instead, the information is saved to the companion **.ctx** binary file. The **.ctl** file (ASCII) will contain references to the .ctx file to load relevant information.

The easiest way to generate standard pages is to use the two wizards discussed above. Use the Control Interface Wizard to generate property procedures involving fonts, colors, or pictures. The resulting procedures may contain words like Font, Picture, or OLE_COLOR. These in turn are used by the Property Page Wizard to do more work.

After the Control Interface Wizard has created public property procedures, these properties enter the host's Properties window. So you may see additional properties like Font, ForeColor, BackColor, or Picture. Each of these will open up a proper dialog box for you to change values at design time.

If you want these properties to be added to the Custom property, use the Property Page Wizard. This wizard reads the property procedures created by the Control Interface Wizard. If it encounters Font, Picture, or OLE_COLOR, its corresponding standard page will be added to the Custom property. When the user opens the Custom property, the resulting Property Pages dialog box may contain a tab named Font, Color, or Picture. Their corresponding entries in the Properties window remain intact. So the user can use either place to change properties.

Standard property pages are saved to a file with the .ctx extension, not to separate modules. Suppose you have a control file named PropDemo.ctl. Adding standard property pages and resaving the same file will automatically create a file named PropDemo.ctx and stored in the same directory. The PropDemo.ctl file will also contain a reference like this:

```
    PropertyPages   =   "PropDemo.ctx":0000
```

This extra file is not created if no standard page is involved (it may be created by other features to store other data.).

You can connect a property page to a custom property name other than Custom (as demonstrated above). This custom name will appear in the Properties window when a control instance is added to a container. Double-clicking this name will display the property page. Use the **Procedure Attributes** dialog box (Tools | Procedure Attributes) to make the connection. Chapter 3 will provide more details when it discusses component attributes..

Magic Square

This section creates a control that will let you display a **magic square**. A magic square has the same (and odd-numbered) number of rows and columns. Each column, row, or diagonal also shares the same sum.

The following steps are used to create a magic square:

1. Enter 1 in the middle of the first row.

2. Enter each subsequent number in each adjacent upper-left cell. (You can also go to the upper-right cell.)

3. If the target cell lies beyond a border, you continue on the other side. The 2 and 5 in Figure 2.26 are examples.

4. If a target cell is already occupied, you enter the next number below the previous number and continue from there. For example, 8 is supposed to go to where 1 is. But since it's already occupied, it goes to below 7 instead.

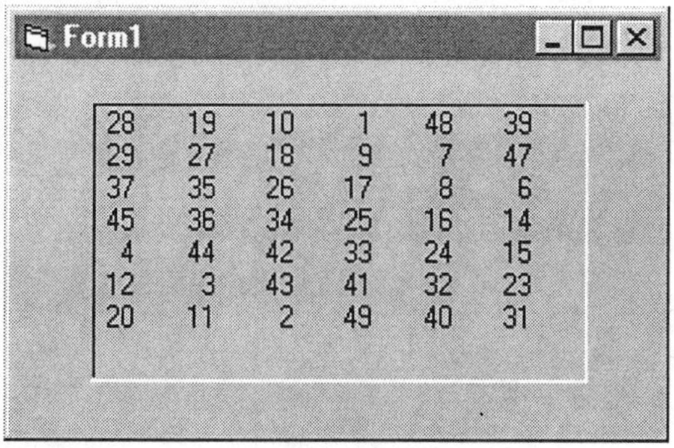

Figure 2.26   A magic square

You can do these on paper, but it's easier to do it with a program. Here we create a control that will prompt you to enter a number to create a magic square based on that number.

The code below produces Figure 2.26. The is the result of supplying 7 when prompted by the input box.

We use a **dynamic array** whose dimensions depend on the number supplied by the user. This array stores all the row and column numbers in the process of creating the square. The array is then used to print out all the numbers.

```
'-----Magic.ctl-----
Private Sub UserControl_Click()
    Dim Num As Integer
    Dim I As Integer
    Dim J As Integer
    Dim Row As Integer
    Dim Col As Integer
    Dim CurrX As Long
    Dim Elm As Integer

    UserControl.BorderStyle = 1
    'EditAtDesignTime set to True at authoring time

    Num = Val(InputBox("Enter an odd number:"))
    If Num = 0 Then Exit Sub    'no entry
    If Num Mod 2 = 0 Then
        Beep
        MsgBox "An even number is illegal."
        Exit Sub
    End If

    Cls        'clear for a new form

    ReDim Arr(1 To Num, 1 To Num)      'dynamic array

    I = 1                              'row 1
    J = (Num + 1) / 2                  'mid column
    Arr(I, J) = 1                      '1st element
    Elm = 2                            '2nd element

    Do While Elm <= Num ^ 2           'up to num square
        Row = (I - 1) Mod Num         'next row
        If Row < 1 Then Row = Row + Num
            'wrap around if 0 or less
        Col = (J - 1) Mod Num         'next col
        If Col < 1 Then Col = Col + Num
            'wrap around if over left
        If Arr(Row, Col) <> 0 Then    'if already assigned
```

```
            I = I + 1
            If I > Num Then I = I - Num
        Else        'move down 1 row, wrap if needed
            I = Row        'move up & left
            J = Col
        End If
        Arr(I, J) = Elm   'assign next element
        Elm = Elm + 1
    Loop

    For I = 1 To Num
        CurrX = 200
        For J = 1 To Num
            CurrentX = CurrX - TextWidth(Arr(I, J))
                    'move printhead right
            Print Arr(I, J);      'print element
            CurrX = CurrX + 500    '500 twips apart
        Next J
        Print                          'new line
    Next I
End Sub
```

The UserControl has no borders by default. Since we use code to change its **BorderStyle** to Fixed Single, the result is like a label control of the same border style.

At authoring time, the **EditAtDesignTime** property is changed to True; this cannot be done by code. So at developer design time, you can right-click a control instance and choose the **Edit** option. The control will go into run mode. If you then left-click it, the UserControl_ Click procedure will be executed. An input box will appear for you to enter a number. The control will then display a magic square at design time.

You can display the numbers with an array of label controls. A practice question will let you try that.

Bridge Game

If you like or are familiar with the bridge game, you'll enjoy this control. Many newspapers and magazines carry columns by famous bridge players. These columns show four hands and advise readers how to win a game. This control doesn't advise you how to play a game, but it does show four hands (Figure 2.27) to let you mull over a strategy.

At developer design time, drawing the control on a form creates only a blank space. At run time, clicking the control (blank space) shows four hands. Each click leads to a new deal.

If the size of the control drawn at design time is not big enough, the hands may be crunched together or some cards may not be shown. In that case, go back to design time and enlarge the control instance.

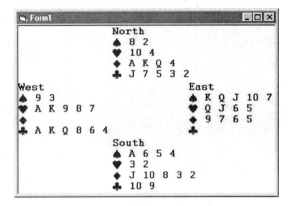

Figure 2.27   A bridge game

At run time, you can enlarge Form1 where the control is sited to enlarge the control. Clicking Form1 will stretch the control to fit the form. This part is controlled by the developer in the Form_Click procedure. After the form and the control are stretched, clicking the control will show a new deal spreading across the new size.

The UserControl_Click procedure is triggered whenever its instance in the container is clicked. This procedure calls a series of other private procedures to create a new deck of 52 cards, distribute them into four hands, sort each hand, and print them out.

The UserControl's BackColor property can be changed by the developer at design time. The property procedures at the end of the following code make that possible. These procedures can be created by the wizard.

```
'-----from Bridge.ctl-----
Dim Deck(1 To 52) As String
Dim Player(1 To 4, 2 To 14)
Dim CdNum As Integer

Private Sub UserControl_Initialize()
    AutoRedraw = True
    BorderStyle = 1        'fixed
End Sub

Public Sub UserControl_Click()
```

```
        Erase Deck        'clear old values
        Erase Player      'a new start
        CdNum = 0

        Call MakeCard("S")
             'call sub and pass S for spade
        Call MakeCard("H")
        Call MakeCard("D")
        Call MakeCard("C")
        Call Shuffle(100)
             'call sub to shuffle 100 times
        Call Deal
End Sub

Private Sub MakeCard(Suit As String)
        Dim I As Integer

        For I = 2 To 14
            CdNum = CdNum + 1
                'each card's index number, 1 - 52
            Deck(CdNum) = Suit & I
                'S1, S2...H1, H2...
        Next I
End Sub

Private Sub Shuffle(SNum)
        Dim CutNum As Integer
        Dim I As Integer, J As Integer
        Dim Tmp As String

        Randomize

        Do While SNum > 0
            CutNum = 20 + Int(Rnd * 7)
                'divide at 20 - 26 midpoint
            For I = 1 To CutNum
                Tmp = Deck(I)
                Deck(I) = Deck(I + CutNum)
                Deck(I + CutNum) = Tmp
            Next I
                'divide deck into 2 nearly equal halves
                'exchange each comparable pair
            SNum = SNum - 1
                'try again if not 0
        Loop
End Sub

Private Sub Deal()
        Dim I As Integer, J As Integer, K As Integer
        Dim SName As String, SNum As Variant
```

```
        Cls

        For I = 1 To 4
            For J = 2 To 14
                K = K + 1    'counter 1 - 52 (4 x 13)
                Player(I, J) = Deck(K)
                    'each player gets a card in turn
            Next J
        Next I
        Call ShowHand(1, "North", ScaleWidth / 3, 0)
        Call ShowHand(2, "East", ScaleWidth * 0.6, _
        ScaleHeight / 3)
        Call ShowHand(3, "South", ScaleWidth / 3, _
        ScaleHeight * (2 / 3))
        Call ShowHand(4, "West", 0, ScaleHeight / 3)
            'player num, side, CurX, CurY
    End Sub

    Private Sub ShowHand(PNum As Integer, _
    Side As String, CurX As Long, CurY As Long)
        Dim SuitCount(1 To 4) As Integer
        Dim Hand(1 To 4, 1 To 13) As Integer
        Dim I As Integer, J As Integer, K As Integer
        Dim Tmp As Integer

    '--divide each player's hand into 4 separate suits
        For I = 2 To 14
            '2 to 14 points, range in Player array
            Select Case Left(Player(PNum, I), 1)
            Case "S"
                SuitCount(1) = SuitCount(1) + 1
                Hand(1, SuitCount(1)) = Val(Right(Player( _
                PNum, I), Len(Player(PNum, I)) - 1))
                    'extract the number from each card
                    'keep track of how many cards in each suit
            Case "H"
                SuitCount(2) = SuitCount(2) + 1
                Hand(2, SuitCount(2)) = Val(Right(Player( _
                PNum, I), Len(Player(PNum, I)) - 1))
            Case "D"
                SuitCount(3) = SuitCount(3) + 1
                Hand(3, SuitCount(3)) = Val(Right(Player( _
                PNum, I), Len(Player(PNum, I)) - 1))
            Case "C"
                SuitCount(4) = SuitCount(4) + 1
                Hand(4, SuitCount(4)) = Val(Right(Player( _
                PNum, I), Len(Player(PNum, I)) - 1))
            End Select
        Next I

    '--sort each separate suit
```

```
    For I = 1 To 4   'four suits
        'sort each suit in descending order
        For J = 1 To SuitCount(I) - 1
            For K = J + 1 To SuitCount(I)
                If Hand(I, K) > Hand(I, J) Then
                    Tmp = Hand(I, J)
                    Hand(I, J) = Hand(I, K)
                    Hand(I, K) = Tmp
                End If
            Next K
        Next J
    Next I

'--print four separate hands
    CurrentX = CurX       'position print head
    CurrentY = CurY       'using passed values
    FontSize = 12
    FontBold = True
    Print Side            'North, East...

    For I = 1 To 4
        FontName = "courier"
        CurrentX = CurX
        FontName = "symbol"

        Select Case I
        Case 1
            ForeColor = vbBlack
            Print Chr(170) & "   ";
        Case 2
            ForeColor = vbRed
            Print Chr(169) & "   ";
        Case 3
            ForeColor = vbRed
            Print Chr(168) & "   ";
        Case 4
            ForeColor = vbBlack
            Print Chr(167) & "   ";
        End Select

        FontName = "courier"

        For J = 1 To SuitCount(I)
            Select Case Hand(I, J)
                Case 14: Print "A ";
                Case 13: Print "K ";
                Case 12: Print "Q ";
                Case 11: Print "J ";
                Case Else: Print Trim(Hand(I, J)) & " ";
            End Select
        Next J
```

```
        Print    'new line
    Next I
End Sub

'MappingInfo=UserControl,UserControl,-1,BackColor
Public Property Get BackColor() As OLE_COLOR
    BackColor = UserControl.BackColor
End Property

Public Property Let BackColor(ByVal _
New_BackColor As OLE_COLOR)
    UserControl.BackColor() = New_BackColor
    PropertyChanged "BackColor"
End Property

'Load property values from storage
Private Sub UserControl_ReadProperties(PropBag _
As PropertyBag)
    UserControl.BackColor = PropBag.ReadProperty( _
    "BackColor", &H8000000F)
End Sub

'Write property values to storage
Private Sub UserControl_WriteProperties( _
PropBag As PropertyBag)
    Call PropBag.WriteProperty("BackColor", _
    UserControl.BackColor, &H8000000F)
End Sub

'-----from Form1-----
Private Sub Form_Click()
    Bridge1.Top = 0
    Bridge1.Left = 0
    Bridge1.Width = Form1.ScaleWidth
    Bridge1.Height = Form1.ScaleHeight
End Sub
```

Clock Control

This section creates a clock control, as shown in Figure 2.28. The control starts running
as soon as you add it to a form. There are three hands with various lengths and colors.
Each hand reflects the current second, minute, and hour. The second hand completes a
circle every 60 seconds. Every second, the second hand moves by 1/60 of the
circumference. Every minute, the minute hand moves by 1/60 of the circumference. The
hour hand also moves by a proper proportion every minute, not every hour.

The tricky part about authoring this control lies in maneuvering the three lines to make them move along the circumference. If you are versed in trigonometry, this should be a fairly easy task. If not, the comments in the following code should help.

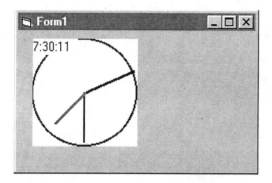

Figure 2.28   A clock control with three moving hands

```
'-----from Clock0.ctl-----
Dim Radius As Single, I As Single, Pi As Single
Dim Min As Integer, Sec As Integer, Hr As Integer

Dim Size As Long

Private Sub UserControl_Resize()
    If Width > Height Then
        Width = Height
    Else
        Height = Width
    End If
        'get smaller of the two, make square
    Size = Width    'get size of width or height
    'setting width/height will trigger Resize event
End Sub

Private Sub UserControl_Show()
    linSec.BorderWidth = 2    'line width
    linSec.BorderColor = vbRed
    linMin.BorderWidth = 2
    linMin.BorderColor = vbBlue
    linHr.BorderWidth = 2
    linHr.BorderColor = vbMagenta

    linSec.X1 = Size / 2    'center second hand
    linSec.Y1 = Size / 2
```

```
    linMin.X1 = Size / 2    'minute hand
    linMin.Y1 = Size / 2
    linHr.X1 = Size / 2    'hour hand
    linHr.Y1 = Size / 2

    Shape1.Top = 0              'move to top left
    Shape1.Left = 0
    Shape1.BorderColor = vbBlue
    Shape1.BorderWidth = 2
    Shape1.Width = Size      'stretch to max
    Shape1.Height = Size
    Shape1.Shape = 3            'change to circle
    Hr = Hour(Now) Mod 12
    Min = Minute(Now)
    Sec = Second(Now)

    Scale (-1, 1)-(1, -1)  'Cartesian scale
    Radius = 1
    Pi = 4 * Atn(1)
    I = Pi / 2 - (2 * Pi) * (Sec / 60)        'interval
        'convert 60-scale to 2pi scale
    linSec.X2 = Radius * Cos(I) 'get x axis
    linSec.Y2 = Radius * Sin(I) 'get y axis
        'position second hand

    linMin.X2 = (Radius - 0.1) * Cos(Pi / 2 - _
    (2 * Pi) * (Min / 60))  'minute hand
    linMin.Y2 = (Radius - 0.1) * Sin(Pi / 2 - _
    (2 * Pi) * (Min / 60))

    linHr.X2 = (Radius - 0.2) * Cos(Pi / 2 - _
    (2 * Pi) * ((Hr + Min / 60) / 12))
    linHr.Y2 = (Radius - 0.2) * Sin(Pi / 2 - _
    (2 * Pi) * ((Hr + Min / 60) / 12))
        'hour hand, adjusted for minute within hour
    Timer1.Interval = 1000
        'set timer interval at 1 second
End Sub

Private Sub Timer1_Timer()
    Sec = Sec + 1        'increment seconds
    If Sec = 60 Then
        Sec = 0
        Min = Min + 1    'increment minutes

        linMin.X2 = (Radius - 0.1) * Cos(Pi / 2 - _
        (2 * Pi) * (Min / 60))  'change minute hand
        linMin.Y2 = (Radius - 0.1) * Sin(Pi / 2 - _
        (2 * Pi) * (Min / 60))

        linHr.X2 = (Radius - 0.2) * Cos(Pi / 2 - _
```

```
        (2 * Pi) * ((Hr + Min / 60) / 12))
      linHr.Y2 = (Radius - 0.2) * Sin(Pi / 2 - _
        (2 * Pi) * ((Hr + Min / 60) / 12))
            'change hour hand every minute
      If Min = 60 Then
            Min = 0
            Hr = Hr + 1
            If Hr = 12 Then
                Hr = 0
            End If
      End If
    End If
    Label1.Caption = Hour(Now) & ":" & Min & ":" & Sec
    I = I - Pi / 30      'clockwise motion
        'interval at 1/60, or 2pi/60
    linSec.X2 = Radius * Cos(I)   'change second hand
    linSec.Y2 = Radius * Sin(I)
End Sub
```

The clock may run slower than it should, due to a great of computing required to move the hands. If you have a fast PC, you may not notice the difference. If you have a slow PC, you may want to adjust the timer's **Interval** property to make the clock move faster.

Calendar Control and Control Array

This section creates a calendar control with a control array. When the control is drawn on a form, it immediately shows the current year/month, as shown in Figure 2.29.

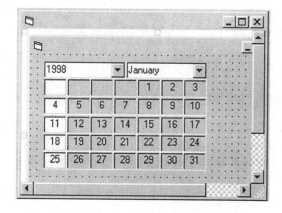

Figure 2.29   Calendar at design time

At run time, the user can choose another year from the left combo box or month from the right combo box. Each action will lead to a new display. Figure 2.30 shows the run time version.

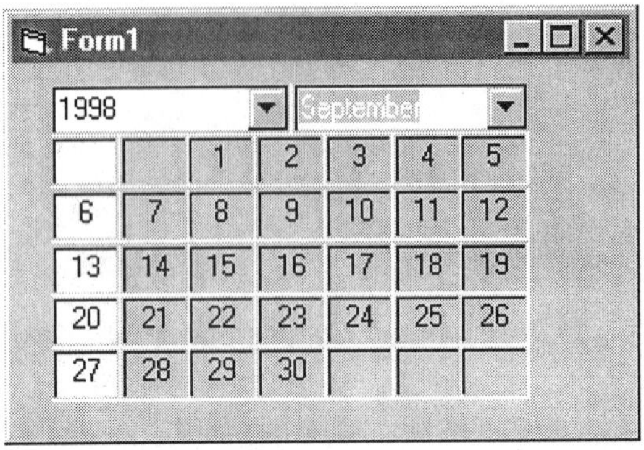

Figure 2.30   Calendar at run time

The year range is from 1990 to 2020. In addition, the User entry at the end of the list lets the user specify another year not in that range. An input box will open up to let you enter a number. This number will be added to the bottom of the list in the combo box for future use.

Our control consists of a UserControl, two combo boxes, and a label control. The last is turned into a control array that will be created on the fly as is necessary. To make it possible for that, we change **Index** value of the label control (lblDays) to 0 at design time.

A **control array** can be created with code at run time. These are the general steps:

1. Add a control to the container (form or UserControl) at design time.

2. Change the control's Name to something meaningful (optional) and Index to 0 (mandatory) at design time.

3. Use the **Load** statement in code to load additional copies of the control. Each copy will have an Index value that is 1 higher than the one before.

4. Use code to move each new copy to a new location so that the copies will not cover up one another.

5. Use the **Visible** property to hide or show each copy.

In the code below, the control array is loaded by the UserControl_Initialize procedure at the control's startup. The others—visibility, sizing, positioning, and coloring—are controlled in the GetLabels sub procedure. This allows the developer at design time to control the container's size. When the UserControl's size is changed at design time, the label controls will change their sizes to fit inside the container.

```
'-----from CalenCtAr.ctl-----
Dim CalArray(36) As Variant
'track 31 days in 7 x 5 grid,
'plus 2 possible extra days

Private Sub UserControl_Initialize()
    Dim I As Integer

    For I = 1990 To 2020
        cboYear.AddItem I
    Next I
    cboYear.AddItem "User"
        'last item, let user enter year
    cboYear.Text = Format(Now, "yyyy")
        'default year is current year
        'default month is current month
    cboMonth.Text = Format(Now, "mmmm")
    cboMonth.AddItem "January"
    cboMonth.AddItem "February"
    cboMonth.AddItem "March"
    cboMonth.AddItem "April"
    cboMonth.AddItem "May"
    cboMonth.AddItem "June"
    cboMonth.AddItem "July"
    cboMonth.AddItem "August"
    cboMonth.AddItem "September"
    cboMonth.AddItem "October"
    cboMonth.AddItem "November"
    cboMonth.AddItem "December"
End Sub

Private Sub UserControl_Resize()
    'rearrange labels when form resized
    'Label1 Name changed to lblDays
    'Index changed to 0
    Static Loaded As Boolean
    Dim I As Integer
    Dim J As Integer
    Dim SW As Long
    Dim SH As Long

    SW = ScaleWidth
    SH = ScaleHeight
```

```
        cboYear.Top = 0
        cboYear.Width = SW / 2
        cboYear.Left = 0
        cboMonth.Top = 0
        cboMonth.Width = SW / 2
        cboMonth.Left = SW / 2

        lblDays(0).Width = SW / 7
        lblDays(0).Height = SH / 6
            'original's size

        If Not Loaded Then
            'load first time, but not later
            For I = 1 To 34
                Load lblDays(I)
            Next I
        End If

        Call GetCalArray
        'cal sub to show initial results
        Call GetLabels

        Loaded = True
    End Sub

    Private Sub GetCalArray()
        Dim MaxDay As Integer
        Dim Mon As Variant
        Dim Yr As Variant
        Dim Day1 As Variant
        Dim I As Integer
        Dim J As Integer

        Erase CalArray
            'erase previous contents
        Yr = cboYear.Text
        Day1 = cboMonth.Text & "/" & Yr   'ex. March/1998
        Mon = Month(Day1)   'get month
        Day1 = WeekDay(Day1) - 1
            'get weekday of 1st day of month

        Select Case Mon        'what month?
        Case 1, 3, 5, 7, 8, 10, 12
            MaxDay = 31
        Case 4, 6, 9, 11
            MaxDay = 30
        Case 2        'leap year
            If Yr Mod 4 = 0 Then
                If Yr Mod 100 = 0 And Yr Mod 400 <> 0 Then
                    MaxDay = 28
                    'if divisible by 100 but not by 400
```

```
            Else
                MaxDay = 29
            End If
        Else
            MaxDay = 28       'if not divisible by 4
        End If
    End Select

    For I = Day1 To MaxDay + Day1 - 1
        'from 1st day of mon (Day1) till
        'max + Day1's number -1
        J = J + 1
        CalArray(I) = J
        'assign sequential number to array element
        If I > 34 Then
        'if flow beyond 5th row, add to last label
            CalArray(34) = CalArray(34) & "/" & J
        End If
    Next I
End Sub

Private Sub GetLabels()
    'change label size and captions
    Dim I As Integer
    Dim J As Integer
    Dim SW As Long
    Dim SH As Long
    Dim FirstTime As Boolean

    SW = ScaleWidth
    SH = ScaleHeight

    FirstTime = True
    If FirstTime Then
        For I = 0 To 34
            lblDays(I).Caption = ""
        Next I
    End If
        'first visit, blank caption
        'skipped in the future
    J = 1
    For I = 0 To 34
        lblDays(I).Width = SW / 7
        lblDays(I).Height = SH / 6
        lblDays(I).Top = (SH / 6) * J
            'change top pos when J changed
        lblDays(I).Left = (SW / 7) * (I Mod 7)
            'move each label to right pos
        lblDays(I).Visible = True     'show result
        If I Mod 7 = 0 Then
            lblDays(I).BackColor = vbCyan
```

```
                'different color for Sundays
            End If

            If CalArray(I) > "0" Then
                lblDays(I).Caption = CalArray(I)
                'put index value in caption
            End If

            If (I + 1) Mod 7 = 0 Then
                J = J + 1
                'to control top position of each row
            End If
        Next I
    End Sub

    Private Sub cboMonth_Click()
        GetCalArray
        'call proc to show result when month changed
        GetLabels
    End Sub

    Private Sub cboYear_Click()
        Dim UserYr As Variant    'track user-entered year
        Dim Flag As Boolean

        If Flag = True Then GoTo GetOut
            'prevents calling itself
        If cboYear.Text = "User" Then
            UserYr = InputBox("Enter a year")
            If UserYr = "" Or Not IsNumeric(UserYr) Then
                Beep
                cboYear.ListIndex = 0
                'if no entry or valid date, show top
                Exit Sub
                Flag = True
                'to prevent calling itself
            End If
            cboYear.AddItem UserYr  'add new item at end
            cboYear.ListIndex = cboYear.ListCount - 1
            'selects last item, calls Click again
        End If

GetOut:
    Call cboMonth_Click
        'call month sub to show new display
    End Sub
```

We also use a different way to determine how many days a month has. In the calendar project in the previous chapter, we tried to provoke an error in order to get that value. Here we tell our program that the months of 1, 3, 5, 7, 8, 10, and 12 have 31 days each.

The others have 30 days, except February. In a leap year, February has 29 days; otherwise, 28. A leap year occurs every four years (divisible by 4), with minor exceptions. Century years (divisible by 100) are leap only if they are divisible by 400.

Drill

Use the following options to answer #1 - 4:
   a.   control class
   b.   control component
   c.   constituent control
   d.   control instance

____   1.   A file with the .ocx extension.
____   2.   A member in an .ocx file.
____   3.   A control added to a form.
____   4.   An existing control added to a UserControl.

____   5.   A UserControl's _____ property determines whether this control can be accessible by other applications.

____   6.   When a control instance is destroyed at design time, you can activate it by choosing the _____ _____ option.

____   7.   Opening a control designer will do this to a control instance:
   a.   remove it from the host
   b.   destroy its design-time cycle
   c.   change it to run mode
   d.   none of the above

____   8.   Suppose a UserControl has the following procedure, clicking a control instance at run time will execute this procedure. True or false?

```
Private Sub UserControl_Click( )
```

____   9.   If a UserControl has the following procedure and its EditAtDesignTime property is set to True, the string in the procedure will be printed to the control at design time. True or false?

```
Private Sub UserControl_Click( )
     Print "I've been clicked."
End Sub
```

_____ 10. In the following arrangement, clicking Form1 will show the message box in UserControl1. True or false?

```
Private Sub Form_Click()      'from Form1
    UserControl1.Do_Click
End Sub

Private Sub Do_Click()        'from UserControl1
    MsgBox "You got me."
End Sub
```

_____ 11. To make a control instance respond to pressing Enter or Esc, you need to set its _____ property to True.

_____ 12. Events, methods, and properties constitute the _____ of a control.

_____ 13. An instance of a control you've authored is automatically given some _____ properties.

_____ 14. When a control instance is disabled at design time, its custom properties appear in its Properties window. True or false?

_____ 15. Standard property pages can include:
  a. font
  b. color
  c. picture
  d. all of the above
  e. none of the above

Connect the following events with the actions in #16-20:
  a. InitProperties
  b. ReadProperties
  c. WriteProperties

_____ 16. Adding a control instance to a form at design time.
_____ 17. Closing a form (where the control has been added) at design time.
_____ 18. Reopening the above form at design time.
_____ 19. Unloading a form by clicking its X button.

_____ 20. When a control instance is switched from run mode to design mode, the first event that occurs is:
  a. Initialize
  b. ReadProperties

      c.   Terminate

      d.   Show

Answers

1.b; 2.a; 3.d; 4.c; 5.Public; 6.Update UserControls; 7.b; 8.T; 9.T; 10.F;
11.DefaultCamcel; 12.Interface; 13.Extender; 14.F; 15.d; 16.a; 17.c; 18.b; 19.b; 20.c

Practice

◙   1.   Create a control named ElapsedTime (Figure 2.31). It should show the elapsed
time, updating every second. The background color should be red and the display
text cyan. The control should consist of two constituent controls: Timer1 and
Label1. The colors and timer interval should be set by code in the control.

Figure 2.31   ElapsedTime control

◙   2.   In the ElapsedTime control, add a method named Pause and make the control
raise an event named Click. When Label1 of the control's instance is clicked at
run time, the timer should pause and unpause alternately.

◙   3.   Add to the ElapsedTime control a new method named StartNew. Call this method
from Form1 at run time to start the timer from 0.

◙   4.   Create a control that has a command button as its constituent control. At run
time, when the hosting Form1 is resized, the button should fill up the form.
(Hint: Use the Move method to move Command1. Put the code in
UserControl_Resize event procedure. Use the form's Resize event to trigger the
control's Resize event.)

☉ 5. In the above control, when the user clicks Command1 at run time, the button's caption should change according to the number clicked, as shown in Figure 2.32. (Hint: You need to raise a Click event and implement a Caption property.)

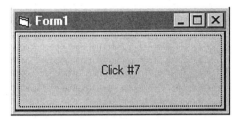

Figure 2.32   Making a class respond to a Click event

☉ 6. Create a control named Color. It should draw a circle and fill it with red color. At run time, when the form where the control is sited is resized, the control instance should fill up the form. (Hint: put the drawing code in UserControl_Paint or UserControl_Resize event procedure.)

☉ 7. Create a control that contains the constituent controls as shown in Figure 2.33. At run time, the focus stays in the top text box. When a number is typed and Enter pressed, it is appended to the list box on the left and added to the sum in the bottom text box. If nothing or a non-numeric is entered, the above does not happen.

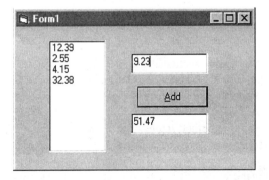

Figure 2.33   Adding numbers in a control

◙ 8. Create a control class named Hi. When added to a form, this control will display a large message "Hi there" for one second, disappear for one second, and then repeat indefinitely.

◙ 9. Create a control that will do the following:

1. Show the initial interface and constituent controls as shown in Figure 2.34.

2. At run time, the user can type a text string in the text box. Clicking Start makes the text start scrolling from left to right.

3. Clicking Pause/Unpause toggles between pausing and continuing the scrolling.

4. The focus should be set on the text box at startup. Pressing Alt+E should also moves the cursor there.

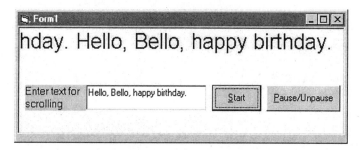

Figure 2.34   Scrolling text displayed by a control

◙ 10. Create a control named PropDemo. It should do.the following:

1. It has one constituent control named Label1.

2. When the control is initialized, the label is stretched to the size of the control and its border is changed to Fixed Single.

3. The control has the Font, BackColor, ForeColor, and Caption properties all mapped to Label1. So when the developer changes these properties of the control, they are reflected in the constituent control.

4. Add PropDemo1 to Form1. When the form is run, use code to change the control's ForeColor, BackColor, FontSize, and assign and show a caption as shown in Figure 3.35.

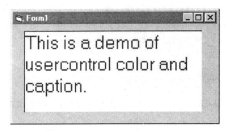

Figure 3.35   Demonstrating control properties

◎   11. Suppose you have two UserControl modules named UC1 and UC2. They have the
     code as shown below. Explain how they differ.

```
'-----from UC1-----
Private Sub UserControl_Click()
    Print "Demo1"
End Sub

'-----from UC2-----
Event Click()

Private Sub UserControl_Click()
    RaiseEvent Click
End Sub

Public Sub ShowDemo()
    Print "Demo2"
End Sub
```

◎   12. Create a control that will draw the U.S. flag as shown in Figure 2.36.

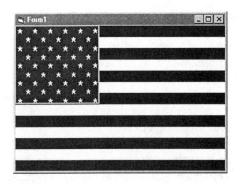

Figure 2.36   The U.S. flag drawn by a class

◉ 13. Create a control that will draw the British flag as shown in Figure 2.37.

Figure 2.37   The U.K. flag drawn by a class

◉ 14. Modify the Dice control (Listing 3) so that when the Dice1_Click and Dice2_Click events occur, the rolled numbers generated in the RollDie sub procedure of the Dice class can be read from Form1. Total these numbers and show the result in Form1's Caption.

◉ 15. Modify the above to create a betting game (Figure 2.38). The user is required to enter a bet number and a bet amount. When Roll is clicked, the two dice are rolled. The sum appears in the form's caption. It that number matches the bet number, the score's value (bottom right) increases by the bet amount, otherwise it decreases by the bet amount.

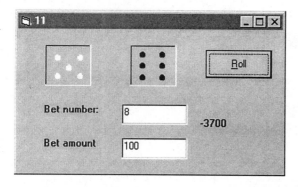

Figure 2.38   A dice game

◙   16. Create a clock (Figure 2.39) with one hand that will move once every second. The hand should start at the 12 o'clock position and moves clockwise. At the end of one minute, it should return to the original position.

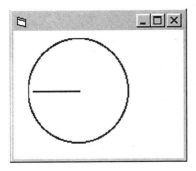

Figure 2.39   A clock with one moving hand

◙   17. Do the following to the preceding control:

1. Add a label control to the UserControl that will display the elapsed minutes and seconds, as shown in Figure 2.40.

2. Add an Enabled property mapped to the Timer control.

3. Add a public sub procedure that will reset the clock to the original position.

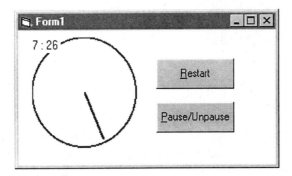

Figure 2.40   A timer clock

○ 18. Create a control that will automatically show a control array of a label control. the labels should show the multiplication table as shown in Figure 2.41.

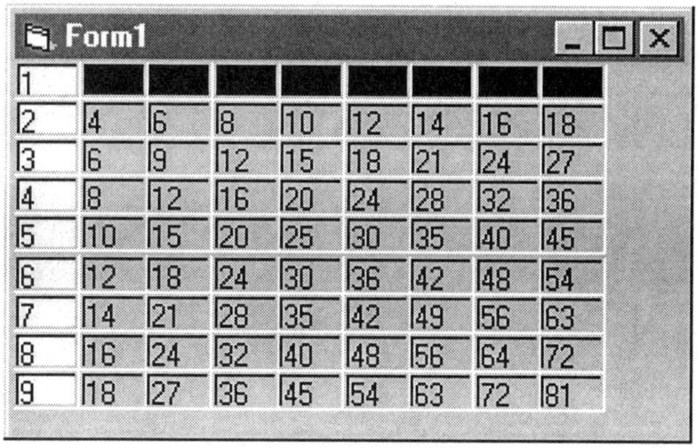

Figure 2.41   A multiplication table

○ 19. In the previous control, change the color of the first row and the first column to red.

○ 20. Create a control that will show a magic square based on the number specified by the user. The control should behave as follows:

1. It should prompt the user at run time to enter an odd number.

2. The numbers should be displayed with a control array of a label control, as shown in Figure 2.42.

3. The control should expose a public sub procedure called ShowMagic.

4. From Form1, use the Form_Click procedure to call ShowMagic. This should allow the user to click the form at run time multiple times to show different squares.

Map the BackColor property to the label control. This will allow the developer to set a new color to display a new square.

Activate the control by using a statement like below:

```
Private Sub Form_Click()
    MagicCtAr1.ShowMagic
End Sub
```

Figure 2.42   A 5 x 5 magic square

Answers

(Note: To load a control module file from the companion disk, right-click the Project window and choose Add | Add File. Then point to the right directory (2Controls) and double-click the desired file (with the **.ctl** extension). Its bitmap will appear in the Toolbox. The control can then be added to a form.)

1.
Private StartTime As Date

```
Private Sub UserControl_Initialize()
    Timer1.Interval = 1000
    Label1.FontSize = 15
    Label1.BackColor = vbRed
    Label1.ForeColor = vbCyan
    StartTime = Now
End Sub

Private Sub Timer1_Timer()
    Label1.Caption = "Elapsed Time = " & _
    Format(Now - StartTime, "hh : mm : ss")
End Sub
```

2.
(ElapsedTime.ctl)

```
'-----from ElapsedTime-----
Public Event Click()

Private Sub Label1_Click()
    RaiseEvent Click
    'transfer Click event to
    'class instances
End Sub

Public Sub Pause()
    'public sub to be called from another module
    'turn off/on elapsed timer
    Static TurnOff As Boolean

    TurnOff = Not TurnOff
    If TurnOff Then
        Timer1.Enabled = False
    Else
        Timer1.Enabled = True
    End If
End Sub

'-----from Form1-----
Private Sub ElapsedTime1_Click()
    ElapsedTime1.Pause
        'call control's method
End Sub
```

3.

```
'-----from ElapsedTime-----
Public Sub StartNew()
    StartTime = Now
End Sub

'-----from Form1-----
Private Sub Form_Click()
    ElapsedTime1.StartNew
End Sub
```

4.
```
'-----from FillDemo module-----
Private Sub UserControl_Resize()
    Command1.Move 0, 0, ScaleWidth, ScaleHeight
End Sub

'-----from Form1-----
Private Sub Form_Resize()
    FillDemo1.Move 0, 0, ScaleWidth, ScaleHeight
End Sub
```

5.
```
'-----from FillDemo module-----
Event Click()

Private Sub Command1_Click()
    RaiseEvent Click
End Sub

Property Let Caption(NewCap As String)
    Command1.Caption = NewCap
    PropertyChanged "Caption"
End Property

Property Get Caption() As String
    Caption = Command1.Caption
End Property

'-----from Form1-----
Private Sub FillDemo1_Click()
    Static Num As Integer
    Num = Num + 1
    FillDemo1.Caption = "Click #" & Num
End Sub
```

6.
```
'-----from Color module-----
Private Sub UserControl_Resize()
    Dim SW As Long, SH As Long
    Dim Radius As Long
```

```
   Cls
   FillStyle = 0   'solid fill
   FillColor = vbRed
   SW = ScaleWidth
   SH = ScaleHeight

   Radius = IIf(SH < SW, SH, SW)
   Radius = Radius / 2
      'use smaller of height or width for radius
   Circle (SW / 2, SH / 2), Radius
End Sub

'-----from Form1-----
Private Sub Form_Resize()
   Color1.Move 0, 0, ScaleWidth, ScaleHeight
End Sub
```

7.

Keep the top text box's TabStop as True and change the others to False. Change the command button's Default property to True. Write the following Click procedure for the command button:

```
'-----from Add.ctl-----
Private Sub cmdAdd_Click()
   If Not IsNumeric(txtEntry.Text) Then
      Beep
      MsgBox "Must enter a number."
      Exit Sub
   End If

   List1.AddItem txtEntry.Text
   txtSum.Text = Val(txtSum.Text) + txtEntry.Text
   txtEntry.Text = ""
End Sub
```

When Enter is pressed, the Click procedure is executed because the command button has the Default property set to True.

8.

```
Private Sub UserControl_Initialize()
   Timer1.Interval = 1000
```

```
End Sub

Private Sub Timer1_Timer()
    Static Go As Boolean

    FontSize = 20
    ForeColor = vbRed
    Go = Not Go
    If Go Then
        Print "Hi there."
    Else
        Cls
    End If
End Sub
```

9.
```
'-----from Scroll.ctl-----
Private Sub UserControl_Initialize()
    FontName = "arial"
    FontSize = 40   'set fontsize for form
End Sub

Private Sub cmdPause_Click()
    Dim Pause As Boolean
    Pause = Not Pause
    If Pause Then
        Timer1.Enabled = Not Timer1.Enabled
    End If
End Sub

Private Sub cmdStart_Click()
    Timer1.Interval = 200
        'activate timer; change every .2 second
End Sub

Private Sub Timer1_Timer()
    Static Pos As Integer
    Static Str As String

    Cls
    Pos = Pos + 1       'starting out
    Str = " " & Text1.Text
```

```
        'put entry in var, add leading space
    Print Mid(Str, Pos); Str;
            'print original string twice
            'then cut the left char each time
            'increment position to move leftward
    If Pos > Len(Str) Then
            'at end of string
        Pos = 1
            'start with 1 again
    End If
End Sub
```

To set the focus on the text box at startup, give 0 to the control's TabIndex value at authoring time. Then at design time, give the control 0 TabIndex value. These steps will make the text box have the initial focus. To enable the user to press Alt+E to go to the text box, there are two ways to do that. 1) Give the label control before it the caption of &Enter and give the text box control the next TabIndex value. 2) Enter E in the UserControl's AccessKeys property.

10.
```
'-----from PropDemo module-----
Private Sub UserControl_Initialize()
    Label1.BorderStyle = 1
    Label1.WordWrap = True
    Label1.Move 0, 0, UserControl.Width, _
    UserControl.Height
End Sub

'MappingInfo=Label1,Label1,-1,BackColor
Public Property Get BackColor() As OLE_COLOR
    BackColor = Label1.BackColor
End Property

Public Property Let BackColor(ByVal New_BackColor As OLE_COLOR)
    Label1.BackColor() = New_BackColor
    PropertyChanged "BackColor"
End Property

'MappingInfo=Label1,Label1,-1,Caption
Public Property Get Caption() As String
    Caption = Label1.Caption
End Property
```

```
Public Property Let Caption(ByVal _
New_Caption As String)
    Label1.Caption() = New_Caption
    PropertyChanged "Caption"
End Property

'MappingInfo=Label1,Label1,-1,Font
Public Property Get Font() As Font
    Set Font = Label1.Font
End Property

Public Property Set Font(ByVal New_Font As Font)
    Set Label1.Font = New_Font
    PropertyChanged "Font"
End Property

'MappingInfo=Label1,Label1,-1,ForeColor
Public Property Get ForeColor() As OLE_COLOR
    ForeColor = Label1.ForeColor
End Property

Public Property Let ForeColor(ByVal _
New_ForeColor As OLE_COLOR)
    Label1.ForeColor() = New_ForeColor
    PropertyChanged "ForeColor"
End Property

'Load property values from storage
Private Sub UserControl_ReadProperties( _
PropBag As PropertyBag)
    Label1.BackColor = PropBag.ReadProperty( _
    "BackColor", &H8000000F)
    Label1.Caption = PropBag.ReadProperty( _
    "Caption", "Label1")
    Set Font = PropBag.ReadProperty("Font", _
    Ambient.Font)
    Label1.ForeColor = PropBag.ReadProperty( _
    "ForeColor", &H80000012)
End Sub

'Write property values to storage
Private Sub UserControl_WriteProperties( _
PropBag As PropertyBag)
```

```
      Call PropBag.WriteProperty("BackColor", _
      Label1.BackColor, &H8000000F)
      Call PropBag.WriteProperty("Caption", _
      Label1.Caption, "Label1")
      Call PropBag.WriteProperty("Font", _
      Font, Ambient.Font)
      Call PropBag.WriteProperty("ForeColor", _
      Label1.ForeColor, &H80000012)
End Sub

'-----from Form1-----
Private Sub Form_Load()
   Show
   With PropDemo1
      .Font.Size = 22
      .BackColor = vbCyan
      .ForeColor = vbRed
      .Caption = "This is a demo of usercontrol color and caption."
   End With
End Sub
```

11.
In UC1, clicking a run-time instance will execute the Private Sub UserControl_Click procedure and print Demo1 on UC11 (the first instance of UC1). Here Private or Public makes no difference.

UC2 raises the Click event with the module-level Event Click( ) declaration. With this declaration in place, when an instance is added to Form1, the Click event becomes available. So you can write an event procedure like this:

```
Private Sub UC21_Click()
   Caption = "Demo2"
   UC21.ShowDemo
End Sub
```

This will print Demo2 on UC21 and make Demo2 the caption of Form1. Clicking UC21 will execute the Private Sub UserControl_Click procedure, which raises an event to make UC21 responsive to clicking. If the RaiseEvent Click statement is absent, the UC21_Click procedure won't execute even if you click UC21. Putting this statement in the Initialize event won't work here.

12.

```
'-----from FlagUS.ctl-----
Private Sub UserControl_Resize()
        'activates when form is changed
    Dim I As Integer
    Dim J As Integer
    Dim PB As PictureBox

    Set PB = Picture1    'use PB for picture box
    PB.Move 0, 0, ScaleWidth, ScaleHeight
        'fill form with picture box

    BackColor = vbWhite 'form color white
    Cls          'clear form
    PB.Cls       'clear picture box
    AutoRedraw = True        'make drawing persistent
    PB.AutoRedraw = True
    PB.Width = 0     'reduce box size
    PB.Height = 0    'to prevent blank when reducing
    Scale (0, 0)-(1, 13)    '13 rows
    FillStyle = 0        'solid pattern
    ForeColor = vbRed    'fill color
    For I = 0 To 13 Step 2
        Line (0, I)-(1, I + 1), , BF
    Next I       '13 stripes, 7 red bands
    ScaleMode = 1 'restore twips mode
    PB.Width = Width * 0.4   'box width is 45% of form
    PB.Height = ScaleHeight * (7 / 13)
        'box height is 7/13 of form's scalable area
    PB.FontName = "wingdings"    'get star char
    PB.FontSize = PB.Width / 210
        'fontsize in proportion to box width
    PB.ForeColor = vbWhite
    PB.BackColor = vbBlue
    For I = 1 To 9       '9 rows
        If I Mod 2 Then
            For J = 1 To 6  '6-star rows
                PB.Print Chr(171); " "; 'star, space
            Next J
        Else
            For J = 1 To 5  '5-star rows
                PB.Print " "; Chr(171); 'space, star
            Next J
```

```
        End If
        PB.Print          'new line
        PB.CurrentY = PB.Height * I / 9
            'adjust new line printing position
      Next I
End Sub


'-----from Form1-----
Private Sub Form_Resize()
    FlagUS1.Move 0, 0, ScaleWidth, ScaleHeight
End Sub



13.
'-----from FlagUK.ctl-----
Private Sub UserControl_Initialize()
    Dim I As Integer
    'At design time, Line1's Name changed to linBar
    'Index changed to 0 for cloning
    linBar(0).Visible = False    'hide original
    For I = 1 To 8
        Load linBar(I)          'create line clones
    Next I
    BackColor = vbBlue  'set form back color
End Sub

Private Sub UserControl_Resize()
    Dim SH As Long
    Dim SW As Long

    SH = ScaleHeight      'get form dimensions
    SW = ScaleWidth
    Call SetBar(1, SW * 0.006, vbRed, 0, SH / 2, SW, SH / 2)
        'middle, left to right bar, red
    Call SetBar(2, SW * 0.006, vbRed, SW / 2, 0, SW / 2, SH)
        'middle, top to bottom
    Call SetBar(3, SW * 0.008, vbWhite, 0, SH / 2, SW, SH / 2)
        'middle, left to right, white
    Call SetBar(4, SW * 0.008, vbWhite, SW / 2, 0, SW / 2, SH)
        'middle, top to bottom, white
    Call SetBar(5, SW * 0.002, vbRed, 0, 0, SW, SH)
        'top-left to bot-right, narrow red
    Call SetBar(6, SW * 0.004, vbWhite, 0, 0, SW, SH)
```

```
        'top-left to bot-right, wide white
     Call SetBar(7, SW * 0.002, vbRed, 0, SH, SW, 0)
        'bot-left to top-right
     Call SetBar(8, SW * 0.004, vbWhite, 0, SH, SW, 0)
End Sub

Private Sub SetBar(I, BW, BC, X1, Y1, X2, Y2)
   linBar(I).BorderWidth = BW   'line width in pixels
   linBar(I).BorderColor = BC    'line color
   linBar(I).X1 = X1
   linBar(I).Y1 = Y1
   linBar(I).X2 = X2            'position line
   linBar(I).Y2 = Y2
   linBar(I).Visible = True     'show line
End Sub
```

14.
```
'-----from Dice module-----
Public Sub RollDie()
   Dim Num As Integer

   Randomize
   Call Hide    'hide all dice
   Num = Fix(Rnd * 6)
   picDie(Num).Visible = True
       'show new die
   mintDieNum = Num
   'assign rolled num to property; can be read by user
End Sub

'-----from Form1-----
Private Sub cmdRoll_Click()
   Dim Num As Integer
   Dice1_Click
   Dice2_Click
   Num = Val(Dice1.DieNum + 1) + Val(Dice2.DieNum + 1)
   Caption = Num
End Sub
```

15.
```
'-----from Form1-----
```

```
Private Sub cmdRoll_Click()
    Dim Num As Integer

    If txtBetAmount.Text = "" Or txtBetNum.Text = "" Then
        Beep
        Exit Sub
    End If

    Dice1_Click
    Dice2_Click
    Num = Val(Dice1.DieNum + 1) + Val(Dice2.DieNum + 1)
    Caption = Num

    If Num = Val(txtBetNum.Text) Then
        lblScore.Caption = Val(lblScore.Caption) + Val(txtBetAmount.Text)
    Else
        lblScore.Caption = Val(lblScore.Caption) - Val(txtBetAmount.Text)
    End If
End Sub



16.
'-----from Clock1.ctl-----
Dim Radius As Single, I As Single, Pi As Single
Dim Size As Long

Private Sub UserControl_Resize()
    If Width > Height Then
        Width = Height
    Else
        Height = Width
    End If
        'get smaller of the two
    Size = Width   'get perfect square
    'setting width/height will trigger Resize event
End Sub

Private Sub UserControl_Show()
    Line1.BorderWidth = 2   'line width
    Line1.BorderColor = vbRed
    Line1.X1 = Size / 2 'center 1st point
    Line1.Y1 = Size / 2
    Shape1.Top = 0          'move to top left
```

```
Shape1.Left = 0
Shape1.BorderColor = vbBlue
Shape1.BorderWidth = 2
Shape1.Width = Size    'stretch to max
Shape1.Height = Size
Shape1.Shape = 3        'change to circle

Scale (-1, 1)-(1, -1) 'Cartesian scale
Radius = 0.9
Pi = 4 * Atn(1)
I = Pi / 2              'interval
    'beginning pos is 12 o'clock
Line1.X2 = Radius * Cos(I) 'get x axis
Line1.Y2 = Radius * Sin(I) 'get y axis
Timer1.Interval = 1000
    'set timer interval at 1 second
End Sub

Private Sub Timer1_Timer()
Static Min As Integer, Sec As Integer

Sec = Sec + 1          'increment seconds
If Sec = 60 Then
    Sec = 0
    Min = Min + 1 'increment minutes
End If
I = I - Pi / 30    'clockwise motion
    'interval at 1/60, or 2pi/60
Line1.X2 = Radius * Cos(I)   'get x axis
Line1.Y2 = Radius * Sin(I)   'get y axis
End Sub
```

17.
From Form1, do the following:

1. Add the Pause/Unpause button and its Click procedure. Clicking it's clicked, the clock will alternately pause and continue from where it left off.

2. Add the Restart button and its Click procedure. Clicking the button will set the hand and the label's caption to their original states.

Add Label1 and place it at the top-right corner so that it will appear regardless of the size of the control. Then add the following statement in the Timer1_Timer procedure:

```
Label1.Caption = Min & " : " & Sec
```

Move the Min and Sec variables to the module level so that they can manipulated in another procedure. Add the following procedures. You can ask the wizard to create the property procedures.

```
'-----from Clock2.ctl-----
Public Sub Restart()
    I = Pi / 2
    Line1.X2 = Radius * Cos(I) 'get x axis
    Line1.Y2 = Radius * Sin(I) 'get y axis
    Min = 0
    Sec = 0
    Label1.Caption = Min & " : " & Sec
End Sub


'WARNING! DO NOT REMOVE OR MODIFY THE FOLLOWING COMMENTED
LINES!
'MappingInfo=Timer1,Timer1,-1,Enabled
Public Property Get Enabled() As Boolean
    Enabled = Timer1.Enabled
End Property

Public Property Let Enabled(ByVal New_Enabled As Boolean)
    Timer1.Enabled() = New_Enabled
    PropertyChanged "Enabled"
End Property

'Load property values from storage
Private Sub UserControl_ReadProperties(PropBag As PropertyBag)
    Timer1.Enabled = PropBag.ReadProperty("Enabled", True)
End Sub

'Write property values to storage
Private Sub UserControl_WriteProperties(PropBag As PropertyBag)
    Call PropBag.WriteProperty("Enabled", Timer1.Enabled, True)
End Sub

'-----from Form1-----
Private Sub cmdRestart_Click()
```

```
        Clock1.Restart
End Sub

Private Sub cmdPause_Click()
        Clock1.Enabled = Not Clock1.Enabled
End Sub
```

18.
```
'-----from MultiTab.ctl----
Private Sub UserControl_Initialize()
        Dim I As Integer, J As Integer
        Dim Indx As Integer
        Dim SW As Long, SH As Long
        SW = ScaleWidth
        SH = ScaleHeight
            'lblNums borderstyle changed
            'to Fixed at design time
        lblNums(0).Visible = False
            'hide first label
        For I = 1 To 9
            For J = 1 To 9
                Indx = Indx + 1   'index for each element
                Load lblNums(Indx)
                lblNums(Indx).Caption = I * J
                    'number to be displayed
                lblNums(Indx).Width = SW / 9
                    'width/height of each label
                lblNums(Indx).Height = SH / 9
                lblNums(Indx).Top = (I - 1) * (SH / 9)
                    'top/left pos of each label
                lblNums(Indx).Left = (J - 1) * (SW / 9)
                lblNums(Indx).Visible = True
                    'show each label
            Next J
        Next I
End Sub
```

19.
Add the following line to just before Next J:

```
    If I = 1 Or J = 1 Then lblNums(Indx).BackColor = vbRed
```

You can have different colors for the two headings. The following changes the row heading to red and the column heading to cyan:

```
If I = 1 Then lblNums(Indx).BackColor = vbRed
If J = 1 Then lblNums(Indx).BackColor = vbCyan
```

20.
```
'-----MagicCtAr.ctl-----
Public Sub ShowMagic()
    Static DidIt As Boolean
    Static PreNum As Integer
    Dim Num As Integer
    Dim I As Integer
    Dim J As Integer
    Dim Row As Integer, Col As Integer
    Dim Elm As Integer
    Dim SW As Long
    Dim SH As Long
    Dim Indx As Integer

    UserControl.BorderStyle = 1

    Num = Val(InputBox("Enter an odd number:"))
    If Num = PreNum Then Exit Sub
        'no change from previous

    If Num = 0 Then Exit Sub   'no entry

    If Num Mod 2 = 0 Then
        Beep
        MsgBox "An even number is illegal."
        Exit Sub
    End If

    Cls     'clear for a new form

    ReDim Arr(1 To Num, 1 To Num)   'dynamic array

    I = 1                       'row 1
    J = (Num + 1) / 2           'mid column
    Arr(I, J) = 1               '1st element
    Elm = 2                     '2nd element
```

```
Do While Elm < = Num ^ 2         'up to num square
   Row = (I - 1) Mod Num        'next row
   If Row < 1 Then Row = Row + Num 'wrap around if 0 or less
   Col = (J - 1) Mod Num         'next col
   If Col < 1 Then Col = Col + Num 'wrap around if over left
   If Arr(Row, Col) < > 0 Then  'if already assigned
      I = I + 1
      If I > Num Then I = I - Num
   Else      'move down 1 row, wrap if needed
      I = Row      'move up & left
      J = Col
   End If
   Arr(I, J) = Elm  'assign next element
   Elm = Elm + 1
Loop

lblNums(0).Visible = False


SW = ScaleWidth
SH = ScaleHeight


Indx = 0
If DidIt Then
'if not 1st time, clear previous control array
   For I = 1 To PreNum
      For J = 1 To PreNum
         Indx = Indx + 1
         Unload lblNums(Indx)
      Next J
   Next I
End If


Indx = 0
For I = 1 To Num
   For J = 1 To Num
      Indx = Indx + 1
      Load lblNums(Indx)
      lblNums(Indx).Width = SW / Num
      lblNums(Indx).Height = SH / Num
      lblNums(Indx).Top = (I - 1) * (SH / Num)
      lblNums(Indx).Left = (J - 1) * (SW / Num)
      lblNums(Indx).Visible = True
```

```
        lblNums(Indx).Caption = Arr(I, J)
    Next J
  Next I

  DidIt = True     'after 1st visit
  PreNum = Num     'previous number
End Sub

'MappingInfo=lblNums(0),lblNums,0,BackColor
Public Property Get BackColor() As OLE_COLOR
  BackColor = lblNums(0).BackColor
End Property

Public Property Let BackColor(ByVal _
New_BackColor As OLE_COLOR)
  lblNums(0).BackColor() = New_BackColor
  PropertyChanged "BackColor"
End Property

'Load property values from storage
Private Sub UserControl_ReadProperties(PropBag _
As PropertyBag)
  lblNums(0).BackColor = PropBag.ReadProperty( _
  "BackColor", &H8000000F)
End Sub

'Write property values to storage
Private Sub UserControl_WriteProperties(PropBag _
As PropertyBag)
  Call PropBag.WriteProperty("BackColor", _
  lblNums(0).BackColor, &H8000000F)
End Sub
```

-3-
ActiveX Documents

TOPIC

Visual Basic is now Internet-enabled. It means that you can use it to handle many things in the World Wide Web (WWW or simply the Web). It's now endowed with many tools to deal with Web-related functions. One of the major Web tools is the ActiveX document.

This chapter covers mostly ActiveX Document. In addition, a number of issues related to ActiveX components in general and their deployment on the Internet will also be addressed. Chapter 4 provides more details about the Internet.

Overview

An ActiveX document is basically a form that behaves like an active Web page. A typical Web page contains text and HTML (Hypertext Markup Language) tags that can lead to multimedia contents, HTML controls, and hyperlinks to other pages (see Chapter 4 for details). An ActiveX document can do those and more. It can include most Visual Basic controls that you normally place on a form. Since it can do more processing, an ActiveX document may be more useful in some situations than a standard Web page.

A Web browser like Internet Explorer treats an ActiveX document as a Web page by reading its contents and interacting with its commands. So when you build a Web site, you might include some typical Web pages and some ActiveX documents. When readers want to do something, such as making a calculation, they can call the ActiveX documents.

The easiest way to build Web pages is to use Microsoft Word 97 and save the document as an **.html** file. You might embed in a page a hyperlink to an ActiveX document. The link will let you and your users reach the ActiveX document to perform some actions.

NOTE   Netscape Navigator, which currently has 50-60% of the browser market, doesn't recognize ActiveX components unless a plug-in (an external add-on program) has been installed on the user's system running Navigator. This could limit the usefulness of ActiveX controls and documents.

To create an ActiveX document, you need to follow these general steps:

1. Start an ActiveX Document DLL or ActiveX Document EXE project. This will automatically add the UserDocument1 module and a companion visual designer window. (The differences between DLL and EXE are the same as in ActiveX code components discussed in Chapter 1.) Each module turns into an ActiveX document. If you want to create multiple documents, you need to use multiple modules.

2. Add controls and write code as you do to a form. The OLE control is dimmed in the Toolbox, so you can't add it to a UserDocument module.

3. Put the project in run mode.

4. Open the Web browser and load the related file. The run-time module will then appear in the browser.

To return to Visual Basic, you need to close the browser and switch to Visual Basic. You can then end the run mode. To run your ActiveX document again, you'll have to repeat steps 3 and 4.

Internet Explorer 3.0 comes with the Visual Basic 5 package. It should be installed on your hard disk during the normal installation process. If you don't have it, you must install it before you can follow the steps discussed here. If you want to use the latest version (4), you can download it from the Microsoft Web site (http://www.microsoft.com); this is a large file that requires many hours (6 hours in my case). Recent releases of Windows 95/98 come with Internet Explorer 4. New PCs also have Internet Explorer 4 installed.

You might consider starting a Standard EXE project and then add a UserDocument module. That will not work. When you are in a Standard EXE or ActiveX Control project, the UserDocument module option is dimmed in the Project menu. On the other hand, this option becomes available when you are in an ActiveX EXE/DLL or ActiveX Document EXE/DLL project. That shows the kinship between these two groups. An ActiveX document can thus be considered a Web-enabled ActiveX server (code component).

A Document Example

Let's create and run an ActiveX document before we discuss more details. Follow these steps:

1. Start an ActiveX Document DLL project. Change the module name to **AXDoc** in the Properties window. This is optional, just as changing a form's name.

2. Add a CommandButton control to the module. Change its Caption to &GoTo and its Name to cmdGoTo.

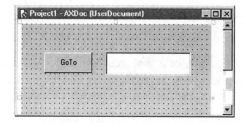

Figure 3.1   An ActiveX document at design time

3. Add a TextBox control and change its Name to txtURL. Erase its Text property content. The user interface should now look like Figure 3.1.

4. Add the following code to the command button's Click event:

```
Private Sub cmdGoTo_Click()
    Hyperlink.NavigateTo txtURL1.Text
End Sub
```

5. Press F5 to put the project in run mode. The UserDocument designer disappears.

6. Open Internet Explorer. This can be done in many ways. If there is a pertinent shortcut on your desktop, just double-click it.

7. In the Address box, type c:\vb\AXDoc.vbd (case makes no difference) and press Enter. (Use the UserDocument's Name property, plus the **.vbd** extension.) If the file can't be found, an error appears. Try a different path. If you have no luck, type c:\ (or the root directory of another hard disk) and press Enter to show the contents of your hard disk's root directory. Navigate from there to various directories. When you find the desired file, copy the string to or type it in the Address box. If the loading is successful, the result should look like Figure 3.2.

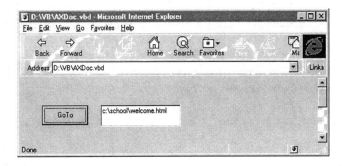

Figure 3.2   An ActiveX document in Internet Explorer

You can now type a URL (Uniform Resource Locator, or a Web address) in the text box and then click the GoTo command button. This will have the same effect as entering an address in the Address box. If your PC is connected to the Web, try Microsoft's home page:

http://www.microsoft.com/

If you're not connected, you can try a local Web page. Our example shows opening a local .html file.

If an error occurs in your code, you'll be taken back to Visual Basic's IDE and break mode will be entered. After fixing errors, press F5 to continue and you'll be back to Internet Explorer. If you wish, you can set a breakpoint or enter a Stop statement in your code. Either will take you back to Visual Basic break mode.

You can now use the taskbar (or many other ways, including Alt+Tab) to switch between Visual Basic and Internet Explorer. If you now click the End button on Visual Basic's Standard toolbar, you'll get once (Internet Explorer 4) or twice (Internet Explorer 3) the error shown in Figure 3.3.

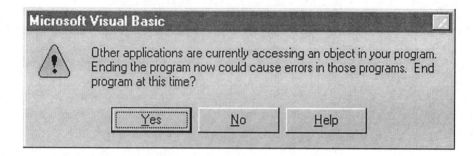

Figure 3.3   Ending execution with document still in Internet Explorer

If you click No, run mode continues and nothing changes. If you click Yes, execution ends. Examine Internet Explorer, and you'll find that the document is gone.

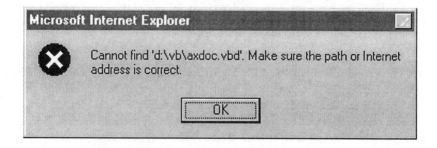

Figure 3.4   Can't find the .vbd file to run

What if you now enter the same file name in Internet Explorer's Address box? The error shown in Figure 3.4 will show up. So now the same file is nonexistent. We'll address this issue in the next section.

What if you now press F5 to put Visual Basic in run mode? If you then go to Internet Explorer and enter the same file name, you'll get no response. You can type something in the Address box, but pressing Enter will lead to no action.

Because of this behavior, Visual Basic manuals advise users to close Internet Explorer before returning to Visual Basic to end run mode. After revising your program, you are supposed to put it in run mode and start Internet Explorer again to test the new version. That makes no sense. There must be a better way.

After playing a while, I've found a better way. This is what you can do:

1. When in Internet Explorer, click Back or Forward, whichever is available. This unloads our document but retains a pointer to it.

2. Return to Visual Basic and click the End button to end run mode. This will cause no error in Internet Explorer 3, but will show Figure 3.3 in Internet Explorer 4. (Another alternative is to click the Break button on the toolbar to put Visual Basic in break mode. This allows you to edit code, but you cannot access the visual objects.)

3. Revise your program, and Press F5 to put Visual Basic in run mode.

4. Go to Internet Explorer, which remains open. Click Forward or Back (opposite of what you did in step 1). Your revised version will appear.

With this technique, you can quickly test new versions without wasting lots of time starting and ending Internet Explorer.

Sometimes Internet Explorer may not work as described above. In that case, enter a root directory (such as c:\) in the Address box. After that, use the Back and Forward button to return to your revised document.

In code, we use the **NavigateTo** method of the **Hyperlink** object to link to another address. Besides NavigateTo, Hyperlink also has the **GoBack** and **GoForward** methods to do the same things as the Back and Forward buttons in Internet Explorer. The Hyperlink object is available to a UserControl or UserDocument module. So we can use an expression like UserDocument.Hyperlink.NavigateTo, instead of just Hyperlink.NavigateTo. Such an expression will cause an error when placed in the Code window of a form because Hyperlink is not available to a form.

Accessory Files

When you create an ActiveX document project, you have a typical project file, plus several other types of files. The main elements are UserDocument modules which are saved to files with the **.dob** extension. You can also add other types of modules that are saved to different extension names.

A **.dob** file contains only ASCII text, just like an .frm file. A companion file with the **.dox** extension saves graphical elements, just as an .frx file does for an .frm file.

In run mode, a UserDocument module has a temporary file saved to disk to be read by a browser. Such a file has the **.vbd** extension. If the current ActiveX document project contains multiple UserDocument modules, each will have its existence on disk. The primary file name is the same as the module name. So if you are using UserDocument1 (the default name), UserDocument1.vbd will be saved to disk when you put the project in run mode. This is the file Internet Explorer can read. When you end run mode, this .vbd file is erased. This is a binary file.

When you compile an ActiveX document project, Visual Basic will create and save two files to the same directory. The **server file** has the .exe or .dll extension, depending on which server project type you've chosen. The companion document file (**client file**) has the .vbd extension. This file stores all the UserDocument modules and their properties, which can change at run time. This file name can be changed to anything after compiling.

A client file contains data which can be manipulated by the companion server. This relationship is comparable to a .doc file and Winword.exe (Microsoft Word). When you double-click a .doc file on your desktop, you'll execute Winword which will then load the data (.doc) file. When you open a .vbd file inside Internet Explorer, the data (.vbd) file will be loaded and its companion server (.dll or .exe) file will also be activated to provide the needed services.

Life Cycle and Attributes

Like an ActiveX control, an ActiveX document can be created and destroyed on several occasions. That in turn will trigger a series of events.

As a demonstration, follow these steps:

1. Start an ActiveX document project.

2. Add the following code. The procedure templates can all be pulled down from the Procedure box in the Code window.

```
Dim mintNum As Integer

Private Sub UserDocument_Initialize()
    GetNum "Initialize"
End Sub

Private Sub UserDocument_InitProperties()
    GetNum "InitProperties"
End Sub

Private Sub UserDocument_Show()
    GetNum "Show"
End Sub

Private Sub UserDocument_Hide()
    GetNum "Hide"
End Sub

Private Sub UserDocument_Terminate()
    GetNum "Terminate"
End Sub

Private Sub GetNum(Msg As String)
    mintNum = mintNum + 1
    Debug.Print mintNum, Msg
End Sub
```

3. Press F5 to put the project in run mode.

4. Open the Immediate window if it's closed.

5. Go to Internet Explorer and load UserDocument1.vbd from the Address box. Three lines appear in the Immediate window (Figure 3.5).

6. If you now click Internet Explorer's Back or Forward button to go to another page, Hide and Terminate will occur. If you reopen (using Back or Forward button) UserDocument1, you'll trigger Initialize, InitProperties, and Show.

Notice that these events are triggered inside Internet Explorer. Putting the project in run mode inside Visual Basic doesn't trigger the Initialize event. Likewise, ending the project inside Visual Basic doesn't trigger the Terminate event.

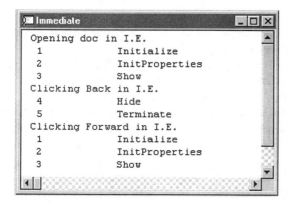

Figure 3.5   A UserDocument's life cycle

If you make the document read and write properties, the ReadProperties and WriteProperties events will be triggered. This will be demonstrated in the next section.

Like a form, there are also Paint and Resize events which may occur depending on what the user does to the document.

An ActiveX UserDocument module shares most events with an ActiveX UserControl module, with minor exceptions. Both have the **EnterFocus** and **ExitFocus** events. The UserControl module has the AccessKeyPress and AmbientChanged events that are not shared by the UserDocument module. The **Scroll** event is unique to the UserDocument module. Scrolling occurs when Internet Explorer's scroll bars are manipulated.

There are these scrolling related properties: **ContinuousScroll** (True), **HScrollSmallChange** (15), and **VScrollSmallChange** (15). The first lets you decide whether scrolling should be continuous or occur only after the scroll box is released. The two Change items let you specify the scrolling speed when an arrow on a scroll bar is clicked. There is no LargeChange property, so you cannot set it. The scrolling speed of clicking an area above or below the scroll box is determined by the Viewport's size relative to the document.

At run time, an ActiveX document adjusts its size to fit in the Internet Explorer window. So its size expands or shrinks as the user expands or shrinks the Internet Explorer window. That leads to a few scrolling issues. The UserDocument module has the **ScrollBars** property that lets you set scroll bars to horizontal, vertical, both (default), or none. If you keep the default Both setting, scroll bars from Internet Explorer will automatically appear or disappear depending on whether there are undisplayed parts to scroll to view.

The **Viewport** is the size of the Internet Explorer window. It may be larger or smaller than the original size of the document being displayed. In the latter case, one or both scroll bars may appear for you to scroll the document to view.

The UserDocument module has these run-time read-only properties: **ViewportTop**, **ViewportLeft**, **ViewportHeight**, **ViewportWidth**. These return the dimensions of the Viewport containing the document. The first two have the value of 0, but the last two can change as the Internet Explorer window is resized. Since these properties are read-only, their values cannot be set by code.

The run-time **MinHeight** and **MinWidth** properties represent the Height and Width properties set at design time. Their values are compared to their Viewport counterparts to determine whether a scroll bar should appear or disappear. For example, if UserDocument.MinWidth is greater than ViewportWidth, then the horizontal scroll bar pops up. You can use code to manipulate these properties against the Viewport to control the document's size and the scroll bars provided by the container. Consider this example:

```
UserDocument.MinHeight = ViewportHeight
```

It will set the document's run-time height to the same as the Viewport's height, and thus clear any vertical scroll bar.

The UserDocument has the **SetViewport** method. It requires two arguments, left position and top position. You can use it to set an object against the Viewport. The following procedure will move Text1 to the top-left corner of the Viewport. To try it, make the Internet Explorer window smaller and scroll Text1 out of view (assuming UserDocument1 contains Text1). When you click the window, the text box will move itself to the top-left corner of the Viewport (the visible area).

```
Private Sub UserDocument_Click()
    UserDocument.SetViewport Text1.Left, Text1.Top
End Sub
```

Multiple Documents and Data Persistence

You can include multiple UserDocument modules in an ActiveX document project. At run time you can navigate from one to another. This section demonstrates how to do that. Follow these steps:

1. Start an ActiveX document project. Change UserDocument1 to UserDoc1.

2. Add Text1. Erase its Text property. Change its Name to txtUD1.

3. Add Command1. Change its Name to cmdGoTo2 and Caption to &GoTo2.

4. Add the following code:

```
Private Sub cmdGoTo2_Click()
    Hyperlink.NavigateTo App.Path & "\" & "userdoc2.vbd"
End Sub
```

5. Add UserDocument2. Change its name to UserDoc2.

6. Repeat steps 2 - 4. Use txtUD2 for the text box. Use GoTo1 (instead of GoTo2) for the command button. Its Click procedure should be as follows:

```
Private Sub cmdGoTo1_Click()
    Hyperlink.NavigateTo App.Path & "\" & "userdoc1.vbd"
End Sub
```

If you now put the project in run mode, you can use Internet Explorer to load UserDoc1.vbd. You can then click the GoTo2 button to load UserDoc2.vbd. From there you can click the GoTo1 button to go back to UserDoc1.vbd.

The **App.Path** statement may be necessary to guide Internet Explorer to find the right directory. An error will occur if Internet Explorer can't find the specified file. Using App.Path will work if both the .dob and the .vbd files are stored in Visual Basic's default directory. If this is not the case, take out App.Path and provide the full path.

Our second Click procedure can be written this way:

```
Private Sub cmdGoTo1_Click()
    Hyperlink.GoBack
End Sub
```

This will work if you start with UserDoc1.vbd. But it won't let you start with UserDoc2.vbd.

If you now type something in each text box and use the command buttons to move back and forth between the two documents, your text box entries will be lost.

What if you want the entries to persist? You need to deploy the **PropertyBag** object to write and read any changes, the same way as you do with an ActiveX control (see Chapter 2). The following procedures added to the two modules' Code windows will ensure data persistence:

```
'-----from UserDoc1 module-----
Private Sub txtUD1_Change()
    PropertyChanged
End Sub

Private Sub UserDocument_WriteProperties(PropBag _
As PropertyBag)
    PropBag.WriteProperty "DocProp", txtUD1.Text, "default"
End Sub

Private Sub UserDocument_ReadProperties(PropBag _
As PropertyBag)
    txtUD1.Text = PropBag.ReadProperty("DocProp", _
    "default")
End Sub

'-----from UserDoc2 module-----
Private Sub txtUD2_Change()
    PropertyChanged
End Sub

Private Sub UserDocument_WriteProperties(PropBag _
As PropertyBag)
    PropBag.WriteProperty "DocProp", txtUD2.Text, _
    "default"
End Sub

Private Sub UserDocument_ReadProperties(PropBag _
As PropertyBag)
    txtUD2.Text = PropBag.ReadProperty("DocProp", _
    "default")
End Sub
```

These all look very complicated. Fortunately, there is plenty of hand-holding as you type code. First off, the procedure templates, complete with the required parameters, can be pulled down from the Object and Procedure boxes in the Code window. Secondly, as you type something meaningful, such as a dot or a space after a keyword, a popup will give you a hint or a list of options.

The **PropertyChanged** statement is triggered whenever you change a pertinent text box in Internet Explorer. This alerts Internet Explorer. When you try to navigate to another document, Internet Explorer displays the message shown in Figure 3.6.

If you choose Yes, the **WriteProperties** event is triggered. The Text property is saved to a name (DocProp in our case) in the pertinent .vbd file. The last argument is optional. It provides an arbitrary default string. If this string matches the text box entry, no saving is made.

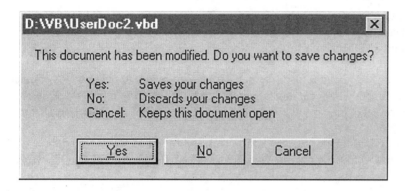

Figure 3.6   Changing a document

When you return to the same document in the future, the **ReadProperties** event occurs and the saved data will be retrieved and redisplayed.

Sometimes you may have two or more sequential documents which you want visitors to follow the correct sequence. You may want them to go to Doc1 before they go to Doc2. They could come to Doc2 accidentally, through a search engine or entering a specific URL. In that case, you want to direct them to Doc1 first. To do this, you need a public variable contained in a standard (code) module.

In the following code, which is a modification of the previous example, we declare Page1 in Module1 as the type UserDoc1. If visitors come to UserDoc1 first, Page1 holds UserDoc1. If not, Page1 is empty. So when visitors come to UserDoc2, the If-Then control structure shows a message box. Then it displays the UserDoc1.vbd page.

```
'-----from Module1-----
Public Page1 As UserDoc1

'-----from UserDoc1-----
Private Sub UserDocument_Initialize()
    Set Page1 = Me
End Sub

'-----from UserDoc2-----
Private Sub UserDocument_Show()
    If Page1 Is Nothing Then
        MsgBox "You must start with Page1."
        Hyperlink.NavigateTo "d:\vb\userdoc1.vbd"
    Else
        Set Page1 = Nothing
    End If
End Sub
```

If you want to add a form to an ActiveX document project, you also need to use global variables to communicate between the form and the UserDocuments. Otherwise, there is no way to transmit data back and forth.

As a demonstration, we intend to use Internet Explorer to read udGrade.vbd. A command button shows frmGrade. The form has three text boxes for entering numbers. A command button on that form lets you close the form and send the result back to the UserDocument.

1.   Start a ActiveX Document project. Add Form1 and Module1. Change the three modules' names to those shown in Figure 3.7. (Their file names are also shown here.)

Figure 3.7   Three modules used in this demonstration

2.   In the mGrade standard module, enter these global variables:

```
'-----Grade.vbp-----
Public gsngAverage As Single
Public gdocNew As udGrade
```

3.   In the udGrade module, add Label1 and Command1. Change Label1's Name to lblGrade. Change Command1's Name to cmdShowForm and Caption to &ShowForm. Add the following code:

```
Private Sub cmdShowForm_Click()
    Set gdocNew = Me 'assign user doc to public var
    frmGrade.Show    'show form
End Sub

Public Sub ShowNew()
    lblGrade.Caption = gsngAverage
    'to be called upon form's exit
End Sub
```

4. In the frmGrade module, add Text1. Change its Name to txtTest and Index to 0. Use copy and paste to make two additional copies of the control array. Arrange them vertically. Add three Label controls to the left of the text boxes, and change their captions to as shown in Figure 3.8. Add Command1 and change its Name to cmdCloseForm and Caption to &CloseForm. Add the following code:

```
Private Sub cmdCloseForm_Click()
    Dim I As Integer
    Dim Sum As Integer
    For I = 0 To 2
        Sum = Sum + txtTest(I).Text
    Next I
    gsngAverage = Format(Sum / I, "#.00")
    frmGrade.Hide
    gdocNew.ShowNew
    'call public sub to refresh user doc
End Sub
```

5. Press F5 to put the project in run mode.

6. Go to Internet Explorer. Open udGrade.vbd. Click ShowForm. The form opens. Enter three numbers as shown in Figure 3.8.

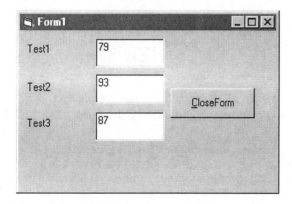

Figure 3.8   Displaying an associated form

7. Click CloseForm. The form is hidden. The public sub procedure in the UserDocument is called, and the label displays the average of the three numbers, as shown in Figure 3.9.

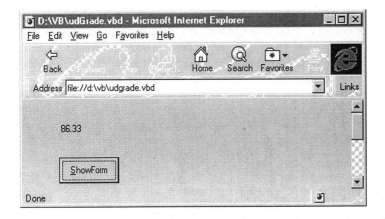

Figure 3.9   Showing a value sent by the form

We use two public variables named gsngAverage and gdocNew to communicate between the form and the UserDocument. The first stores a numeric value that is visible globally. The second is assigned the UserDocument. Then we use it to call a public sub procedure in the UserDocument. Without this public object variable, there is no way to refresh the UserDocument with the new label caption.

ActiveX Document Migration Wizard

You can convert an existing form to an ActiveX document. It's not complicated, but somewhat tedious. If you don't want to do it manually, use the **ActiveX Document Migration Wizard** to do the work for you.

You can access this wizard by choosing Add-Ins | ActiveX Document Migration Wizard. If this option doesn't appear, use Add-Ins | Add-In Manager to bring it up first.

After the wizard is loaded, the initial dialog box appears. It tells you that it can only convert existing forms to UserDocuments. Click Next to go to the next dialog box. All the forms in the current project are listed. You can check/uncheck one or more. Check the desired form(s) and click Next.

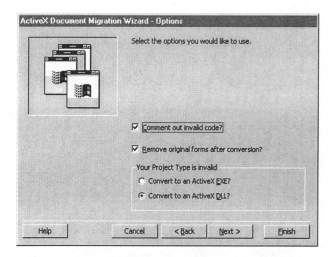

Figure 3.10   The third dialog box of the wizard

Figure 3.10 appears next. Here you can choose to create either a DLL or an EXE project—if you started with an invalid project. (The Project | Project Properties dialog box will be changed to reflect your option made here). You can choose to remove the original forms after conversion. If you choose not to, they will remain intact and you can do whatever you want with them, including removing them manually.

You can choose to comment out invalid code. If you do, some conspicuous comments may be added to your code. You can do whatever you want with these comments. If you choose not to comment out invalid code, they will remain and may cause errors at run time.

After clicking Next, the fourth dialog box (Figure 3.11) appears. Here you can ask the wizard to show you a summary report, which you can save or discard. You can also save the settings you've made here as the default for the future (they'll be used for future sessions).

A summary report appears—if you chose to generate one. It tells you what you can do with an ActiveX document. You can choose Save or Close. A final dialog box informs you that the forms have been converted.

The wizard will change the startup object from the original form to **Sub Main**. If you have no Sub Main procedure, an error will occur at run time. To avoid this error, use Project | Project Properties and change from Sub Main to None. If you want to start with Sub Main, add a standard module and put the initializing code there.

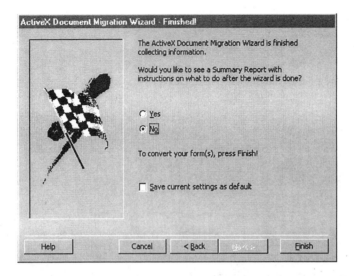

Figure 3.11   The fourth dialog of the wizard

Examine the Project window. A ActiveX document is added here for each form you try to convert. You can now test the document as explained before. If you want to save this new document, go through the regular saving routine.

Creating a Web Browser

Internet Explorer comes with a **WebBrowser control** which you can add to a Visual Basic application. By adding this control, your application can act like a Web browser, which can browse a remote Web site as well as a local folder.

To access this control, go to the **Components** dialog box (Project | Components). Check Microsoft Internet Controls (from the Shdocvw.dll file) and click OK. Two controls will be added to the Toolbox. The one that looks like an emerald globe is known as WebBrowser. You can now draw this control on a form.

The WebBrowser control acts as a container to display the contents of a Web page. It features more than 20 events, which are common occurrences in the course of Web browsing. Their names can be displayed in the Code window's Procedure box. It bristles with methods, which pop up when in the Code window you type the control's name followed by a dot. The most common methods are deployed in this project.

We intend to use a WebBrowser control to fill up a form. At run-time, the browsing area changes as the form is resized. The control is invisible at design time. But at run time, scroll bars are automatically added whenever necessary. But it cannot be resized at run time. So our code will use the **Move** method to make the control fill up the form whenever the latter is resized.

Figure 3.12   The menu options for the Web browser

To provide the user some options, we'll use a menu, which takes up minimal space and doesn't interfere with the display of Web contents. We have one File menu, which has the options shown in Figure 3.12. Each option has the same name as shown here, except preceded by *mnu*. These names are used in the code shown below.

```
'-----MyBrowser.vbp-----
Private Sub Form_Load()
    Caption = "My Browser"
    WebBrowser1.Navigate "http://www.microsoft.com/"
End Sub

Private Sub Form_Resize()
    WebBrowser1.Move 0, 0, ScaleWidth, ScaleHeight
    'stretch control to fill up form
```

```
End Sub

Private Sub mnuHome_Click()
    WebBrowser1.GoHome
    'home page set by user
End Sub

Private Sub mnuBack_Click()
    On Error Resume Next
    'if there is no place to go
    WebBrowser1.GoBack
End Sub

Private Sub mnuForward_Click()
    On Error Resume Next
    WebBrowser1.GoForward
End Sub

Private Sub mnuGoTo_Click()
    Dim URL As String
    URL = InputBox("Enter a Web address.", _
    "URL", "http://www.")
    If URL = "" Then Exit Sub     'if cancel
    WebBrowser1.Navigate URL
End Sub

Private Sub mnuRefresh_Click()
    WebBrowser1.Refresh
    'refresh the current page
End Sub

Private Sub mnuSearch_Click()
    WebBrowser1.GoSearch
    'activate browser's Search button
End Sub

Private Sub mnuStop_Click()
    WebBrowser1.Stop
    'stop current action
End Sub

Private Sub mnuQuit_Click()
    End
End Sub
```

The WebBrowser1 name, which we use in our code, is the default name for the first
control instance you add to a form. At run time, when a menu option is clicked, an
appropriate method of the control is executed. That allows the user to do a number of
common tasks in Web browsing.

Our Form_Load procedure loads Microsoft's home page. You can use any URL you want. If you wish, you can use WebBrowser1.GoHome to start with the URL you set in your Internet Explorer. If your PC is connected to the Internet, the specified page will appear inside the browser. If not, the message shown in Figure 3.13 will appear.

Figure 3.13   Running the project without Internet connection

If you choose Stay Offline, an error message will appear inside the browser window. The project stays in run mode. You can now use the menu to browse a local source. Just choose the GoTo option from the File menu. An input box will prompt you to enter a new URL. If you supply a local destination, C:\ for example, the browser will display its contents, as shown in Figure 3.14. The browser now behaves like My Computer.

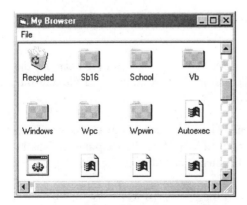

Figure 3.14   Browsing a local source

You can make your browser look like Internet Explorer. Just add some images to a picture box control and place this control at the top. When an image is clicked, its Click procedure will then trigger a method of the WebBrowser control.

This browser will also display an ActiveX document. To do that, you need to compile the browser into an executable file. Then run it. Then put an ActiveX document in run mode from inside Visual Basic. From the browser's File menu, choose GoTo and enter the full path and file name of the ActiveX document (if don't specify a local path, the Navigate method assumes that you want to go to a URL). This will work if you put both the compiled browser and the .vbd file in the same directory. It may not work if they are in different directories. Another way is to put this browser in offline mode. Then use My Computer to find the .vbd file. Drag the file to inside the browser. This will load the document. Figure 3.15 shows the Dice ActiveX document (see later in this chapter) shown inside MyBrowser.

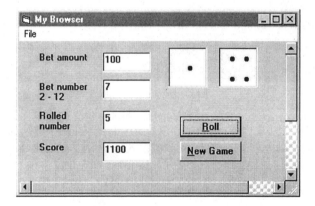

Figure 3.15   MyBrowser showing an ActiveX document

What happens if you convert MyBrowser to an ActiveX DLL project (you can use the wizard discussed earlier to do the conversion) and load the resulting .vbd file into Internet Explorer? The result is shown in Figure 3.16.

Notice that the Edit and View menus are gone. The File menu in our browser (different from Internet Explorer's own File menu) is now added before the Help menu. This is known as **menu merging**. If you pull down this menu, our previous options will appear.

Also notice the extra scroll bars which come with our own browser. We now have a browser inside another browser.

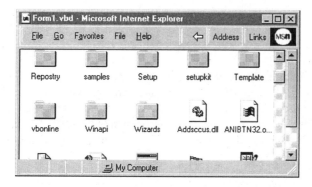

Figure 3.16   Menu merging

Windows Registry and Component IDs

When you use the Object Browser, or go to the Components dialog box (Project | Components) or the References dialog box (Project | References), lots of information about components are made available to you. Where do they come from? The answer is the **Windows Registry**. It's a database that contains a great deal of information about your system and installed components.

Chapter 1 talks about COM (Component Object Model) as the infrastructure that makes it possible for components to work together. The mechanism that makes this possible is also the Windows Registry.

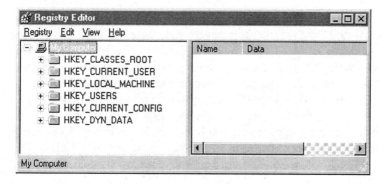

Figure 3.17   The Registry's main sections

You can run the **Registry Editor** to show you what's stored in the Registry. From Windows 95, choose Start | Run and enter **regedit** (regedit.exe). Figure 3.17 appears. The Registry Editor now shows different root sections, also known as hives.

There are several ways you can find out a component installed on your system. One way to do that is to open the HKEYS_CLASSES_ROOT section and scroll to the desired component. Suppose you scroll all the way to MSFlexGridLib.MSFlexGrid and click the + sign to open it. A **CLSID** folder shows up (the next section explains CLSID). Click it to open. The right pane (Figure 3.18) now shows the class ID of the MSFlexGrid control as follows:

$$\{6262D3A0\text{-}531B\text{-}11CF\text{-}91F6\text{-}C2863C385E30\}$$

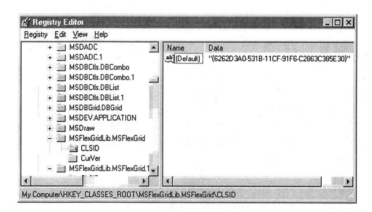

Figure 3.18   The CLSID of an ActiveX control

If you now double-click the Default name shown in the right pane, an input box pops up with the ID string ready for you to edit. You're not supposed to change anything here, unless you know what you're doing. You can, however, search for this string. So press Ctrl+C to copy it to the Clipboard. Then click Cancel to clear this input box. Then choose Edit | Find and press Ctrl+V to paste the copied string into the text box (Figure 3.20). If you click Find Next and wait (you may have to wait a long time if you system is slow and contains many installed components), you'll eventually get Figure 3.19. The left pane shows our control's CLSID (together with all the other components' CLSIDs. The right pane shows our control's descriptive string. So these items are cross-referenced in the Registry.

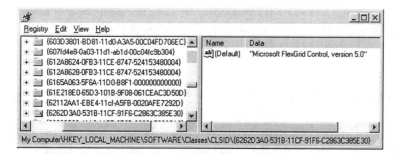

Figure 3.19   A control's CLSID and descriptive string

If you know a component's descriptive string, you can also find its CLSID. Start by choosing Edit | Find. Figure 3.20 appears. Type the string in the Find What box. Uncheck "Match the whole string only" because the descriptive string may not be precise. Then click Find Next.

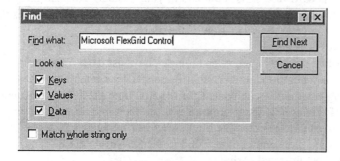

Figure 3.20   Using a descriptive string to find a CLSID

If you keep choosing Find Next, you'll dig into all the sections and IDs related to the MSFlexGrid control. You can use the same techniques to search for the information related to other components.

Interface Issues

A component must expose itself for its services to be accessible from outside. Its **interfaces** are the openings that allow other applications to access the component's services. Think of a vending machine. It has a slot for you to insert money and a keypad for you to make selections. These are the machine's interfaces. A component operates in a similar fashion.

Component and Member IDs

A component's interfaces consist of public methods, properties, and events. These public members are exposed, so users can use the Object Browser to see them. Some of their attributes are entered into the Windows Registry discussed in the previous section.

To identify items and distinguish one from another, Visual Basic generates a **GUID** (Globally Unique IDentifier) alphanumeric string for each project (type library), each public class, and each interface. The last two are known as CLSID (Class ID; yes, this is the same thing discussed in the previous section) and IID (Interface ID). These IDs are generated when you compile a component project. They are 16-byte (128-bit) strings based on an algorithm established by the Open Software Foundation (OSF). The algorithm relies on the current date and various hardware serial numbers in your system. This can mostly make each ID unique from another that may be generated from the same machine or from another machine by another author on the other side of the globe.

To enable communication between servers and clients, these IDs must enter Windows Registry. When you run a component module in Visual Basic's IDE, a temporary registration is made. Running a compiled component for the first time makes a permanent registration in your system. Running the Setup program will do the same thing. You can also use the **Regsvr32.exe** program to register (with no switch) or unregister (with the /u switch) it. Various ID strings and numbers can be found in the Registry's HKEY_ CLASSES_ROOT section as demonstrated earlier.

When you compile a project (which can be a component project) that contains an existing component, the component's IDs are added to the project's new IDs. This enables the new project to access the component's services. The project's new IDs make it possible for other applications to enlist the services of the project.

When you instantiate an class, you create an object, which is an instance of the class. Such an object contains pointers to the class. Clients can then use these pointers to access the services (events, methods, and properties) in the class. That raises the issue of early binding and late binding.

Early binding occurs when you use the **New** keyword with a specific class name to reference a class. The class ID is bound (connected) to the client at compile time. This can speed up the client's execution at run time because it doesn't have to look for the class's ID at run time.

Late binding occurs when you use the generic object type known as **Object** to reference a class, such as the following:

```
Dim objX As Object
Set objX = New ClassName
```

Here we use Object instead of *ClassName* to reference a class. In this situation, the client has to look for the class's ID in the Registry. This will slow down its execution.

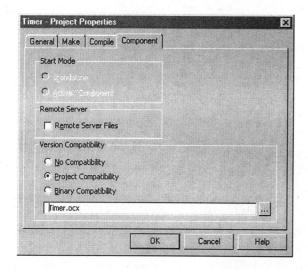

Figure 3.21   The Component tab of the Project Properties dialog box

The **Project Properties** dialog box (Project | Project Properties) and the Procedure Attributes dialog box (Tools | Procedure Attributes) let you set attributes to identify a component's interface and its various members.

From the General tab of the Project Properties dialog box, you can set a type/library name, description, and an accompanying help file. From its Component tab (Figure 3.21), you can select No Compatibility, Project Compatibility (default), or Binary Compatibility. In the first case, a new set of ID numbers will be generated each time you compile. In the second option, the compiled version appears in the bottom text box. Keeping this option checked can avoid the problem of missing references while testing your component. Compiling another time will lead to a new set of IDs except the type library ID. Select the last option if you want to make sure that the new version you are developing will be compatible with the previous compiled one; the old IDs are kept and reused.

If you compile many times with the first two options discussed above, you'll clutter the Windows Registry with lots of entries. Unless you turn on Binary Compatibility, each compiling generates a new set of IDs that are entered into the Registry. This could make it quite cluttered. To clean up, use the **RegClean** program. This program was included on the Visual Basic 4 CD. It's not on the Visual Basic 5 CD. You can download it from the Microsoft Web site.

Procedure Attributes

The **Procedure Attributes** dialog box (Tools | Procedure Attributes), shown in Figure 3.22, plays an important role in identifying your component's members. From the top portion (before the Advanced button is clicked), you can give the selected member a description and a help file, if you have created one. The Advanced button opens up the bottom portion for you to set lots of attributes.

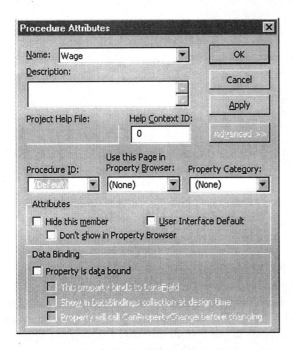

Figure 3.22   Procedure Attributes dialog box

The Procedure Attributes dialog box can be bewildering. It contains many items, which can change according to the component type or procedure type selected. The following observations may help you sort things out:

- The Procedure Attributes option is dimmed (not available) from the Tools menu unless the Code window of a module has the focus.

- All the public members in the current module appears in the Name combo box. Public members include events, methods (sub and function procedures), properties (variables and property procedures). Private items don't appear here. Select a member from this list to set its attributes.

- The Description text box lets you add a descriptive string to the selected member. This string appears in the Object Browser to tell users what you're up to. In the Visual Basic IDE, it also appears in the Components and References (both from the Project menu) dialog boxes.

- You can click the Advanced button to open up the bottom portion where you can set more attributes, particularly those related to properties (public variables and property procedures).

- The bottom portion has three parts and various options whose availability depends on the type of member you've selected. When a method is selected, there are only two available options: *Procedure ID* and *Hide this member*. In the case of an event, *User Interface Default* becomes available also. If a property is involved, all the options are made available.

Every public member of a class has a procedure ID. **The Procedure ID** combo box lets you choose a **standard member ID**. This exercise is to inform the host container about a component's type; it doesn't change the behavior of a procedure.

All procedure types have the (None) or (Default) ID options. The former is the default. Members marked (None) will be assigned procedure IDs by Visual Basic rather than by the author.

Only one member can be marked as **Default** (or 0 value for Procedure ID, also known as DISPID). If you try to assign that value to another member method or property, a message box will let you choose to accept or reject the new assignment. An example of default property is the Text property in the TextBox control. So it allows you to use Text1 or Text1.Text as equivalent.

If an event is involved, the Procedure ID combo box contains events related to click, key, mouse, and Error.

In the case of a method (sub or function procedure), the options include **AboutBox**. You can use this option to add an About property to a control. First, add a procedure like the following (you can use any name for this procedure) in the Code window of the UserControl module:

```
Public Sub About()
    MsgBox ("Authored by . .  .")
End Sub
```

Then go to the Procedure Attributes dialog box and choose AboutBox in the Procedure ID combo box to assign it to the Sub About procedure.

After that, a control instance's Properties window will contain the **About property**, together with an ellipsis. Clicking the ellipsis will execute the procedure.

Your About feature can be more elaborate. You can load a form and then unload it. This form can contain labels, bitmaps, and command buttons to show more information about your control.

If a property (variable or property procedure) is involved, a long list of properties appears in the Procedure ID combo box.

A public property in a component can be connected to a **property page**; this is relevant in the case of an ActiveX control. To make the connection, select the property in the Procedure Attributes dialog box and then open up the **Use this Page in Property Browser** combo box. Your custom property pages and the standard property pages will appear. Select one to associate with this property. After that, a control instance's Properties window will display this property's name with an ellipsis. Clicking the ellipsis will open up the property page.

You can also use the **Property Category combo box** to place a property in one of the available categories. That way when the Categorized button in the Properties window is clicked, this property will be displayed in the specified category.

In the **Attributes frame**, you can hide a member, thus not showing it in the Properties window (*Don't show in Property Browser*) and the Object Browser (*Hide this member*, which can be an event, method, or property); these two options are mutually exclusive— checking one will uncheck the other. A hidden member can still be manipulated by code. You can also make a property or event the user interface default (by checking the **User Interface Default** check box). A default property appears highlighted when you open the Properties window. A default event appears highlighted when you pull it down in the Code window's Procedure box. You can't make a method default.

In the **Data Binding frame** (bottom), you can make the current member capable of binding to a data field. After you check the only check box, the three suboptions will appear for you to select one.

Many of the items discussed above are also available the Class Builder add-in. If you make a change here, it will also be reflected in the other places. These items can be read, but not changed, in the Object Browser.

Packaging Components for the Internet

To distribute your components, you need to use the **Application Setup Wizard** to package them. For components to be used on individual machines, the wizard will create a setup file which users can run to install your components on their systems. For distribution via the Internet, the wizard will create a number of accessory files to facilitate downloading and installation.

The following steps package a component for Internet distribution:

1. From Windows 95, choose Start | Programs | Microsoft Visual Basic 5 | Application Setup Wizard. The Introduction screen appears.

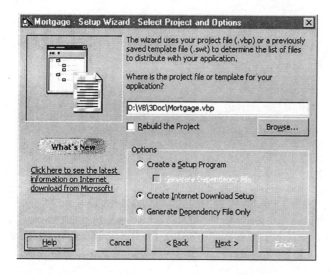

Figure 3.23   The second screen of the Setup Wizard

2. Click Next. Figure 3.23 appears. You are now asked to enter a project name and choose some options. Use the Browse button to enter a project file name. If you want to visit the Microsoft site (assuming you're connected to the Internet), click What's New. In the Options frame, click Create Internet Download Setup.

3. Click Next. Figure 3.24 appears. You're now asked to specify a location where your component will be stored. This is the source from which a Web browser will download to a user's local drive. You can use the suggested default folder for the time being, and copy the resulting files to a server directory later.

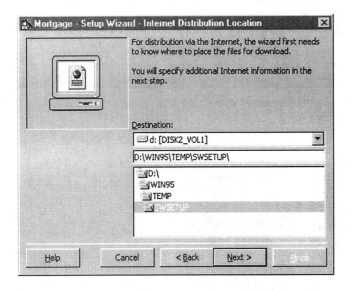

Figure 3.24   Specifying the location for storing the component

4. Click Next. Your screen will go through a series of flashes as the wizard collects relevant information from your system. Then Figure 3.25 appears. You're here asked to specify where run-time components will be downloaded from. The default Microsoft site is a good choice. If you intend to deploy your component on your intranet, it's better to specify a local location for easier download. In that case, click the second option and enter the required URL (or blank for the same location where your component will be stored).

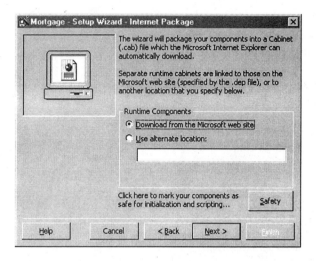

Figure 3.25   The source location for downloading runtime components

5. Click Safety to display an optional dialog box. Figure 3.26 appears. All the public modules appear in the left box. You can check one or both check boxes on the right. By checking each, you're pledging (guaranteeing) your component to be safe for use on the Internet. When you're done, click OK to close this new dialog box. The previous dialog box reappears.

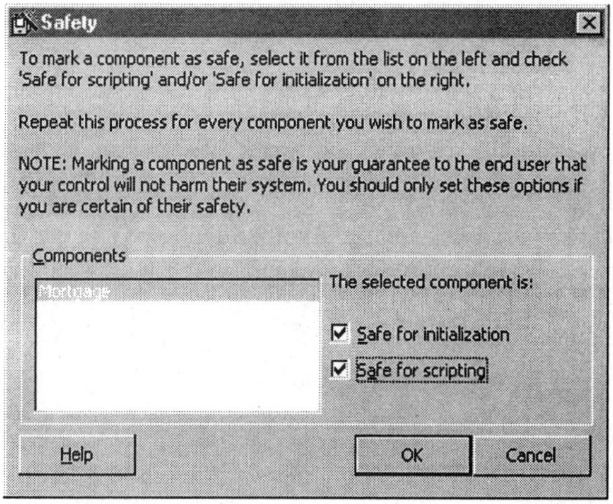

Figure 3.26   Safety checking

6. Click Next. The wizard tells you whether your component includes ActiveX server components. You're given a chance to add existing .dll or .exe files so that they can be incorporated into the current component.

7. Click Next. The dialog box shows all the dependent files in your component. You can click File Details to show details.

8. Click Next. The File Summary dialog box (Figure 3.27) appears. The files listed here are necessary for your components to run.

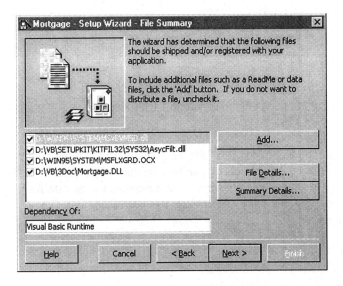

Figure 3.27   The File Summary dialog box

9. Click Next. The Finished dialog box appears. You can optionally click the Save Template button for reuse in the future. Click Finish. Another dialog box shows the final message. It's finally over.

The above steps will create the following files:

    Mortgage.CAB
    Mortgage.HTM
    Mortgage.VBD

The Mortgage.HTM file is a Web page with the following lines:

```
<HTML>
<OBJECT ID="Mortgage"
CLASSID="CLSID:DE71F4A8-A6FA-11D1-8EAC-92EBE0817E3F"
CODEBASE="Mortgage.CAB#version=1,0,0,0">
</OBJECT>

<SCRIPT LANGUAGE="VBScript">
Sub Window_OnLoad
    Document.Open
    Document.Write "<FRAMESET>"
    Document.Write "<FRAME SRC=""Mortgage.VBD"">"
    Document.Write "</FRAMESET>"
    Document.Close
End Sub
</SCRIPT>
</HTML>
```

When a browser loads this file, the code inside will load the ActiveX document file to replace this Web page.

When the user's browser encounters the Mortgage.vbd component, it checks to see whether the user's Registry has the matching ID and CLSID. If so, the **CODEBASE** attribute is ignored. If not, the ID strings are used to download the component and registers it on the user's system.

Since a Visual Basic component requires a run-time engine, that engine must also be available in the local drive. That requires some dependency files. Because of that, the wizard also creates a folder named SUPPORT. It contains three files:

Mortgage.DDF
Mortgage.DLL
Mortgage.INF

The second is the server file that provides the services needed by the VBD file, as explained at the beginning of this chapter. The other two are ASCII files to help downloading. The INF file contains several URLs, including the following:

```
http://activex.microsoft.com/controls/vb5/MSFlxGrd.cab
http://activex.microsoft.com/controls/vb5/MSVBVM50.cab
```

This is the Microsoft site for downloading the dependency files in order to run your component.

The INF file also contains this string:

```
clsid={6262D3A0-531B-11CF-91F6-C2863C385E30}
```

You probably remember this CLSID when we discuss the Windows Registry. This is the ID for the MSFlexGrid control.

If you store all the above folder and files in one directory on the server, you should not have any problem. When the browser loads the HTM file, all the necessary files are accessible or can be downloaded.

Distributing components via the Internet can also involve licensing and digital signing. The former requires a **license package file** created by the Lpktool.exe file. This application file is stored in the Tools directory of the Visual Basic CD. **Digital signing** (to trace the culprit in case a component causes havoc) requires the ActiveX SDK. It's available from the following Microsoft site:

> http://www.microsoft.com/devonly/

You can reach that site directly from inside Visual Basic—if your PC is connected to the Internet. Just choose Help | Microsoft on the Web | For Developers Only Home Page.

Inserting and Scripting Controls

ActiveX components can be deployed on the Internet. An ActiveX document can be loaded like a typical Web page, as demonstrated earlier. An ActiveX control can be inserted into a Web page. If you wish, you can embed a script into the Web page to manipulate this control.

To run applications on the Internet, Sun Microsystems invented a cross-platform language called **Java**. Programs written in Java are known as **Java applets**. These are stored on a Web server. A Web page can contain instructions to run the applet in the client's browser.

Microsoft's response to this technology is ActiveX. The old OLE technology is repackaged to operate on the Internet. The new ActiveX controls (from the old OLE controls) work in a fashion comparable to Java applets.

If you want to do something fancier than the HTML language and a scripting language like VBScript or JavaScript can do, you can insert ActiveX controls into a Web page. When a visitor loads the page, the control will provide more capabilities.

How do you insert an ActiveX control into a Web page? The easiest way is to use the **ActiveX Control Pad**. This application can be downloaded from the Microsoft Web site (see Chapter 4 for more details). While that chapter will provide a fuller coverage of the

World Wide Web, HTML, and the VBScript language, this section briefly discusses adding ActiveX controls to a Web page.

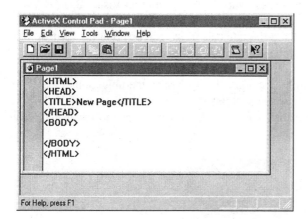

Figure 3.28   ActiveX Control Pad's initial screen

Run ActiveX Control Pad. The initial screen appears (Figure 3.28). Notice that an HTML page named Page1 appears in the caption. The skeleton HTML tags are automatically added. the cursor now appears between <BODY> and </BODY>, ready for you to enter tags or objects (controls). If you already have an existing HTML page where you want to insert a control, use File | Open to retrieve it first.

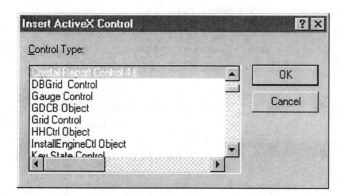

Figure 3.29   Inserting an ActiveX control

To insert a control, choose Edit | Insert ActiveX Control. Figure 3.29 appears. All the controls found in the Registry are now displayed in this dialog box. Scroll to the desired one and double-click it. In our case, we intend to insert the Microsoft FlexGrid control. Two items are then displayed: a Properties window (resembling its Visual Basic counterpart) and a visual designer with the grid control inside. You can now use the former to set design-time properties and the latter to resize and position the control. When you are done, close the windows by clicking their X buttons.

Figure 3.30 shows the code written by the control pad. Notice the ubiquitous CLSID string. It's the same one shown earlier in the Registry. So instead of typing this ID manually or getting it from the Registry, you can ask the control pad to insert it for you.

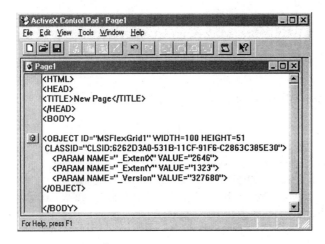

Figure 3.30   The code inserted by ActiveX Control Pad

The various numbers specify the physical dimensions of the control. If you change them in the designer window, these numbers will change.

Notice the icon on the left of the <OBJECT> tag. If you click it, the visual designer and the Properties window will pop up for you to graphically edit this control. After you make changes, the code will change to reflect your new settings. If you wish, you can enter code manually. In the end, it's the code, not the visual objects, that determines the control's appearance and behavior.

You can use VBScript to programmatically manipulate an ActiveX control inserted into a Web page. You can also use ActiveX Control Pad to insert a script. Just choose Tools |

Script Wizard. In the following steps, we intend to insert a command button into a Web page and use a script to manipulate the button:

1. Choose Edit | Insert ActiveX Control. Double-click Microsoft Form 2.0 CommandButton. In the Properties window, enter Hello as the command button's Caption (this is empty by default). Close the additional windows. The <OBJECT> tag is now inserted into the HTML document (Page1).

2. Choose Tools | ScriptWizard to open the wizard. As shown in Figure 3.31, the top-left box shows all the available objects. You can click the +/- before each to open/close each object's available list of events. The top-right box shows all the available methods and properties that can be inserted into your code (by double clicking). The bottom box shows existing code.

3. In the Select an Event list (top left), click the + sign next to CommandButton1 to open up its events. Click the Click event to select it.

4. At the bottom, change List View to Code View. The CommandButton1_ Click( ) appears in the bottom box.

5. Move the cursor there and type the code as shown. Don't include End Sub; it will be automatically added.

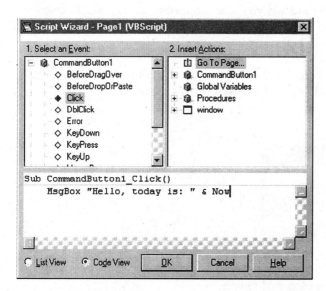

Figure 3.31   Inserting an event procedure in Script Wizard

The result now appears in Figure 3.32. You have written a Click procedure for CommandButton1. If you open up Procedures in the Insert Actions box (top right), the new procedure will be listed. If you wish, you can insert it into your code shown at the bottom. Doing so will have the effect of calling the procedure.

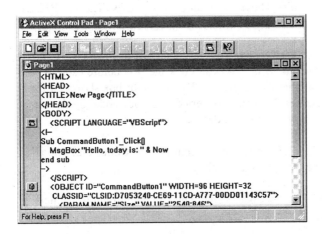

Figure 3.32   The procedure inserted by ScriptWizard

Click OK to close the Script Wizard and you'll be returned to the HTML document window. As shown in Figure 3.32, a script is inserted in the right place. If you wish to make changes, you can just do it in this window.

Notice that an icon appears next to the <SCRIPT> tag. Clicking it will open up the Script Wizard. You can then edit the script or add new procedures.

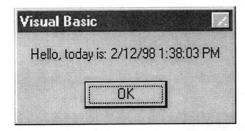

Figure 3.33   Demonstrating a command button

To see how your page will play out, save it with the default Page1 name. An .htm extension will be automatically added. Launch Internet Explorer and load Page1.htm. A command button will appear. Clicking the button will display Figure 3.33.

If you prefer JavaScript over VBScript, you can use Tools | Options | Script to change the default script language.

If you don't want to use the Script Wizard to write code, you can simply use Notepad. Here we demonstrate how to script a MSFlexGrid control. Go to ActiveX Control Pad and insert MSFlexGrid1. Save Page1 (after a control is inserted) from ActiveX Control Pad as Grid.htm. Run Internet Explorer and load Grid.htm. The control now appears. Right-click an empty area inside the Internet Explorer window and choose View Source from the popup menu. Notepad is launched and Grid.htm's source code appears inside. Modify the file as shown below. (If you don't understand these tags, just type as shown. Chapter 4 will explain all of them.)

```
<HTML>          <!-- Grid.htm -->
<HEAD>
<TITLE>New Page</TITLE>
</HEAD>
<BODY>

<H2>Scripting an ActiveX control</H2>

<OBJECT ID="MSFlexGrid1" WIDTH=1000 HEIGHT=300
 CLASSID="CLSID:6262D3A0-531B-11CF-91F6-C2863C385E30">
    <PARAM NAME="_ExtentX" VALUE="2646">
    <PARAM NAME="_ExtentY" VALUE="1323">
    <PARAM NAME="_Version" VALUE="327680">
</OBJECT>

<SCRIPT LANGUAGE=VBScript>
<!--
    Sub Window_OnLoad()
      Dim I, J, Grid

      Set Grid = MSFlexGrid1

      Grid.Rows = 10          '10 rows
      Grid.Cols = 10          '10 cols

      For I = 1 To 9
          Grid.Col = I
          Grid.ColWidth(I) = 500
          Grid.Row = 0
          Grid.Text = Chr(I + 64)
            'letters for top row
          Grid.Col = 0
```

```
        Grid.Row = I
        Grid.Text = I          'numbers for left col
    Next

    For I = 1 To 9
      For J = 1 To 9
        Grid.Row = I   'write multiplication
        Grid.Col = J   'table to grid
        Grid.Text = I * J
      Next
    Next
  End Sub
-->
</SCRIPT>
</BODY>
</HTML>
```

Notice that the items between <OBJECT> and </OBJECT> are from the ActiveX Control Pad. The only change here is the Width and Height. The rest is added.

After typing the code as shown above, save it over the original. Go back to Internet Explorer and press F5 to refresh the page (retrieve the new copy from disk). The result is shown in Figure 3.34.

Figure 3.34   **Scripting an ActiveX control**

The Control Pad does not insert the CODEBASE attribute. Its presence may be necessary. If the user's system doesn't contain the MSFlexGrid control, the following line (inserted after the CLSID line and before the closing > of the OBJECT tag) will guide the browser to download from the Microsoft site:

```
CODEBASE="http://activex.microsoft.com/controls/vb5/
MSFlxGrd.cab"
```

Dice Game

This section demonstrates how to create an ActiveX document that will let the user play a dice game. We intend to create two pictures resembling two physical dice that you can roll. We then will let the user place a bet amount on a number and roll the dice. If the two numbers don't match, the bet amount is deducted. If they do, the player gets an amount based on the probability of getting that number in rolling two dice.

Here are the steps for creating the user interface:

1. Start a new project and choose ActiveX Document DLL from the New Project dialog box.

2. Change UserDocument1 to docDice in the Properties window.

3. Add four label controls, four text boxes, and three command buttons as shown in Figure 3.35.

4. Add a picture box control. Change its size as shown. Change its BackColor to cyan. Change its name from Picture1 to P and its Index to 0. This is necessary to make it the first element of a **control array**.

5. Select the picture box. Choose Edit | Copy. The picture box control is now copied to the Clipboard.

6. Right-click an empty area inside the UserDocument and choose Paste from the popup menu. The top-left of the container now shows a new picture box. Its Index property is 1.

7. Repeat step 6 ten times to create 12 dice altogether.

8. Drag the last six dice to the top row, and the first six to the bottom row, as shown at the bottom of Figure 3.35. The bottom dice are number 0 to 5 and the top 6 to 11.

9. Add dots inside each die. This can be done many ways. Add a shape control inside the first die. Change its Shape to circle and FillStyle to solid. Resize the shape to fit inside the picture box. You can then copy this dot and paste it into all the dice. These dots can be either a control array or individual objects. They are used for decorative purposes; we are not going to programmatically maneuver them.

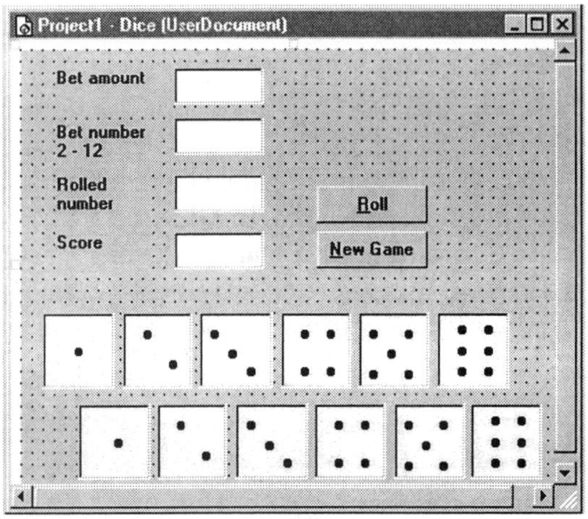

Figure 3.35   The dice game at design time

In the following code, the Initialize procedure hides all the dice. The user is expected to make entries in the first two text boxes and then click Roll. The cmdRoll_Click procedure then generates two random numbers and displays their corresponding dice.

```
'-----Dice.vbp-----
Dim K          'counter
    'Picture1 changed to P at design time
    'it's also a control array with index 0-11
Private Sub UserDocument_Initialize()
    Dim I As Integer

    For I = 0 To 11
        P(I).Visible = False
    Next I       'hide all 12 dice
End Sub

Private Sub cmdNew_Click()
    K = 0
    txtAmount.Text = ""
```

```
        txtBetNum.Text = ""
        txtRollNum.Text = ""
        txtScore.Text = ""
        txtAmount.SetFocus
End Sub

Private Sub cmdRoll_Click()
        Static P1 As PictureBox       'hold pic boxes
        Static P2 As PictureBox
        Dim Roll1 As Integer
        Dim Roll2 As Integer
        Dim PayRate As Single

        If Val(txtAmount.Text) < 1 Or _
        txtBetNum.Text = "" Then
            Beep           'if no entry, 0, or negative
            MsgBox "You must enter numbers in the top 2 text boxes."
            Exit Sub
        End If

        If Val(txtBetNum.Text) < 2 Or _
        Val(txtBetNum.Text) > 12 Then
            Beep            'if entry <2 or >12
            MsgBox "The bet number must be 2 - 12."
            Exit Sub
        End If

        Select Case txtBetNum.Text
        Case 2, 12        'determines payoff rate
            PayRate = 36
        Case 3, 11
            PayRate = 36 / 2
        Case 4, 10
            PayRate = 36 / 3
        Case 5, 9
            PayRate = 36 / 4
        Case 6, 8
            PayRate = 36 / 5
        Case 7
            PayRate = 36 / 6
        End Select

        K = K + 1          'show round # in form caption

        If K > 1 Then    'after 1st round, hide previous
            P1.Visible = False
            P2.Visible = False
        End If

        Randomize          'get new Rnd seed
        Roll1 = Int(Rnd * 6)       '1st roll, 0-5
```

```
P(Roll1).Left = 3000      'show 1st die
P(Roll1).Top = 100
P(Roll1).Visible = True
Set P1 = P(Roll1)
    'assign to P1, to be erased (made invisible)

Roll2 = Int(Rnd * 6) '2nd roll of die

If Roll2 = Roll1 Then   'if double, load 2nd copy
    P(Roll1 + 6).Left = 4000
    P(Roll1 + 6).Top = 100
    P(Roll1 + 6).Visible = True
    Set P2 = P(Roll1 + 6) 'assign to P2, to be erased
Else            'if not double, show another die
    P(Roll2).Left = 4000
    P(Roll2).Top = 100
    P(Roll2).Visible = True
    Set P2 = P(Roll2)   'assign to P2, to be erased
End If

txtRollNum.Text = Roll1 + Roll2 + 2
    'sum of rolled dice

If txtBetNum.Text = txtRollNum.Text Then
    txtScore.Text = Val(txtScore.Text) + _
    txtAmount.Text * PayRate
        'if match, ?? times of bet
Else
    txtScore.Text = Val(txtScore.Text) - _
    txtAmount.Text  'if not, deduct bet amount
End If
End Sub
```

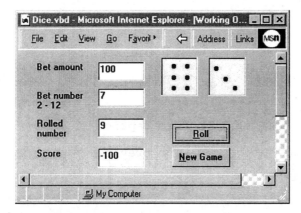

Figure 3.36   The dice game shown in Internet Explorer

You can now put the UserDocument in run mode and go to Internet Explorer to show it as demonstrated before. The result should be as shown in Figure 3.36.

Another way to show the same result is to use a regular Web page to load this file. Try the following steps:

1. Open Noptepad.

2. Type the text as shown below:

```
<SCRIPT LANGUAGE=VBScript>
<!--
    Sub Window_OnLoad
        Document.Open
        Document.Write "<FRAMESET>"
        Document.Write "<FRAME SRC='d:\vb\dice.vbd'>"
        Document.Write "</FRAMESET>"
        Document.Close
    End Sub
-->
</SCRIPT>
```

3. Save the text with any legal name but with the **.html** or **.htm** extension.

4. Go to Internet Explorer and load the above file. The result should be the same as shown in Figure 3.36.

If this file is in the same directory as the .vbd file to be loaded, then the extra path is not needed. Otherwise, you must tell Internet Explorer where to find the file.

Our script in the Web page creates a frame and loads the ActiveX document into it. The document then replaces the original page. See Chapter 4 for details of creating Web pages and using the VBScript language.

Interactive Tutorial

This section provides an interactive tutorial. This is a standalone executable. The next section will adapt this project to the Internet.

Figure 3.37 shows the user interface. Each question is displayed in the top-left label control. A feedback instruction is displayed in the label control on the right. The label control at the bottom shows the score. A text box in the middle lets the user type answers.

The OK button lets the user register an answer. The four command buttons with arrows let the user navigate to any question.

To accomplish this project, you need to supply one or more source files that provide the contents. Then you need an engine that can drive the contents to provide the interactive mechanism.

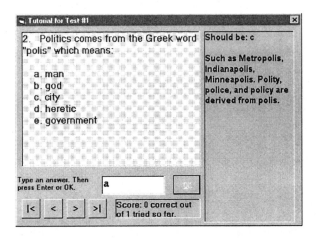

Figure 3.37   An interactive tutorial

There are many ways to supply the contents, including databases or binary files. The simplest way is to use an ASCII file; such a file can be easily changed with a text editor. This is the model we'll follow here. This file needs a uniform structure that can be manipulated by the engine.

The structure we plan to use here follows this format:

    1.   Question 1 text goes here . . . .
         a. choice 1
         a. choice 2
         . . .
    //correct answer
    This kicks in if the user supplies an incorrect answer.
    //
    2.   Question 2 goes here . . . .
         . . .

NOTE   To test this project, you need to provide your own text file named Tutor1.txt. It has to follow the above format.

So we use // as the marker to mark the end of a question's text. The correct answer is placed after the first // marker and in the same line. The feedback instruction is placed in a new line and before the final // marker, which occupies a separate line by itself. Each ensuing question then follows the same format.

Our engine will read the contents and divide them into three groups: question text, correct answers, and feedback instructions. Each group will then be stored in its own array. These arrays can then be used to respond to user actions.

In addition, we have two more arrays to interact with the user. One array stores the answers supplied by the user. The other contains the program's response to a user answer. These can be used to display previous results if the user scrolls to previously-answered questions.

```
'-----Tutor.frm-----
Option Compare Text      'ignore case
Option Base 1            '1-based array

Dim QuesNum As Integer
Dim TotNum As Integer
Dim Ques(10) As String    'hold questions
Dim Ans(10) As String     'hold stu answers
Dim Keys(10) As String      'hold correct answers
Dim FeedBack(10) As String
Dim ShowFeedBack(10) As String

Private Sub cmdStart_Click()
    Dim Temp1 As String      'read one line
    Dim Temp2 As String      'add read lines
    Dim FBack As String      'temp for holding feedback msg

    cmdStart.Visible = False     'hide Start button
    cmdUp.Visible = True         'show navigation buttons
    cmdDown.Visible = True       'set to False at design time
    cmdFirst.Visible = True
    cmdLast.Visible = True
    cmdOK.Visible = True
    txtAns.Visible = True
    lblAns.Visible = True

    txtAns.SetFocus

    On Error GoTo ErrTrap

    Open "tutor1.txt" For Input As #1
```

```
    'you need to create this file first
    'use a list box if there are multiple files
    Do While Not EOF(1)
        Line Input #1, Temp1      'read one line
        If Left(Temp1, 2) = "//" Then
            QuesNum = QuesNum + 1
            Ques(QuesNum) = Temp2
            Keys(QuesNum) = Mid(Temp1, 3, Len(Temp1))
                'put each question & key in arrays
            Temp2 = ""        'clear for reuse

            Do While FBack <> "//"  'read feedback into array
                Line Input #1, FBack
                If FBack = "//" Then Exit Do    'exclude //
                FeedBack(QuesNum) = FeedBack(QuesNum) & FBack
            Loop
            FBack = ""
        Else
            Temp2 = Temp2 & Temp1 & vbCrLf    'add lines
        End If
    Loop
    Close #1

    TotNum = QuesNum
    QuesNum = 1
    lblQues.Caption = Ques(QuesNum)
    Exit Sub

ErrTrap:
    MsgBox Err.Description
End Sub

Private Sub cmdOK_Click()
    Static Answered As Integer
    Static Score As Integer

    If txtAns.Text = "" Then
        MsgBox "You must type an answer."
        txtAns.SetFocus      'put cursor in text box
        Exit Sub
    End If

    Answered = Answered + 1
    'number of questions already answered
    If txtAns.Text = Keys(QuesNum) Then
        lblFeedBack.Caption = "You are right!"
        ShowFeedBack(QuesNum) = "You are right!"
        Score = Score + 1
    Else
        FeedBack(QuesNum) = "Should be: " & _
        Keys(QuesNum) & vbCrLf & vbCrLf & FeedBack(QuesNum)
```

```
                    'add key to feedback
        lblFeedBack.Caption = FeedBack(QuesNum)
        ShowFeedBack(QuesNum) = FeedBack(QuesNum)
    End If

    Ans(QuesNum) = txtAns.Text
    lblScore.Caption = "Score: " & Score & " correct out of " &
Answered & " tried so far."
    cmdOK.Enabled = False
    txtAns.SetFocus        'for next answer
End Sub

Private Sub cmdUp_Click()
    QuesNum = QuesNum - 1
    ShowChange
End Sub

Private Sub cmdDown_Click()
    QuesNum = QuesNum + 1
    ShowChange
End Sub

Private Sub cmdFirst_Click()
    QuesNum = 1
    ShowChange
End Sub

Private Sub cmdLast_Click()
    QuesNum = TotNum
    ShowChange
End Sub

Sub ShowChange()
    If QuesNum < 1 Then
        Beep
        QuesNum = 1
    End If
        'prevent going beyond 1st and last question

    If QuesNum > TotNum Then
        Beep
        QuesNum = TotNum
    End If

    lblFeedBack.Caption = ShowFeedBack(QuesNum)
    lblQues.Caption = Ques(QuesNum)
    txtAns.Text = Ans(QuesNum)
    If txtAns.Text = "" Then
        cmdOK.Enabled = True
    Else
        cmdOK.Enabled = False
```

```
            'if no entry yet, allow entry
        End If
        txtAns.SetFocus
        SendKeys "{end}"
End Sub

Private Sub txtAns_KeyDown(KeyCode As Integer, _
Shift As Integer)
        If KeyCode = vbKeyPageUp Or _
        KeyCode = vbKeyUp Then cmdUp_Click
            'respond to pressing PgUp and PgDn
        If KeyCode = vbKeyPageDown Or _
        KeyCode = vbKeyDown Then cmdDown_Click
End Sub
```

Clicking an arrow button or pressing PgUp/PgDn will bring up an appropriate question
and, if available, the corresponding user answer and program feedback. These mouse and
keyboard actions will increment or decrement a form-level counter and then call the
ShowChange procedure to display the appropriate contents.

Our arrays are limited to 10 elements each. If your file contains more elements, you need
to change that.

Our example opens a fixed file from the default directory. If you want the engine to drive
multiple files, use a list box (or combo box) control that shows all the file names. Then
write a Click procedure that will open the file being clicked. A common dialog control
will be more appropriate if the files are stored in another directory.

Internet Tutorial

In the previous tutorial, we use the **Open** statement to open a text file. This statement goes
to a local drive to load the specified file. It won't work if the text file is located on a
remote server.

To read a file from a remote site, you need to use the **Inet** ActiveX custom control
(Microsoft Internet Transfer Control 5.0) that comes with the Professional Edition. You
can use its methods and properties to access and manipulate files stored on an **FTP** (File
Transfer Protocol) server. There are many FTP servers that let you read and download
files. But to write to one, you need a permission and have a user name and a password.

The Inet control lets you set properties at design time or run time. The required property
settings are done at run time in the following example. The example won't work unless

you have the permission to access the specified server. If you do, use the example shown here but make necessary changes.

To read a file, our previous example uses the **Line Input** statement to read one line at a time. That allows us to detect and intercept markers and place different parts in different arrays. That strategy won't work here. So we need to make a change also.

We can use the **Input** statement to read an entire file, like the following:

```
Temp = Input(LOF(1), #1)
```

The file (#1) opened with the Open statement is now read in its entirety and assigned to the Temp variable. After that you need to parse the Temp variable's contents to find where the markers are.

In the following example, we use the Inet control to open a remote file. The file is assigned to the Temp variable. We then use the **InStr** function to find each // marker and the **Mid** function to extract the text before the next // marker (or the next carriage return). The extracted text is then assigned to a proper array. After the arrays are assigned, all the other routines will work as in the previous example.

```
'-----TutorNet.vbp-----
Private Sub cmdStart_Click()
    Dim Temp As String
        'to store all the text read
    Dim P1 As Integer, P2 As Integer
        'get pos of each marker
    cmdStart.Visible = False    'hide Start button
    cmdUp.Visible = True        'show navigation buttons
    cmdDown.Visible = True
    cmdFirst.Visible = True
    cmdLast.Visible = True
    cmdOK.Visible = True
    txtAns.Visible = True
    lblAns.Visible = True

    txtAns.SetFocus

    On Error GoTo ErrTrap

    With Inet1
        .URL = "ftp://www.tulsa.cc.ok.us"
        'online help says URL must come first
        .Password = "forestlin00019"
        .UserName = "forestlin"
        .RemotePort = 21
        .Document = "/forestlin/tutor1.txt"
```

```
        .RequestTimeout = 10
    End With

    Temp = Inet1.OpenURL(Inet1.URL)
        'open file and assign it to var

    P2 = -3        'to initialize P1 to 1 below
    Do
        QuesNum = QuesNum + 1
            'start QuesNum with 1, add 1 each time
        P1 = P2 + 4
        'P1 is 4 characters after P2
        'after // and Cr and Lf
        'i.e., start with a new line
        P2 = InStr(P1, Temp, "//")
        'find the pos of first / char
        Ques(QuesNum) = Mid(Temp, P1, P2 - P1)
        'extract from P1 up to before 1st /
        'store result in question array
        P1 = P2 + 2
        'move P1 to after //
        P2 = InStr(P1, Temp, Chr(13))
        'find pos of carriage return

        Keys(QuesNum) = Mid(Temp, P1, P2 - P1)
        'extract string and put in keys array
        P1 = P2 + 2
        'move P1 after Cr and Lf, or to new line
        P2 = InStr(P1, Temp, "//")
        'find the pos of //
        FeedBack(QuesNum) = Mid(Temp, P1, P2 - P1)
        'extract string and put in feedback array
    Loop While (P2 + 3 <= Len(Temp))
        'continue if not end, last //,
        'including possible carriage return
    Temp = ""
    'clear the var storing file
    TotNum = QuesNum
    QuesNum = 1
    lblQues.Caption = Ques(QuesNum)
    Exit Sub

ErrTrap:
    MsgBox Err.Description
End Sub
```

The Inet control can be used to upload files to a server. You can also use it to manage the files you've stored on that server. See the online help for more details.

Drill

_____ 1. From a Visual Basic form, you can use the Hyperlink object to link to another location. True or false?

_____ 2. The Hyperlink object has this/these method(s):
   a. NavigateTo
   b. GoBack
   c. GoForward
   d. all of the above
   e. none of the above

_____ 3. A UserDocument module can be added to this/these project(s).
   a. Standard EXE
   b. ActiveX Control
   c. ActiveX DLL
   d. ActiveX EXE
   e. both c and d

_____ 4. You can add this/these module(s) to a UserDocument project:
   a. standard (code) module
   b. class module
   c. UserControl module
   d. all of the above

_____ 5. A form can be added to an ActiveX Document project. True or false?

_____ 6. Suppose that an ActiveX Document DLL project includes Form1, Doc1, and Doc2, and that loading Doc1 will display Form1. When you navigate to Doc2,
   a. both Form1 and Doc1 disappear
   b. Form1 remains but Doc1 disappears
   c. Doc1 remains but Form1 disappears
   d. all three are displayed

_____ 7. A compiled ActiveX document project contains a client file with this extension:
   a. .vbd
   b. .dob
   c. .exe
   d. .dll

Choose one or more events in the following list to answer #8 - 10:

      a.   Initialize
      b.   Show
      c.   Hide
      d.   Terminate
      e.   none of the above

____ 8.   When a document inside Visual Basic is switched to run mode.

____ 9.   When a document is loaded into Internet Explorer.

____ 10.   When another document is displayed.

____ 11.   An ActiveX document is contained in the Internet Explorer window known as the _____ .

____ 12.   If you set a UserDocument's ScrollBars property to Both, both scroll bars always automatically appear at run time. True or false?

____ 13.   A UserDocument, like a form, maintains the same size at both design time and run time. True or false?

____ 14.   A document's design-time Width property becomes the _____ property at run time.

____ 15.   If you set a UserDocument's BackColor property to red, loading it to Internet Explorer will enable you to distinguish the UserDocument from the rest of the Internet Explorer window. True or false?

____ 16.   A menu attached to a UserDocument
      a.   disappears at run time
      b.   appears inside the document
      c.   merges with Internet Explorer's menus
      d.   is illegal

____ 17.   It's not possible to pass information from one ActiveX document to another when they are run by Internet Explorer. True or false?

____ 18.   When a component's public property is designated as the user interface default at authoring time, it will become this at developer design time:
      a.   the default property in the Properties window
      b.   the default item in the Procedure combo box
      c.   the default caption

      d.   none of the above

___ 19. When a component's public property is designated as the procedure ID default at authoring time, it will become this at developer design time:
      a.   highlighted in the Properties window
      b.   redundant in code
      c.   hidden from view
      d.   none of the above

___ 20. When Internet Explorer encounters a Web page with an ActiveX component, it automatically downloads the component to the user's system. True of false?

Answers

1.F; 2.d; 3.e; 4.d; 5.T; 6.b; 7.a; 8.e; 9.a/b; 10.c/d; 11.Viewport; 12.F; 13.F; 14.MinWidth; 15.F; 16.c; 17.F; 18.a; 19.b; 20.F

Practice

◙   1.   Suppose you have an ActiveX Document DLL project consisting of two UserDocument modules. What happens when the following procedures are executed?

```
'-----from UserDocument1-----
Private Sub UserDocument_Click()
    UserDocument.Hyperlink.NavigateTo App.Path & "\" &
"userdocument2.vbd"
End Sub

'-----from UserDocument2-----
Private Sub UserDocument_Click()
    UserDocument.Hyperlink.NavigateTo App.Path & "\" &
"userdocument1.vbd"
End Sub
```

◙   2.   Suppose you add a text box to each of the above modules. What happens to the text box contents you typed if you navigate to the other module and return?

◙   3.   In the above scenario, add code to save a text box entry at run time so that it will return after you return to that module.

◉   4.   Assuming that the following procedure is added to UserDocument1 in the previous question, explain the resulting consequences.

```
Private Sub UserDocument_InitProperties()
    Text1.Text = "11111111"
End Sub
```

◉   5.   How can you enable two ActiveX documents to communicate with each other?

◉   6.   Modify the Grade.vbp project so that the three numbers entered in the form will also be displayed in the UserDocument, as shown in Figure 3.38.

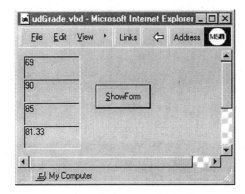

Figure 3.38   Returning data from a form

◉   7.   In an ActiveX control you're authoring, how do you make the name of a property page (which you've created) appear in the control instance's Properties window so that users of the control can use this property name to open up the property page?

◉   8.   Find the class ID (CLSID) of the CommonDialog control in the Windows Registry.

◉   9.   Find the type library GUID of the above control.

◉   10.   Use the ActiveX Control Pad to insert the CommonDialog control's CLSID into a Web page.

◉   11.   Write a Click procedure for the grid control shown in Figure 3.34. When the user clicks a cell inside the grid, a message box will pop up to show the row number, column number, and their product, as shown in Figure 3.39.

Figure 3.39   Showing information in a grid cell

12. Create an ActiveX document (Figure 3.40) that will let the user enter an Arabic number and convert it to a Roman number.

These are the Roman numerals and their Arabic equivalents: I (1), V (5), X (10), C (100), D (500), and M (1000).

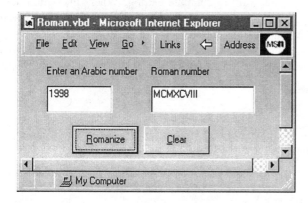

Figure 3.40   Converting an Arabic number to a Roman number

13. Create an ActiveX document that will convert a Roman number to an Arabic number (Figure 3.41).

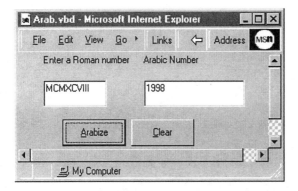

Figure 3.41   Converting a Roman number to an Arabic number

◎   14. Create an ActiveX document that simulates a slot machine (Figure 3.42). You
enter a wager amount and click Turn to show three flags. If they all match, your
payoff is 30 times; otherwise, you lose your bet. The bottom label shows three
numbers reflecting your performance (luck). If you don't want to change the
wager amount, you can just click Turn to continue betting. When this button has
the focus, you can also continue to press the Enter key to keep going. If you want
to improve your odds, you can increase the 30 factor in the code.

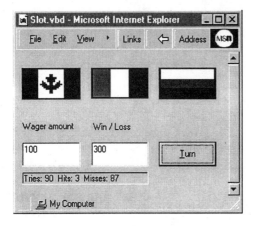

Figure 3.42   A slot machine

(This program uses two image control arrays. At design time, Image1's Index value is
changed to 0. At run time, its Visible property is set to False and five invisible clones are
created. Each is also loaded with an icon. These icons are copied at run time to three

members of the Image2 control array. These members are properly arranged at design time and their Stretch properties are also set to True so that the icons can be enlarged at run time.)

◉ 15. Create an ActiveX document that will create a magic square that appears inside a grid control (Figure 3.43).

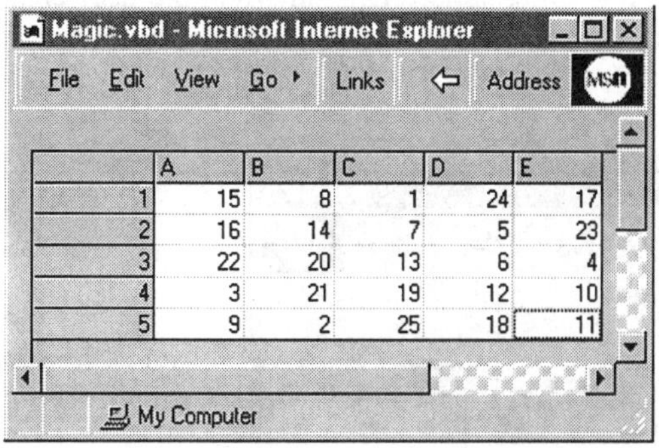

	A	B	C	D	E
1	15	8	1	24	17
2	16	14	7	5	23
3	22	20	13	6	4
4	3	21	19	12	10
5	9	2	25	18	11

Figure 3.43   A magic square inside a grid control

◉ 16. Write an ActiveX document that uses a grid control to display the mortgage payments for various interest rates and durations. Figure 3.44 shows 7% to 10% interest rates at a 0.5% interval and 15 to 30 years in durations at a 5-year interval. The result is based on $1000 mortgage. For example, a 30-year mortgage at 7% requires $6.65 monthly payment. So a $100,000 mortgage will lead to a monthly payment of $665.

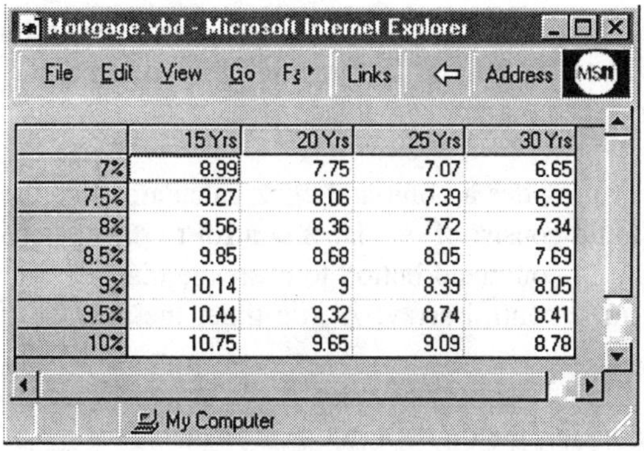

	15 Yrs	20 Yrs	25 Yrs	30 Yrs
7%	8.99	7.75	7.07	6.65
7.5%	9.27	8.06	7.39	6.99
8%	9.56	8.36	7.72	7.34
8.5%	9.85	8.68	8.05	7.69
9%	10.14	9	8.39	8.05
9.5%	10.44	9.32	8.74	8.41
10%	10.75	9.65	9.09	8.78

Figure 3.44   A mortgage calculator

◉ 17. Modify the previous document so that the total monthly payment will be displayed when the user supplies the total amount of mortgage and choose a cell in the grid.

Figure 3.45 shows that a 30-year $200,000 mortgage at 7% interest requires $1330 monthly payment.

The program should respond to the user clicking a different cell by showing a different monthly payment. The same thing should happen when the user changes the number in the top-right text box.

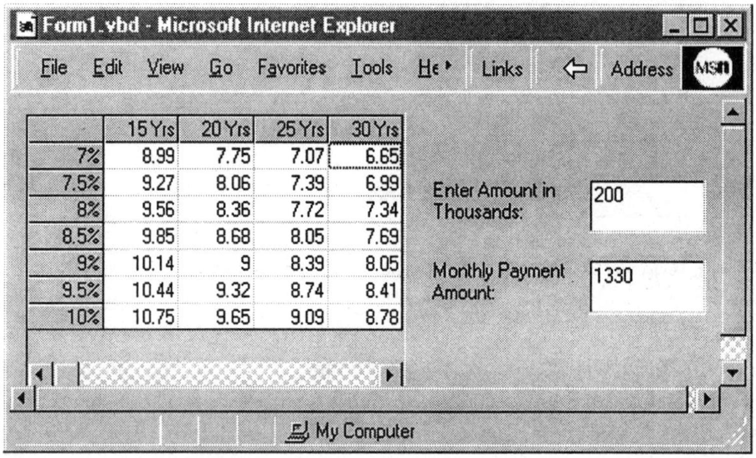

Figure 3.45   Calculating monthly mortgage payment

◉ 18. In the Dice project, add the feature to save the data in the text boxes. With this new feature, when the user navigates to another location and then returns, the previous numbers should be displayed.

◉ 19. Create an ActiveX document that provides a point-and-click calculator like the one shown in Figure 3.46. It should consist of one label control to display entered digits as well as calculated output, a command button to clear the display, and a panel of command buttons that are a control array. At run time, the user is expected to follow these steps:

1. Enter the first operand by clicking the digits in the right panel.

2. Enter an operator by clicking an appropriate sign in the panel.

3. Enter the second operand.

4. Click the = sign to show the result in the label control.

The calculator should respond to the user doing each of the above steps.

Figure 3.46   Point-and click calculator

◙   20. Create an ActiveX document that will let users play a one-person or two-person
tic-tac-toe game, as shown in Figure 3.47. In a two-person game, players take
turns to click the 9-piece board consisting of a control array of 9 command
buttons. In a one-player game, the user starts by clicking a piece and the program
responds by choosing a piece.

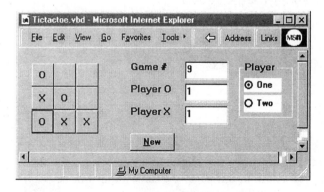

Figure 3.47   A tic tac toe game in Internet Explorer

Answers

1. You can load either UserDocument1.vbd or UserDocument2.vbd into Internet Explorer. When the window is clicked, it will load the other.

2. It will be erased. The default entry, if any, will return. Anything you enter at run time will be gone.

3.
```
'-----from UserDocument1-----
Private Sub Text1_Change()
    PropertyChanged
End Sub

Private Sub UserDocument_ReadProperties(PropBag As PropertyBag)
    Text1.Text = PropBag.ReadProperty("text", Text1.Text)
End Sub

Private Sub UserDocument_WriteProperties(PropBag As PropertyBag)
    PropBag.WriteProperty "text", Text1.Text, "xx"
End Sub

'-----from UserDocument2-----
Private Sub Text1_Change()
    PropertyChanged
End Sub

Private Sub UserDocument_ReadProperties(PropBag As PropertyBag)
    Text1.Text = PropBag.ReadProperty("text", Text1.Text)
End Sub

Private Sub UserDocument_WriteProperties(PropBag As PropertyBag)
    PropBag.WriteProperty "text", Text1.Text, "xx"
End Sub
```

4.
The text string appears in the Text1 box as soon as the document is shown. This also triggers the Text1_Change event. When you try to navigate to another page, you'll be asked to save the change. When you return to this page, the same string will be loaded—regardless of whether you've saved the previous string.

5. Use global (public) variables in a standard module. These variables can be assigned objects or data. These variables are visible to all the modules (documents) in the same project. They persist even after a document is replaced or erased.

6.

```
'-----Grade2.vbp-----
'-----from mGrade2.bas-----
Public gsngAverage As Single
Public gdocNew As udGrade
Public gintTest(2) As Integer


'-----from udGrade2.dob-----
Private Sub cmdShowForm_Click()
    Set gdocNew = Me
    frmGrade.Show
End Sub

Public Sub ShowNew()
    Dim I As Integer
    For I = 0 To 2
    lblGrade(I).Caption = gintTest(I)
    Next I
    lblGrade(I).Caption = gsngAverage
End Sub

'-----from frmGrade2.frm-----
Private Sub cmdCloseForm_Click()
    Dim I As Integer
    Dim Sum As Integer
    For I = 0 To 2
        gintTest(I) = txtTest(I).Text
        Sum = Sum + txtTest(I).Text
    Next I
    gsngAverage = Format(Sum / I, "#.00")

    frmGrade.Hide
    gdocNew.ShowNew
End Sub
```

7. Use the Procedure Attributes dialog box to connect the property page to the Properties window. If a public property has been selected from the Name combo box, the "Use this Page in Property Browser" combo box becomes available. If you open it up,

you'll find standard property pages and your custom property pages. Select one in the list. After that, when you add a control instance to the form, its Properties window will show the property's name, complete with an ellipsis. Clicking the ellipsis will open up the property page, where various properties can be set at design time.

8. Choose Start | Run from Window 95 and enter regedit. Open the Find menu and choose Find. Type Microsoft Common Dialog Control in the *Find what* box, uncheck "Match whole string only," and click Find Next.

    {F9043C85-F6F2-101A-A3C9-08002B2F49FB}

9. After the above steps, choose Edit | Find Next. The second time you'll get the following ID:

    {6E16EBC1-F4B8-11D0-8EAA-444553540000}

    If you scroll upward to see where this ID below, you'll find TypeLib.

10. Run the ActiveX Control Pad as explained in the text. A Web page named Page1 is automatically created. If you have an existing page, you can open it to replace this default page. Move the insertion point to the desired location (where you want to insert an ActiveX control). Choose Edit | Insert ActiveX Control. The dialog box of that name appears. A list box shows all the controls registered on your system. Scroll to Microsoft Common Dialog Control and double-click it. You can now set the design-time properties. After you close the Properties window, code lines, including necessary IDs will be inserted into your Web page.

11. Add the following procedure just before --> in the Grid.htm code:

```
Sub MSFlexGrid1_Click()
    MsgBox MSFlexGrid1.Row & " x " & MSFlexGrid1.Col _
    & " = " & MSFlexGrid1.Text
End Sub
```

12.
```
'-----Roman.vbp-----
Dim RomanNums As Variant

Private Sub cmdRomanize_Click()
    Dim ArabNum As Integer
    ArabNum = Val(txtArab.Text)
    txtRoman.Text = ""       'clear previous display
```

```
      RomanNums = Array("M", "D", "C", "L", "X", "V", "I")
         'put all Roman numerals in array
         '1000, 500, 100, 50, 10, 5, 1
      ArabNum = Romanize(ArabNum, 1000, 0)
         'call function and pass 3 numbers
         '1st argument is the original value
         '2nd argument is 1000
         '3rd argument is 0, 1st element in
         'RomanNums array, namely M
         'assign returned value to variable
      ArabNum = Romanize(ArabNum, 500, 1)
      ArabNum = Romanize(ArabNum, 100, 2)
      ArabNum = Romanize(ArabNum, 50, 3)
      ArabNum = Romanize(ArabNum, 10, 4)
      ArabNum = Romanize(ArabNum, 5, 5)
      ArabNum = Romanize(ArabNum, 1, 6)
End Sub

Private Function Romanize(Num1, Num2, Num3)
   Do While (Num1 > = Num2)
      txtRoman.Text = txtRoman.Text & RomanNums(Num3)
      'add each Roman numeral of the num3 pos
      'in the RomanNums array to text box
      Num1 = Num1 - Num2
      'subtract value, after adding to text box
   Loop

   If Int(Num1 * 10 / Num2) = 9 Then      'if 9
      txtRoman.Text = txtRoman.Text & _
      RomanNums(Num3 + 2) & RomanNums(Num3)
      'add 3rd pos down and the current numeral
      Num1 = Num1 - Num2 * 0.9
   ElseIf Int(Num1 * 10 / Num2) = 4 And _
   (Num3 Mod 2) = 0 Then      'if 4 but not 2
      txtRoman.Text = txtRoman.Text & _
      RomanNums(Num3 + 2) & RomanNums(Num3 + 1)
      'add 3rd pos down and 2nd pos down
      Num1 = Num1 - Num2 * 0.4
   End If

   Romanize = Num1      'return remaining value
End Function
```

```
Private Sub cmdClear_Click()
    txtArab.Text = ""
    txtRoman.Text = ""
    txtArab.SetFocus
End Sub
```

13.
```
'-----Arab.vbp-----
Private Sub cmdArabize_Click()
    Dim I As Integer
    Dim StrLen As Integer
    Dim Total As Integer
    Dim Deduct As Integer

    StrLen = Len(txtRoman.Text)
        'get the number of characters
    ReDim RomanNums(StrLen) As String
        'set dynamic array's dim

    For I = 1 To StrLen
        RomanNums(I) = Mid(txtRoman.Text, I, 1)
    Next    'put each char in entry into array

    'convert all roman to arab and add them up
    For I = 1 To StrLen
        Select Case RomanNums(I)
        Case "M", "m"
            Total = Total + 1000
        Case "D", "d"
            Total = Total + 500
        Case "C", "c"
            Total = Total + 100
        Case "L", "l"
            Total = Total + 50
        Case "X", "x"
            Total = Total + 10
        Case "V", "v"
            Total = Total + 5
        Case "I", "i"
            Total = Total + 1
        End Select
    Next I
```

```
'C before M or D, X before C or L
'I before X or V--add them up
For I = 1 To StrLen - 1
    Select Case RomanNums(I)
    Case "C", "c"
        If RomanNums(I + 1) = "M" Or _
        RomanNums(I + 1) = "m" Or _
        RomanNums(I + 1) = "D" Or _
        RomanNums(I + 1) = "d" Then _
        Deduct = Deduct + 100
        'if c before m or d, deduct 100
    Case "X", "x"
        If RomanNums(I + 1) = "C" Or _
        RomanNums(I + 1) = "c" Or _
        RomanNums(I + 1) = "L" Or _
        RomanNums(I + 1) = "l" Then _
        Deduct = Deduct + 10
    Case "I", "i"
        If RomanNums(I + 1) = "X" Or _
        RomanNums(I + 1) = "x" Or _
        RomanNums(I + 1) = "V" Or _
        RomanNums(I + 1) = "v" Then _
        Deduct = Deduct + 1
    End Select
Next I

txtArab.Text = Total - Deduct * 2
    'all digits were added, so the last group
    'must be subtracted twice to get total
End Sub

Private Sub cmdClear_Click()
    txtArab.Text = ""
    txtRoman.Text = ""
    txtRoman.SetFocus
End Sub


14.
'-----Slot.vbp-----
Private Sub UserDocument_Initialize()
    Dim I As Integer
```

```
    Image1(0).Visible = False    'hide original image
    On Error GoTo ErrTrap        'if fail to load icons
    For I = 1 To 5
        Load Image1(I)  'load five clones
    Next I
        'load a picture to each image box
    Image1(0).Picture = LoadPicture _
    ("graphics\icons\flags\flgcan.ico")
    Image1(1).Picture = LoadPicture _
    ("graphics\icons\flags\flgfran.ico")
    Image1(2).Picture = LoadPicture _
    ("graphics\icons\flags\flggerm.ico")
    Image1(3).Picture = LoadPicture _
    ("graphics\icons\flags\flgitaly.ico")
    Image1(4).Picture = LoadPicture _
    ("graphics\icons\flags\flgrus.ico")
    Image1(5).Picture = LoadPicture _
    ("graphics\icons\flags\flgusa02.ico")
    Exit Sub

ErrTrap:
    MsgBox Error
End Sub

Private Sub cmdTurn_Click()
    Dim I As Integer
    Dim Amt As Integer
    Dim RndNum As Integer
    Dim Sum As Integer
    Static Try As Integer
    Static Hit As Integer
    Dim Num(2) As Integer

    Randomize
    If Text1.Text = "" Then
        Beep    'if no bet
        Text1.SetFocus
        Exit Sub
    End If

    For I = 0 To 2
        RndNum = Fix(6 * Rnd)    'random number 0 - 5
```

```
    Image2(I).Picture = Image1(RndNum).Picture
        'load 1 of 6 images to 1 of 3 boxes
    Num(I) = RndNum      'put random number in array
Next I

If Num(0) = Num(1) And Num(1) = Num(2) And _
Num(0) = Num(2) Then
    'if all 3 numbers match, 30 times payoff
    Text2.Text = Val(Text2.Text) + Text1.Text * 30
    Hit = Hit + 1
Else
    Text2.Text = Val(Text2.Text) - Text1.Text
End If      'deduct wager amount
Try = Try + 1
lblScore.Caption = "Tries: " & Try & "  Hits: " _
& Hit & "  Misses: " & (Try - Hit)
    'show score in label
End Sub



15.
'-----Magic.vbp-----
'before running, add MSFlexGrid1 to form and enlarge it
Dim Num As Integer
Private Sub UserDocument_Initialize()
    Dim I As Integer, J As Integer

    Num = Val(InputBox("Enter an odd number:"))

    If Num = 0 Then Exit Sub
    If Num Mod 2 = 0 Then
        MsgBox "Can't use an even number."
        Exit Sub
    End If

    MSFlexGrid1.Rows = Num + 1
    MSFlexGrid1.Cols = Num + 1
        'total row and col numbers
    MSFlexGrid1.FixedRows = 0
    MSFlexGrid1.FixedCols = 0
        'allow writing to border
    For I = 1 To Num
        MSFlexGrid1.Col = I
```

```
        MSFlexGrid1.Row = 0
        MSFlexGrid1.Text = Chr$(I + 64)
            'letters for top row
        MSFlexGrid1.Col = 0
        MSFlexGrid1.Row = I
        MSFlexGrid1.Text = I
            'numbers for left col
    Next I

    MSFlexGrid1.FixedRows = 1
        'border col and row
    MSFlexGrid1.FixedCols = 1
    ShowMagic
        'call sub to show numbers
End Sub

Sub ShowMagic()
    Dim I As Integer, J As Integer
    Dim Row As Integer, Col As Integer
    Dim Elm As Integer

    ReDim Arr(1 To Num, 1 To Num) As Integer
        'dynamic array to store magic numbers

    I = 1                        'row 1
    J = (Num + 1) / 2            'mid column
    Arr(I, J) = 1                '1st element
    Elm = 2                      '2nd element

    Do While Elm < = Num ^ 2         'up to num square
        Row = (I - 1) Mod Num        'next row
        If Row < 1 Then Row = Row + Num 'wrap around if 0 or less
        Col = (J - 1) Mod Num        'next col
        If Col < 1 Then Col = Col + Num 'wrap around if over left
        If Arr(Row, Col) < > 0 Then  'if already assigned
            I = I + 1
            If I > Num Then I = I - Num
        Else     'move down 1 row, wrap if needed
            I = Row      'move up & left
            J = Col
        End If
        Arr(I, J) = Elm  'assign next element
        Elm = Elm + 1
```

```
    Loop

    For I = 1 To Num
        MSFlexGrid1.ColWidth(I) = 700
        For J = 1 To Num
            MSFlexGrid1.Row = I
                'set current row & col
            MSFlexGrid1.Col = J
            MSFlexGrid1.Text = Arr(I, J)
            'enter magic number in current cell
        Next J
    Next I
End Sub

Private Sub MSFlexGrid1_Click()
    Dim R As Integer, C As Integer
    Dim I As Integer, J As Integer
    Dim RSum As Integer, CSum As Integer

    R = MSFlexGrid1.Row
    C = MSFlexGrid1.Col   'get current row/col

    For I = 1 To Num
        MSFlexGrid1.Row = R   'current row
        MSFlexGrid1.Col = I   'each col
        CSum = CSum + Val(MSFlexGrid1.Text)
            'add current cell to col sum
        MSFlexGrid1.Col = C   'current col
        MSFlexGrid1.Row = I   'each row
        RSum = RSum + Val(MSFlexGrid1.Text)
            'add current cell to row sum
    Next I
End Sub


16.
'-----Mortgage.vbp-----
Private Sub UserDocument_Initialize()
    Dim I As Integer
    Dim J As Integer
    Dim Amt As Single
    Dim IntRate As Single
    Dim Yr As Integer
```

```
grdMort.Rows = 8     'define rows/cols
grdMort.Cols = 5

grdMort.FixedRows = 0
grdMort.FixedCols = 0
    'free up borders for entries

grdMort.Row = 0      'entering row 0
Yr = 15    'year starts with 15
For I = 1 To 4
    grdMort.Col = I
    grdMort.Text = Yr & " Yrs"
    Yr = Yr + 5
Next I

grdMort.Col = 0      'entering col 0
IntRate = 7
For I = 1 To 7
    grdMort.Row = I
    grdMort.Text = IntRate & "%"
    IntRate = IntRate + 0.5
Next I

IntRate = 0.07
For I = 1 To 7 'each row
    Yr = 15     'year starts with 15
    grdMort.Row = I
    For J = 1 To 4 'each column
        grdMort.Col = J
        Amt = Pmt(IntRate / 12, Yr * 12, -1000)
            'monthly payment, "-" to rid - sign
        Amt = Format(Amt, "#.00")
            'format to 2 decimal places
        grdMort.Text = Amt 'put in cell
        Yr = Yr + 5 'increment year by 5
    Next J
    IntRate = IntRate + 0.005
        'increment interest rate by 5%
Next I
grdMort.FixedRows = 1
grdMort.FixedCols = 1
    'restore fixed border
End Sub
```

17.

```vb
'-----Mortgage1.vbp-----
Private Sub UserDocument_Initialize()
    Dim I As Integer
    Dim J As Integer
    Dim Amt As Single
    Dim IntRate As Single
    Dim Yr As Integer

    grdMort.Rows = 8     'define rows/cols
    grdMort.Cols = 5

    For I = 0 To 4
        grdMort.ColWidth(I) = 700
    Next I 'set column width

    grdMort.FixedRows = 0
    grdMort.FixedCols = 0
        'free up borders for entries

    grdMort.Row = 0      'entering row 0
    Yr = 15     'year starts with 15
    For I = 1 To 4
        grdMort.Col = I
        grdMort.Text = Yr & " Yrs"
        Yr = Yr + 5
    Next I

    grdMort.Col = 0      'entering col 0
    IntRate = 7
    For I = 1 To 7
        grdMort.Row = I
        grdMort.Text = IntRate & "%"
        IntRate = IntRate + 0.5
    Next I

    IntRate = 0.07
    For I = 1 To 7 'each row
        Yr = 15     'year starts with 15
        grdMort.Row = I
        For J = 1 To 4 'each column
            grdMort.Col = J
            Amt = Pmt(IntRate / 12, Yr * 12, -1000)
```

```
                    'monthly payment, "-" to rid - sign
              Amt = Format(Amt, "#.00")
                 'format to 2 decimal places
              grdMort.Text = Amt  'put in cell
              Yr = Yr + 5 'increment year by 5
         Next J
         IntRate = IntRate + 0.005
             'increment interest rate by 5%
      Next I

      grdMort.FixedRows = 1
      grdMort.FixedCols = 1
         'restore fixed border

      grdMort.Row = 1     'move to top left
      grdMort.Col = 1
End Sub

Private Sub grdMort_Click()
   If txtAmount.Text = "" Then
      MsgBox "You must enter a number in the" _
      & " first text box."
      Beep    'if no number to calculate
      Exit Sub
   End If
   txtShow.Text = txtAmount.Text * grdMort.Text
      'if a cell in the grid is clicked
      'show monthly mortgage payment
End Sub

Private Sub txtAmount_Change()
   Call grdMort_Click
      'if textbox content changed
End Sub
```

18.
Add the following procedures:
'-----Dice2.vbp-----
```
Private Sub txtAmount_Change()
   PropertyChanged    'notify change
End Sub
```

```
'the following is optional
'Private Sub txtBetNum_Change()
'    PropertyChanged "Text"
'End Sub
'

'Private Sub txtRollNum_Change()
'    PropertyChanged "Text"
'End Sub
'

'Private Sub txtScore_Change()
'    PropertyChanged "Text"
'End Sub


Private Sub UserDocument_WriteProperties(PropBag As PropertyBag)
    PropBag.WriteProperty "Text", txtAmount.Text, "x"
    PropBag.WriteProperty "Text", txtBetNum.Text, "x"
    PropBag.WriteProperty "Text", txtRollNum.Text, "x"
    PropBag.WriteProperty "Text", txtScore.Text, "x"
    'save text box data
End Sub


Private Sub UserDocument_ReadProperties(PropBag As PropertyBag)
    txtAmount.Text = PropBag.ReadProperty("Text", "x")
    txtBetNum.Text = PropBag.ReadProperty("Text", "x")
    txtRollNum.Text = PropBag.ReadProperty("Text", "x")
    txtScore.Text = PropBag.ReadProperty("Text", "x")
    'retrieve data to text boxes
End Sub



19.
'-----Calc.vbp-----
Dim Op1 As String
Dim Op2 As String
Dim Optr As String


Private Sub UserDocument_Initialize()
    'Command1 Name changed to Cmd
    'Index changed to 0

    Dim I As Integer

    Cmd(0).Visible = False  'invisible
```

```
Cmd(0).Width = 500        'each 500 twips square
Cmd(0).Height = 500
Cmd(0).FontSize = 12
For I = 1 To 9
   Load Cmd(I)    'create 9 copies of button

   Select Case I      'horizontal position
   Case 1, 2, 3                'bottom row
      Cmd(I).Top = 1500
   Case 4, 5, 6                'middle row
      Cmd(I).Top = 1000
   Case 7, 8, 9                'top row
      Cmd(I).Top = 500
   End Select

   Select Case I      'vertical position
   Case 1, 4, 7                '1st col
      Cmd(I).Left = 1500
   Case 2, 5, 8                '2nd col
      Cmd(I).Left = 2000
   Case 3, 6, 9                '3rd col
      Cmd(I).Left = 2500
   End Select

   Cmd(I).Caption = I      'show number in caption
   Cmd(I).Visible = True   'show button
Next I

Load Cmd(10)
Cmd(10).Left = 3000
Cmd(10).Top = 500
Cmd(10).Caption = "+"
Cmd(10).Visible = True

Load Cmd(11)
Cmd(11).Left = 3000
Cmd(11).Top = 1000
Cmd(11).Caption = "-"
Cmd(11).Visible = True

Load Cmd(12)
Cmd(12).Left = 3000
Cmd(12).Top = 1500
```

```
        Cmd(12).Caption = "*"
        Cmd(12).Visible = True

        Load Cmd(13)
        Cmd(13).Left = 3000
        Cmd(13).Top = 2000
        Cmd(13).Caption = "/"
        Cmd(13).Visible = True

        Load Cmd(14)
        Cmd(14).Left = 1500
        Cmd(14).Top = 2000
        Cmd(14).Caption = "0"
        Cmd(14).Visible = True

        Load Cmd(15)
        Cmd(15).Left = 2000
        Cmd(15).Top = 2000
        Cmd(15).Caption = "."
        Cmd(15).Visible = True

        Load Cmd(16)
        Cmd(16).Left = 2500
        Cmd(16).Top = 2000
        Cmd(16).Caption = "="
        Cmd(16).Visible = True

End Sub

Private Sub Cmd_Click(Index As Integer)
    Dim Entry As String
    Dim Tmp As String

    Entry = Cmd(Index).Caption
        'get clicked caption into Entry

        'trap wrong entries
    Select Case Entry
    Case "+", "-", "*", "/"
        'can't enter operator before Op1 or after Op2
        If Op1 = "" Or Op2 <> "" Then Beep: Exit Sub
    Case "="
        'can't use = unless Op1 or Op2 is entered
```

```
        If Op1 = "" Or Op2 = "" Then Beep: Exit Sub
    End Select

    If Entry = "=" Then        'if =, then finish up
        Select Case Optr
        Case "+"     'calculate and display
            lblOutput.Caption = Val(Op1) + Val(Op2)
        Case "-"
            lblOutput.Caption = Val(Op1) - Val(Op2)
        Case "*"
            lblOutput.Caption = Val(Op1) * Val(Op2)
        Case "/"
            lblOutput.Caption = Val(Op1) / Val(Op2)
        End Select

        Op1 = Val(lblOutput.Caption)
            'assign output to Op1 for next operation
            'clear other variables
        Op2 = ""
        Optr = ""
        Exit Sub
    End If

    Select Case Entry
    Case "0" To "9", "."
        Tmp = Entry
    Case Else
        Optr = Entry
        Exit Sub
            'get out if +, -, *, /
    End Select

    If Optr = "" Then
        Op1 = Op1 & Tmp
            'if no operator, add to Op1
        lblOutput.Caption = Op1
    Else    'if operator clicked, add to Op2
        Op2 = Op2 & Tmp
        lblOutput.Caption = Op2
    End If
End Sub

Private Sub cmdClear_Click()
```

```
    Op1 = ""     'clear variables and output display
    Op2 = ""
    Optr = ""
    lblOutput.Caption = ""
End Sub
```

20.

```
'-----Tictactoe.vbp-----
Dim Score(1 To 9) As Integer
    'keep track of X or O to determine winner
Dim Player As Integer
    '1 if O wins, 2 if X wins
Dim Ind(1 To 8, 1 To 3) As Integer 'to index pieces
Dim XTurn As Boolean
Dim I As Integer     'for looping
Dim J As Integer
Dim K As Integer     'counter

Private Sub UserDocument_Initialize()
    'Command1 Name changed to cmdTile
    'Index changed to 0 at design time

    cmdTile(0).Visible = False  'invisible
    cmdTile(0).Width = 500      'each 400 twips in width

    'to give each piece an index number
    'so that they can be looped with For
    Ind(1, 1) = 1   'rows
    Ind(1, 2) = 2
    Ind(1, 3) = 3
    Ind(2, 1) = 4
    Ind(2, 2) = 5
    Ind(2, 3) = 6
    Ind(3, 1) = 7
    Ind(3, 2) = 8
    Ind(3, 3) = 9

    Ind(4, 1) = 1    'columns
    Ind(4, 2) = 4
    Ind(4, 3) = 7
    Ind(5, 1) = 2
    Ind(5, 2) = 5
```

```
Ind(5, 3) = 8
Ind(6, 1) = 3
Ind(6, 2) = 6
Ind(6, 3) = 9

Ind(7, 1) = 1    'diagonal
Ind(7, 2) = 5
Ind(7, 3) = 9
Ind(8, 1) = 3
Ind(8, 2) = 5
Ind(8, 3) = 7

For I = 1 To 9
   Load cmdTile(I)    'create 9 copies of button

   Select Case I      'horizontal position
   Case 1, 2, 3                '1st row
      cmdTile(I).Top = 300
   Case 4, 5, 6                '2nd row
      cmdTile(I).Top = 800
   Case 7, 8, 9                '3rd row
      cmdTile(I).Top = 1300
   End Select

   Select Case I      'vertical position
   Case 1, 4, 7                '1st col
      cmdTile(I).Left = 300
   Case 2, 5, 8                '2nd col
      cmdTile(I).Left = 800
   Case 3, 6, 9                '3rd col
      cmdTile(I).Left = 1300
   End Select

   cmdTile(I).Caption = ""      'no caption
   cmdTile(I).Visible = True   'show button
Next I

txtGameNum.Text = 1      'game number starts with 1
txtPlayer0.Text = 0     'score 0
txtPlayerX.Text = 0
optOne.Value = True      'default one-player
End Sub
```

```
Private Sub cmdTile_Click(I As Integer)
    Static Tie As Integer    'track tie game
    If cmdTile(I).Caption < > "" Then
        Beep            'if button already clicked
        Exit Sub
    End If

'****2 players****
  If optTwo.Value Then
    If XTurn Then        'X turn
        cmdTile(I).Caption = "X"
        Score(I) = 2    'player 2 score
    Else                 'O turn
        cmdTile(I).Caption = "O"
        Score(I) = 1    'player 1 score
    End If
    XTurn = Not XTurn    'switch between O and X
  End If
'*********

'****1 player****
  If optOne.Value Then
    cmdTile(I).Caption = "O"    'enter player O's score caption
    Score(I) = 1               'player1 score

    If K = 0 Then       'player not allowed to enter 5 in 1st round
        If Score(5) = 1 Then
            Beep
            cmdTile(I).Caption = ""
            Score(I) = 0
            Exit Sub
        End If
    End If
  End If

  Tie = Tie + 1

  For I = 1 To 8  'try to win
     If Score(Ind(I, 1)) = 2 And Score(Ind(I, 2)) = 2 And _
     Score(Ind(I, 3)) = 0 Then cmdTile(Ind(I, 3)).Caption = "X": _
     Score(Ind(I, 3)) = 2: GoTo Test
     If Score(Ind(I, 1)) = 2 And Score(Ind(I, 3)) = 2 And _
     Score(Ind(I, 2)) = 0 Then cmdTile(Ind(I, 2)).Caption = "X": _
     Score(Ind(I, 2)) = 2: GoTo Test
```

```
         If Score(Ind(I, 2)) = 2 And Score(Ind(I, 3)) = 2 And _
         Score(Ind(I, 1)) = 0 Then cmdTile(Ind(I, 1)).Caption = "X": _
         Score(Ind(I, 1)) = 2: GoTo Test
      Next I

      For I = 1 To 8  'try to block
         If Score(Ind(I, 1)) = 1 And Score(Ind(I, 2)) = 1 And _
         Score(Ind(I, 3)) = 0 Then cmdTile(Ind(I, 3)).Caption = "X": _
         Score(Ind(I, 3)) = 2: GoTo Test
         If Score(Ind(I, 1)) = 1 And Score(Ind(I, 3)) = 1 And _
         Score(Ind(I, 2)) = 0 Then cmdTile(Ind(I, 2)).Caption = "X": _
         Score(Ind(I, 2)) = 2: GoTo Test
         If Score(Ind(I, 2)) = 1 And Score(Ind(I, 3)) = 1 And _
         Score(Ind(I, 1)) = 0 Then cmdTile(Ind(I, 1)).Caption = "X": _
         Score(Ind(I, 1)) = 2: GoTo Test
      Next I

         'if no match, then generate a random response
      Do While K < 4
         'don't get in after 5th turn, to prevent infinite loop
         J = Int(8 * Rnd) + 1
         If cmdTile(J).Caption = "" Then
            cmdTile(J).Caption = "X"    'show X in caption
            Score(J) = 2               'put in array
            Exit Do     'get out
         End If
      Loop
   End If
'**********

'****determine if there is winner****
Test:
   For I = 1 To 8
      If Score(Ind(I, 1)) * Score(Ind(I, 2)) * _
      Score(Ind(I, 3)) = 1 Then
         Player = 1   'player 0 wins
         GoTo Fin
      End If
   Next I
   For I = 1 To 8
      If Score(Ind(I, 1)) * Score(Ind(I, 2)) * _
      Score(Ind(I, 3)) = 8 Then
         Player = 2   'player X wins
```

```
            GoTo Fin
        End If
    Next I

'****game over****
Fin:
    If Player = 1 Then
        Tie = 0
        'clear static var used to track game's end
        txtPlayer0.Text = txtPlayer0.Text + 1
        MsgBox "O wins"
        ClearUp     'call sub to clear array var
        FinishUp    'call sub to disable buttons
    End If

    If Player = 2 Then
        Tie = 0
        txtPlayerX.Text = txtPlayerX.Text + 1
        MsgBox "X wins"
        ClearUp
        FinishUp
    End If

    If Tie > = 9 Then     'game over
        Tie = 0
        MsgBox "Tie"
        ClearUp
        FinishUp
    End If

    Tie = Tie + 1
    K = K + 1
End Sub

Private Sub ClearUp()
    For I = 1 To 9
        Score(I) = 0         'clear array variables
        cmdTile(I).Enabled = True
    Next I
    Player = 0
    Beep
End Sub
```

```
Private Sub cmdNew_Click()
    For I = 1 To 9
        cmdTile(I).Caption = ""
    Next I              'clear all captions
    XTurn = False    'new round for 2 players
    K = 0
    txtGameNum.Text = txtGameNum.Text + 1
    ClearUp     'call sub to clear array var
End Sub

Private Sub FinishUp()
    For I = 1 To 9
        cmdTile(I).Enabled = False    'disable buttons
    Next I
End Sub
```

-4-

The Internet, HTML, and VBScript

TOPICS

This chapter covers a few topics related to the Internet and the World Wide Web.
Knowing these topics enables you to apply your Visual Basic knowledge to the Internet.

The coverage here provides considerable breadth but not much depth. A few related books
are being planned and may be available in the near future.

Internet Overview

The Internet (Net for short) is a global network of computer networks. It's a network that enables connected computers to communicate with one another. In its most elementary level, it's like a telephone system that enables people to verbally communicate with one another. Once connected to the Internet, a computer can transmit and receive text, voice, graphics, and motion pictures—the whole multimedia gamut.

The Internet had its origin in the Cold War. Researchers in major universities working on different military projects needed to communicate with one another. To increase the chances for these communications to go through, researchers devised the **TCP/IP** (they stand for Transmission Control Protocol and Internet Protocol) **protocol**, which is a set of rules. This protocol requires a message to be divided into smaller units known as **packets**, each of which containing a sequential number and the addresses of the sender and the recipient. These packets can go through different telephone routes in a web-like structure (think of a spider web or a fishnet). If one route is blocked (maybe by a nuclear attack), packets can find alternative ways (think of highway detours) to reach the same destination. When the packets arrive, they will be reassembled and delivered to the recipient.

This history molded the Internet to what it is today. As the U.S. government relegated its control to the market place, today's Internet is a vast loosely structured network of networks. There are rules set by some international bodies (one of them is **W3C** or the **World Wide Web Consortium**) with members coming from major user groups. These rules don't always apply because users continue to do innovative and sometimes insidious things (such as attempting and succeeding in paralyzing a major network like America Online). That's why the Net continues to grow and change. It's like the Wild West all over again.

To handle numerous types of users, it was necessary to divide them into different **domains**. Think of the name *microsoft.com*. The notation after the dot is a domain type. It can be **com** (commercial, most common), **edu** (education), **gov** (government of the U.S.), **mil** (military of the U.S.), **org** (organization, noncommercial), **net** (network), **us** (United States, or many other abbreviations for other countries), and some new types from time to time.

The Internet provides different kinds of services, each following its own protocol. Most are now replaced by the Web (short for World Wide Web), which follows the **HTTP** (Hypertext Transfer Protocol) protocol. A **URL**, or Uniform (or Universal) Resource Locator, is used by the Web to find a site. When a browser sees an address that starts with http://, it follows the HTTP protocol to find the site. Most Web sites start with the

WWW name to signify it as a Web site. However, there are some sites that don't use that prefix, including home.microsoft.com and home.netscape.com.

As the Internet becomes the global information superhighway, companies and individuals get on the highway to do business and visit one another. Companies maintain their own internal networks that comply with the IP protocol. These are known as **intranets**. To protect themselves, companies deploy **firewalls** (proxy servers) to prevent access by unauthorized outsiders. But this arrangement allows them to venture out to touch the world. Once they venture beyond their firewalls, they are reaching the **extranet**. So now company employees can follow the same common rules and standards to communicate with anyone else, inside or outside the company.

Besides the above company scenario, the Net is teeming with two other types of activities: billboards and information stores. Most Web sites (see the next section about this) today are like billboards advertising services/merchandise and soliciting shoppers/patrons. This is also the fastest growing activities. Since it's relatively inexpensive to open and maintain a Web site, more and more businesses and individuals are opening up shops on the Web.

There are other Web sites which offer vast amount of information waiting for visitors to peruse. These are usually offered by nonprofit organizations. There are also commercial outfits offering substantial useful information free to visitors. They do this to promote their images or products. Some magazines, for example, let you read their summarized versions for free or give you a one-month free subscription. They will charge your if you want other services.

The Web and the Internet are now treated by many as synonymous. Technically there is a difference. The Internet is the vast infrastructure containing all the interconnected highways. The Web is a particular type of vehicle that uses the highway to provide multimedia communications.

If you are an individual user, you can pay a monthly fee (about $20) to an **ISP** (Internet service provider) to connect to the Internet. You use a modem to connect from your PC to the ISP's modem via the telephone line. Modem connections are relatively slow, mostly at 28.8, 33.6, or 56 Kbps (kilobits per second). Coaxial cables and satellite connections are finding more subscribers who are willing to pay higher prices to cruise the Net at a higher speed. Large companies also use expensive T1 and T3 lines to connect their computers. These fiber-optic cables can carry data at 1.544 and up to 44.736 Mbps.

In spite of the increasing **bandwidth** (capacity to carry data, such as the number of lanes in a highway), the Internet is still slow and may be getting slower due to more and more users crowding it. A new high-speed highway known as **Internet2** is being opened. In late 1997 about a dozen major U.S. universities began their connections to this new system. How this experiment will affect ordinary users is hard to predict at this time.

World Wide Web and Browsers

The Internet gained its widespread popularity largely due to the World Wide Web and two major Web browsers.

The Internet was strictly text-based at the outset. The content may be rich, but the media was boring. Then the HTML (see the next section) came along to display fancy fonts and brilliant colors. Multimedia capabilities were later added to make the Net glitzier and livelier, looking more and more like television.

Ease of use was also an issue. Anyone wanting to access the Net in the earlier days had to use abstruse UNIX commands. It was like DOS before the arrival of Windows. It was not for green horns or timid hearts.

Then came **Mosaic**. It was the first graphical Web browser developed at NCSA (National Center for Supercomputer Applications, a tax-payer funded institution located at the University of Illinois). This GUI point-and-click browser was a vast improvement over arcane UNIX commands. Besides, it was free for anyone to download. Vast number of people began to flock to the Web.

A graduate student working on Mosaic would make the next leap. A venture capitalist lured him and his colleagues to Silicon Valley to start a Web browser company. The result was **Netscape**. The browser, an improvement upon Mosaic, was an instant success. More and more people all over the world began to cruise the Net with Netscape.

Netscape's phenomenal success began to shake up the computer world. Netscape officials and many computer pundits began to foresee a future in which Windows and Microsoft would become irrelevant. In that world, Netscape, the universal browser, would replace the Windows operating system, and computers of all kinds would talk with one another with the new universal language known as **Java**. Sun, which invented Java by modifying and simplifying the C++ language, would then co-rule computerdom with Netscape.

The alarmed Microsoft began to see its very survival at stake. It began to reverse itself and wholeheartedly embrace the Internet. Microsoft's entry into the Internet made big waves. The biggest computer event in 1996 was Microsoft's joining the Web browser battle. It rapidly released **Internet Explorer** 2 and 3; version 4, the latest, became available in late 1997. It also lets anybody download the browser free of charge. Its battery of popular applications and development tools, including Office 97, Visual C++, Visual J++, and Visual Basic, are all given capabilities to handle Web functions.

Microsoft's embracing the Web has profound effects on users of Microsoft products. Most of these products let you create Web pages with a minimum of efforts. Web-enabled compound documents can be assembled quickly and transmitted via the Internet. Web pages can be manipulated with **VBScript**, a slimmed-down version of Visual Basic's language component. If you want to develop and manipulate Web sites, you can use Visual Basic 5 to do many things, including creating executables that behave like Web pages.

Microsoft's most effective tactic to gain market share for its browser is to integrate the browser (Internet Explorer 4) into Windows 95/98. This integration now makes your desktop just another Web site. Or, to look at it from another angle, a remote Web site can be treated as a part of your desktop. The net result is that instead of Netscape Navigator reaching in to grab every desktop, Windows is reaching out to grab the Internet. As Internet Explorer's market share (about 40% in early 1998) increased dramatically, reducing Netscape's dominance, the alarmed Netscape convinced the U.S. Justice Department to force Microsoft to untie Windows 95/98 and Internet Explorer 4 on the ground that this combination would lock out competitors. This legal battle is not over as of early 1998.

The future of the Web is bright, but Microsoft's role in it is at the moment clouded by a number of celebrated lawsuits. Besides the above-mentioned U.S./Netscape vs. Microsoft fight, Sun is also suing Microsoft on the ground that Internet Explorer 4 doesn't fully support Java, which, controlled by Sun, is seen by Microsoft as a weapon to wipe out Microsoft. Various State Attorney Generals and even the European Union are also investigating the charges that Microsoft is monopolistic and predatory.

Web battles notwithstanding, the Web marches on. The popularity of the Web and Web browsing has also increased **Web publishing**. That's putting your contents in a Web site for others to access. To let others access your data, you can run a computer 24 hours a day running a Web server program and connecting to the Internet with a domain name. Web browsers can then log on to your site. You can put up free contents to attract viewers and then sell advertisements to earn income, all similar to the way a magazine or newspaper is run. A cheaper way is to pay an ISP extra fees to provide you a specific name and some hard disk space to store your contents. Browsers can then log on to your name (address) to access your contents. This low-cost alternative is attracting lots of individual entrepreneurs to open up shops on the Web.

Hypertext Markup Language (HTML)

The Web is closely related to HTML. A **Web page**, or Web document, is an HTML file. When a Web browser loads a disk file that follows the HTML rules, the browser interprets the **tags** (commands) embedded in the file and displays the contents accordingly. When the browser is asked to navigate to a URL, it goes to the specified address to load the specified file. If no file is specified in the URL, the default file or the one with the name of **Default.html** or **Index.html** is loaded. The URL is a Web site, and the default page is the **home page**. The site may have many other pages stored in the same or related directory; the home page then provides links to the other pages.

The sections below explain the basics of HTML and demonstrate the concrete steps of using Notepad to create Web pages and show them in Internet Explorer.

Editing and Displaying Text

Internet Explorer will display plain text just as a text editor does. To change contents, however, you have to use a text editor. Internet Explorer uses **Notepad** by default. So you can use Notepad to create a text file and Internet Explorer to show its contents. After the text is displayed, you can go from the Internet Explorer window to the Notepad window to change text and then return to the Internet Explorer window to view the new version.

To make it easier to write code/text and display results, follow these steps:

1. Run Notepad (Start | Programs | Accessories | Notepad). Inside Notepad, type some text (anything) and use File | Save to save a file with the **.htm** or **.html** extension to the desired folder. Exit Notepad.

2. Find the browser shortcut. Your desktop should show a shortcut named "The Internet." This shortcut was created when Internet Explorer was installed.

3. Right-click the above icon to pop up its shortcut menu, and then choose Properties. The **Internet Properties** dialog box appears.

4. Click the Navigation tab. Enter a full path (the file name and folder of the file saved in step 1) in the Address field, such as the following:

    file://c:\my documents\calc.htm

5. Click OK to exit the Internet Properties dialog box.

6. Double-click The Internet shortcut. The browser is launched, and the page created in step 1 appears.

7. Right-click anywhere inside the browser window to pop up its shortcut menu. Click **View Source**. Notepad is launched, and the text entered in step 1 is displayed.

8. Edit text and save it over the old file (File | Save).

9. Go to the browser by using the Windows taskbar or by clicking its exposed window.

10. Press **F5** to refresh the screen. The new (edited) file is displayed.

11. If you want to edit the contents again, go to the Notepad window by clicking its exposed portion or using the taskbar. Don't use the browser's View Source option from the popup menu unless you want to open up another Notepad window.

This arrangement makes it easy to test a file again and again. If you want to test another file, repeat steps 1 - 5 with a different file name. If you want to save the revised edition without erasing the old one, use Notepad's File | Save As and supply a new name.

If you want to use the browser to display another .html file, type its full path in the browser's Address field. If you don't know where the file is located, enter the root directory (such as c:\) to display its contents, navigate to the desired folder, and double-click the desired file when it's shown (the file must have the .htm or .html extension) to show its contents in the browser. You can then use View Source to launch Notepad and change its contents. After you've displayed a file, you can use the browser's History button or the down arrow in the Address field to show a list of files, and then click one of them to show its contents.

Notepad has limited editing capabilities. You may want to use other editors such as Word or WordPad. Word is slow because it bristles with features you don't need. WordPad is a good choice; it's fast and has more editing features than Notepad.

The following steps show you how to **associate** an .html file with **WordPad**. When you right-click a file with the .html extension, the popup menu shows these options at the top of the list: Open, Open with Word, and Edit.

If you click Open, Internet Explorer will be loaded and the file will be displayed in it. (The same thing happens when you double-click an .html file.) If you click Edit or Open with Word, Word will open and the file will be loaded. If you wish, you can change Edit's setting so that clicking it will open WordPad instead.

Use **My Computer** to show any .html file. Select the file and choose View | Options from the menu. The Options dialog box appears. Open the **File Types** tab. All the registered file types appear in a list box. Scroll the list to Microsoft HTML Document 4.0 and select it. The bottom of the dialog box shows related details. Click the Edit button to change the default settings. The Actions list box now shows all the available options (this is the same list that pops up when you right-click a file of this type in My Computer). Click the Edit option to select it. Then click the Edit button below it. The new dialog box shows you Winword.exe and its path. Use the Browse button to find Wordpad.exe and open it. The new string will replace the old one. Go to this string and add "%1" at the end. The result should be as shown below:

        "C:\Program Files\Accessories**Wordpad.exe**" "%1"

Below this string there is also the Use DDE check box. Uncheck it. Finally, click a series of OKs to exit. If you now right-click an .html file and choose Edit, the file will be opened in WordPad. After making changes, make sure to resave it as a text document (no formatting). This file can then be viewed in a browser.

In the above steps, you can use the New (instead of Edit) button to create a new entry for the popup menu. In that case, you can use a new name such as "Edit with WordPad." This name will then appear when you right-click an .html file in the future. You can also use the Set Default button to make an entry the default. In that case, when you double-click an .html file in the future, WordPad will be launched.

You can also use Visual Basic's Code window to do text editing. The simplest way is to copy from the Notepad window to Visual Basic. Then do editing there, such as setting tabs, changing case, replacing variables, commenting/ uncommenting an entire block, etc. Then copy the edited text back to the Notepad window.

Basic Structure

A browser will read and display plain ASCII text. If you want it to display text in fancier ways, however, you'll have to add a series of **tags** to mark up the text. When the browser encounters these tags, it will interpret them according to their specified meanings and act on them to display different results.

An **HTML tag** is enclosed in a pair of angle brackets. Most have an opening tag and an closing tag, although a few don't have the latter. A closing tag is the same as the opening counterpart, except with the / sign added.

To tell the browser to go act on these tags, you normally follow this basic framework:

```
<HTML>
<BODY>
Enter text here.
</BODY>
</HTML>
```

The whole thing starts with <HTML> and ends with </HTML>. The body text appears between the <BODY>-</BODY> pair. Before this pair, you can embed text in the <TITLE>-</TITLE> pair to enter a text string in the browser's title bar. This title pair is normally enclosed inside the <HEAD>-</HEAD> pair, like this:

```
<HTML>
<HEAD>
<TITLE>My Page</TITLE>
</HEAD>
<BODY>
This is the body text of my page.
<!--This comment line is not shown.-->
</BODY>
</HTML>
```

The title will appear in the caption of the browser window. The body text appears inside the window. And the comment is not shown. **Comments** are placed between <!-- and -->.

NOTE Internet Explorer ignores the <HTML>, <HEAD>, and <BODY> tags. They are not required to create a Web page. Other browsers may not behave the same way. So it's a good idea to follow the common practice of including them. Besides, having these makes a Web page's source code self-documenting.

Web browsers **parse** (interpret) a Web page before displaying or acting on it. In parsing, browsers act on the HTML tags they can understand and ignore those they don't understand. Those not understood may also be treated as literals and displayed as they are. If there are errors in your tags, browsers may produce unexpected results. For example, if you embed a title tag without the matching closing tag, all the remaining text will be shown in the caption rather than inside the window.

In parsing HTML tags, browsers ignore case. You can use any case in a Web page. So <BODY>, <Body>, and <body> are treated as equivalent. For readability, many Web authors use uppercase for keywords that have special meanings to a browser.

A Web page's text and tags can be in any shape you want. In our earlier example, we could have lumped all the separate lines into a single continuous line (by taking away all the carriage returns) and the result (output display) would not change. However, by arranging the source document in a logical manner, you enhance readability and can more easily modify and debug errant tags.

Some codes that a text processor can act on are ignored by browsers. They include tabs, carriage returns, and extra spaces. A two-line text separated by a hard return will be displayed in one line, with a space separating the two. Tabs and multiple spaces will be replaced by one space. Browsers manage text flow by wrapping long text lines and supplying scroll bars when necessary. As you change the size of the browser window, the text inside may change shape. If you want to control text flow or display some unusual characters, you need to use tags or special codes, as explained in the following section.

Finally, Web browsers are not all equal. They may not recognize some tags. They may render identical tags in slightly different ways. The resulting colors, font styles, etc. may appear differently in different browsers or different versions of the same browser. Fortunately, there are enough commonality between the two major browsers (Netscape Navigator and Internet Explorer) that you can produce substantially similar results under most circumstances.

Document Formatting

You can control text display in a browser by embedding a series of tags in your Web page. The list below shows the most commonly used tags. Most require opening and closing tags, except where noted.

<Hn>	Heading; H1 (largest) and up to H7 (smallest).
<HR>	Horizontal rule (line); no closing tag; use <HR WIDTH=70%> to shorten the line.
<CENTER>	Horizontal centering.
 	Line break; hard return; no closing tag.
<P>	Paragraph break; two hard returns; closing tag optional.
<I>	Italic.
<U>	Underline.

\<S\>	Strikethrough.
\<STRIKE\>	Same.
\<B\>	Boldface.
\<STRONG\>	Same.
\<BIG\>	Font one size larger.
\<SMALL\>	Font one size smaller.
\<PRE\>	Preformatted text; maintains original shape of text and controls; displays text with monospace font.
\<XMP\>	Example; monospace font.
\<TT\>	Teletype; monospace font.
\<BLOCKQUOTE\>	Indent text as well as controls from both left and right margins; can be nested to provide multiple levels of indentation.
\<SUB\>	Subscript.
\<SUP\>	Superscript.
\<OL\>	Ordered list; sequential numbers added.
\<UL\>	Unordered list; bullets added.
\<DIR\>	Same.
\<MENU\>	Same.
\<LI\>	List; indented; placed inside the above four; no closing tag.

Some of the above tags have the ALIGN attribute. You can use it to align text RIGHT, LEFT, or CENTER. Here are two examples:

```
<H2 ALIGN=RIGHT>This line will be right-aligned.</H2>
<P ALIGN=CENTER>This paragraph will be centered.</P>
```

The \<LI\> tag is used inside \<OL\>-\</OL\>, \<UL\>-\</UL\>, \<DIR\>-\</DIR\>, and \<MENU\>-\</MENU\> pairs to create a list of items, each shown in a separate line and indented from the left margin. Such a list can be anything, including hyperlinks.

\<OL\> can include two parameters: START and TYPE. START is used to specify the beginning number other than the default beginning number. TYPE can be 1 (default, Arabic numerals), A (uppercase letters), a (lowercase letters), I (uppercase Roman numerals), or i (lowercase Roman numerals).

The code below produces the result shown in Figure 1. Notice that in the ordered list, we start with 2 of the lowercase alphabetic letters. Without the START and TYPE attributes, the default would be 1, 2, 3, etc. If you prefer to use Roman numerals, use I or i for the TYPE attribute.

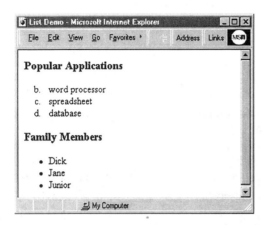

Figure 4.1   Ordered and unordered lists

```
<HTML>
<HEAD><TITLE>List Demo</TITLE></HEAD>
<BODY>
<H3>Popular Applications</H3>
<OL START=2 TYPE=a>
   <LI>word processor
   <LI>spreadsheet
   <LI>database
</OL>
<H3>Family Members</H3>
<UL>
   <LI>Dick
   <LI>Jane
   <LI>Junior
</UL>
</BODY>
</HTML>
```

The <LI> tag has a built-in indentation and carriage return. The output indentation is not affected by indenting the source code. Adding a <BR> tag at the end has no effect. Adding two such tags or one <P> will insert an extra line. If no text appears after <LI>, only a bullet is displayed in a separate line.

If you want to insert some unusual **characters** that are not available from the keyboard or that are used by HTML, you need to resort to special codes. These codes start with &# followed by a number, which may be the same as an ASCII value. In some cases, you can use & followed by a pnemonic shorthand. For example, &#192 or &Agrave will produce the letter A with a grave accent (À). If there is text immediately following such a code, use a semicolor (;) to mark the end of the code.

The following table produces a short list of useful characters. You can use either the first column or the second column to produce the characters shown in the third column.

&#34	&quot	"	
&#60	&lt	<	Less than
&#62	&gt	>	Greater than
&#64		@	
			Non-breaking space
&#169		©	
&#174		®	

The last section in this chapter will tell you where you can find a complete list of all the available characters and their corresponding codes.

You are supposed to use "	" to force a horizontal tab. It works in Word 97, but Internet Explorer ignores it. One alternative is to add **non-breaking spaces**. So " " (the semicolons are optional) placed at the beginning of a paragraph will insert five extra spaces and thus indent the first line.

Anchors and Hyperlinks

A **hyperlink** is a mechanism that allows a browser user to load another page, thus linking from the current page to another. Clicking a hyperlink can take you to one of the following:

- Another location within the same page
- The beginning of another page in the same site
- The beginning of another page in another site
- A specific location in another page in any site

Depending on the browser and the settings specified by the browser user, a hyperlink appears underlined and/or in a different color. When the mouse pointer goes over it, the pointer turns into a pointing hand.

To embed a hyperlink in a Web page, you use the <A> (**anchor**) tag together with the HREF (hypertext reference) attribute. Here is an example:

```
You can visit the
<A HREF="http://www.microsoft.com">
Microsoft</A> site to get more details.
```

The above will be displayed in a single line. The text between < A > and < /A > will be colored and underlined. As you point to it, the status bar of the browser will show the specified URL, which doesn't appear inside the browser window. If your PC is connected to the Internet, clicking this hyperlink will take you to Microsoft's home page. If it's not, you'll get an error message instead.

What if you want to let the user move to another spot in the same page? Use < A > and the NAME attribute to name the target spot (also known as a **bookmark**). Then embed in the source location a hyperlink pointing to the target location. Here is an example:

```
You can see our
<A HREF="#report">
annual report
</A> for details.
lines of text here
<HR>
<A NAME="report">
<H1>Annual Report</H1>
</A>
```

In this case, "annual report" becomes a hyperlink. Pointing to it displays its target name ("#report") in the status bar. Clicking it displays the new area at the top of the browser window, assuming there are many lines of text in between.

Notice that the source uses the HREF attribute and a name preceded by the # character. The target, on the other hand is specified with the NAME attribute and the name string doesn't have the # character.

What if you want let your user to quickly return to the original spot? Use < A > to name that spot and embed another hyperlink in the new location, like this:

```
You can see our
<A NAME="top">
<A HREF="#report">
annual report
</A> for details.
lines of text here
<HR>
<A NAME="report">
<H1>Annual Report</H1>
</A>
```

```
<P>
Return to the <A HREF="#top">top</A>.
```

We now embed a hidden name (top) in the beginning and a hyperlink at the bottom. When this new link is clicked, the top of the browser window will show the spot named *top*.

What if you want to direct the user to another spot in another page, which may be in the current site or another site? Use the following examples:

```
<A HREF="PageName#LocationName">
<A HREF="../NewDir/PageName#LocationName">
<A HREF="URL#LocationName">
```

In the first example, the page is located in the current server's current directory. In the second case, the page is stored in another directory that is up one level and then down one level to a specified name. In the third case, the URL specifies a Web site. If that page doesn't have the specified location name, the top is displayed. In all cases, a # character separates a page and a named location inside that page.

You can also use a hyperlink to let a visitor send e-mail to a specific address. In the following example, the text between the opening and closing tags will be displayed and highlighted (if you wish, you can replace the actual address with any descriptive string). When it's clicked, the user's e-mail editor (if any) will be activated and the address specified after **mailto** will enter the To field, ready for composing a message.

```
<A HREF="mailto:flin@usa.net">flin@usa.net</A>
```

Colors and Multimedia

You can deploy colors, sound, graphics, and animation to jazz up your Web pages. Using HTML, it's surprisingly easy to do these seemingly complicated things.

The simplest way to spice up a page is to use the opening <BODY> tag to specify a series of attributes. You can use BGCOLOR to specify a background color, BACKGROUND to load a background image file, BGPROPERTIES to specify FIXED to make the loaded picture fixed (non-scrolling, thus acting as a watermark), or designate a color for TEXT (foreground), LINK (unvisited link), and VLINK (visited link).

The following shows an example. The fixed background picture is loaded from a local directory (you can also specify a remote URL to load a picture from there). The other items are assigned different color values.

```
<BODY BACKGROUND="watermark.gif"
BGPROPERTIES=FIXED BGCOLOR=#FFFFFF TEXT=#000000
LINK=#FF6600 VLINK=#330099>
```

To assign a **color** value, follow the #RRGGBB format. Start with the # character (this character is optional), followed by a red value, a green value, and a blue value—each expressed in a 2-digit hexadecimal number.

Here are some examples:

#000000	Black, no color
#FFFFFF	White, all colors present
#FF0000	Red
#00FF00	Green
#0000FF	Blue
#00FFFF	Cyan, combining green and blue
#FF00FF	Magenta, combining red and blue
#FFFF00	Yellow, combining red and green

You can also use one of these words to replace an RGB value: aqua, black, blue, fuchsia, gray, green, lime, maroon, navy, olive, purple, red, silver, teal, white, and yellow. There are also other words. These values are fixed, so you cannot customize them.

Another way to add color to a block of text is to use the <FONT> tag. In the following example, the text after this tag and before </FONT> will be displayed in red:

```
<FONT
   SIZE=+2
   FACE="century, garamond"
   COLOR=#FF0000>
```

You can use the <BASEFONT SIZE=n> to specify a base font size from 1 (smallest) to 7 (largest). If this tag is not used, the default font size is 3. When you use SIZE with a + or -, you are increasing or decreasing from the base size. So a +2 value will increase the font size by 2 from the base size.

The FACE attribute can be used to designate a series of font names. If the first is found, it's used. Otherwise, the next available one is used. If nothing in the list is found, the default font is used.

You can add sound to a Web page. When the page is loaded, the sound will be automatically played. Use the <BGSOUND> tag (no closing tag) to specify a source file and the number of times to play the file, such as this syntax:

```
<BGSOUND SCR="url" LOOP=INFINITE>
```

Here you use SCR to specify the source file, which can be a file with the extension of AU, WAV, or MID (based on my experience, an RMI file will also work). Use LOOP to specify the number of times to play the file; it could be -1 or INFINITE for continuous playing. Playing begins when a page is loaded and ends when the loop is finished or the page is unloaded (when you load another page).

In the following examples, files are loaded from the local drive (the Media subdirectory of where Window 95 is installed); such files can also be downloaded from a remote site. In the first example, the ding sound will be repeated indefinitely. In the second case, the music will be played only once. If the LOOP attribute is absent, the default is 1.

```
<BGSOUND SRC="d:\win95\media\ding.wav" LOOP="infinite">
<BGSOUND SRC="d:\win95\media\beethoven's fur elise.rmi" LOOP=1>
```

If you don't get any sound, it may be due to typing errors or wrong directory. Based on my experience, the above examples work well in Internet Explorer 4, but not in Internet Explorer 3. Of course, your system must be equipped for multimedia.

Figure 4.2   Playing an audio file

When the following hyperlink is clicked, the File Download dialog asks you whether you want to open the file from its current location or save it to disk. If you choose the former, The **ActiveMovie** control (Figure 4.2) pops up and begins to play the music file. The total play time is shown on the left and a timer in the middle shows the elapsed time. This control is bundled with Internet Explorer and other applications.

```
<A HREF="d:\win95\media\beethoven's fur elise.rmi">
Play F&uuml;r Elise.</A>
```

We've also added an umlaut (Für). The following is the equivalent:

```
<A HREF="d:\win95\media\beethoven's fur elise.rmi">
Play F&#252;r Elise.</A>
```

Do you want to play video clips from your browser? Try the following. It will open a file from the local drive and display the clip in a separate window, again using the ActiveMovie control.

```
<A HREF="d:\vb\graphics\avis\findfile.avi">
Play FindFile AVI.</A>
```

Any AVI files in you local drive or a remote Web site can be played this way. The Help subdirectory of the Windows 95 directory contains a few video clips (AVI files). If you have the Internet Explorer 4 CD-ROM, you can play with dozens of video clips promoting Microsoft products. These short movies each lasts about one minute.

You can display a static or animated picture in your Web page. Use the <IMG> tag to specify a source (SCR) and an optional ALIGN location. Here is an example:

```
<IMG SRC="e:\cdsample\catalog\products\baseball\
features.gif" ALIGN=RIGHT>
```

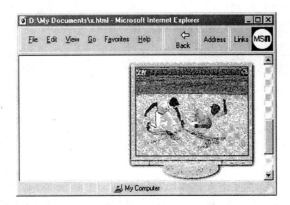

Figure 4.3   A GIF picture

The specified picture (Figure 4.3; it's included on the Internet Explorer 4 CD) will appear as soon as the page is loaded. You can also use LEFT, MIDDLE, TOP, or BOTTOM with ALIGN to control the picture's position and the text around it.

In the following example, the picture is not shown until the hyperlink is clicked. A separate window will open to display the picture.

```
<A HREF="e:\cdsample\catalog\products\baseball\
features.gif">Show Baseball GIF.</A>
```

Two types of graphics are popular on the Internet, **GIF** (Graphics Interchange Format) and **JPEG** (Joint Photographic Experts Group, used mostly for photos). GIF files can also be animated. In our example picture above, three frames will be shown one after another infinitely.

A graphic can be used as a hyperlink. When the picture is clicked, another page will be loaded. Here is an example:

```
Click the picture to show Play Ball.
<A HREF="playball.htm">
<IMG SRC="e:\cdsample\catalog\products\baseball\
features.gif" ALIGN=MIDDLE>
</A>
```

We use the same picture as before, except placing the left-side text line in the middle (from top to bottom) of the picture. Since the picture is included in the <IMG> tag, it's shown as soon as the page is loaded. However, since the picture is inside the <A> and </A> tags, it's treated as a hyperlink and enclosed in a box. When you point to it, the target address appears in the status bar at the bottom. Clicking the picture cum hyperlink loads the target file.

Controls, Forms, and CGI Scripts

HTML provides **intrinsic controls**, which are comparable to the intrinsic controls in Visual Basic. They can be embedded in a Web page to provide interaction between the browser user and the remote Web server hosting the page.

There are nine intrinsic controls (there are different ways to count them). They can be created with the following three tags and their various attributes:

<INPUT TYPE= >
    TEXT　　　　　　Default type, same as text box; events: OnBlur, OnChange,
    　　　　　　　　OnFocus, OnSelect.
    PASSWORD　　　Same as TEXT, but hides user entry; events: OnBlur, OnFocus.

CHECKBOX	Same as check box; events: OnClick, OnFocus.
RADIO	Same as option button; events: OnClick, OnFocus.
BUTTON	Similar to command button; events: OnClick, OnFocus.
RESET	Clears user entries and restores defaults; events: OnClick, OnFocus.
SUBMIT	Sends user input to server; events: OnClick, OnFocus.
<TEXTAREA>	Multiline text box; events: same as TEXT.
<SELECT>	Same as list/combo box; use <OPTION> to add options; events: OnBlur, OnChange, OnFocus.

These controls behave very much like Visual Basic's counterparts, as noted in the comments above.

A control may respond to one or more events. A check box, radio button, and command button (BUTTON, RESET, or SUBMIT) each can respond to the most common **OnClick** event. An option change (another option is clicked) can trigger the **OnChange** event of a combo/list box (created with <SELECT>). You can write code to respond to these events.

The first seven controls are created with the <INPUT> tag. You use the TYPE attribute to distinguish one from another. If no TYPE is specified, the default is TEXT.

```
<HTML>
<BODY>
<FORM>
One-line text box <INPUT TYPE=TEXT><BR>
Check box <INPUT TYPE=CHECKBOX>
Option button <INPUT TYPE=RADIO><BR>
Password box <INPUT TYPE=PASSWORD><BR>
Command buttons <INPUT TYPE=RESET>
<INPUT TYPE=SUBMIT><BR>
<TEXTAREA>Multi-line text box</TEXTAREA><BR>
Combo box:
<SELECT>
    <OPTION>Option 1</OPTION>
    <OPTION>Option 2</OPTION>
</SELECT>
</FORM>
</BODY></HTML>
```

The above code produces the page shown in Figure 4.4. You can now handle these controls as you can with Visual Basic controls at run time. Press Tab repeatedly to go to various controls and do something, such as typing an entry in a text box. Then click Reset to clear your entries. (In Internet Explorer 4, unlike version 3, the Reset button won't clear entries unless the controls are enclosed between the <FORM> and </FORM> tags.)

If you want to use a script to manipulate a control, you'll need to use the NAME attribute to specify a name; this will be demonstrated in the sections below. You can also use the VALUE attribute to specify a command button's caption or a TEXT control's initial text entry. For TEXTAREA, the default entry is placed between the opening and closing tags (use VALUE to manipulate a run-time entry). With TEXT, you can use SIZE to change its default width based on the number of characters. With TEXTAREA, use COLS and ROWS to change its width and height. In both, you can use MAXLENGTH to limit the number of characters entered at run time.

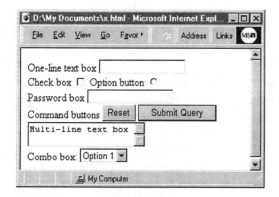

Figure 4.4   Intrinsic controls

NOTE   You can put attributes inside quotes or in any case combination. They make no difference to browsers. However, if there are spaces, quotes are necessary to tell the browser where an attribute ends.

NOTE   TEXTAREA is implemented differently by Netscape and Internet Explorer. The latter by default provides a vertical scroll bar and wraps long lines. Netscape provides both horizontal and vertical scrolling and doesn't wrap long lines. To force wrapping, add WRAP=1 in the opening tag.

If you want a check box or radio (option) button checked by default, just add CHECKED (no parameter) inside its tag. In the case of radio buttons, if you use the same name for a group of them, only one can be selected. When another is selected at run time, the previously selected one will be deselected.

You can use the <SELECT> tag to create a combo box or a list box. The following code will create a list box with three options. The first will also be selected. At run time, when the user clicks another option, it will be selected instead. If you remove the SIZE attribute, the list box will change to a combo box. You can then click the down arrow to open up the available list.

```
< SELECT NAME=Card SIZE=3 >
    < OPTION SELECTED > Visa
    < OPTION > MasterCard
    < OPTION > Discovery
< /SELECT >
```

You can use the VALUE attribute inside an < OPTION > tag to assign a value to a particular option. When this option is selected and the form is submitted (see below), this value can be processed by the server.

In many Web sites, you see the Reset and Submit buttons. When Reset is clicked, your entries are cleared. What happens when you click Submit? The information gathered from various controls in that page is sent to that site's Web server, which processes the information and may send you a response.

For the Web server to do **form processing**, you need to use the < FORM > tag to run a program or script stored on the server. When the Submit button is clicked, the information gathered by the controls located between < FORM > and < /FORM > is processed by that program. In this arrangement, you can have multiple *forms* (these are different from Visual Basic forms), each with a distinct name and a separate set of intrinsic controls.

NOTE   Netscape won't display intrinsic controls unless the tags to create them are preceded by the <FORM> tag.

If you are an administrator of a Web server, you'll need to write (or acquire) a program (compiled) or script (interpreted) to respond to user inputs. These programs are commonly known as **CGI** (Common Gateway Interface) scripts. They are usually written in a C-like language called **Perl**. If you want to pursue this subject further, there are many books and online resources.

VBScript

As browsers become more sophisticated, they can do more and more. One of their new important functions is **client-side processing**.

Instead of sending raw data to the Web server, the browser can process the data on the user side and then send the result to the server. This can reduce the load on the Internet because less information is sent, as well as on the server because much of the work is done on the client side.

To do client-side processing, a browser has to be equipped with a scripting language, an interpreter that can execute commands contained in an ASCII file. The browser can then follow the instructions to process the data supplied by the user. A Web page author can embed such commands to make the page livelier and more useful.

The two most popular scripting languages are **JavaScript** (created by Netscape, based on the C++/Java syntax; Microsoft's comparable offering is known as **JScript**) and **VBScript** (a subset of Visual Basic). Internet Explorer can handle both JavaScript (JScript) and VBScript.

VBScript may become the universal language for office automation. The entire Microsoft Office 97 suite can be automated with VBScript. Web pages can be done the same way. Many vendors have also licensed it from Microsoft to automate their applications. So, if you become good at it, you may find many uses for it.

If you are already familiar with the VBA (language) component in Visual Basic, you already know most of VBScript. It's basically VBA with some elements taken out. Those that are taken out mostly relate to input/out functions. These functions are considered dangerous on the Internet because they can destroy files.

To instruct your browser to execute VBScript code, you use the <SCRIPT>-</SCRIPT> tags to define the executable section, and the LANGUAGE attribute to specify the scripting language. Then embed code to process data. Here is an example:

```
<HTML>
<HEAD>
<TITLE>Hello</TITLE>
</HEAD>
<BODY>
<H1>Hello</H1>
<SCRIPT LANGUAGE=VBScript>
<!--
    MsgBox "Hello, world."
-->
</SCRIPT>
<H2>world</H2>
</BODY>
</HTML>
```

Run the code and observe how the browser handles the situation. Normally the browser parses a page sequentially. First, the title appears in the browser's caption. Then the first text line appears in the window. The script is processed next. Any code not inside a procedure (sub or function), also known as **inline code**, is executed at parsing time in sequential order. That leads to a beep and the appearance of a message box. After you click OK to clear the box, the second text line finally appears.

The <SCRIPT>-</SCRIPT> section can be placed anywhere within the <HTML>-</HTML> tags. Some people prefer to put it at the beginning (in the <HEAD>-</HEAD> block) while others prefer the end. You can have multiple such sections. It's advisable to put all or most of the procedures in one section and place them in an easily identified area. When you have lengthy code, this arrangement lets you more easily manage it.

The comment tags of HTML may be redundant. They are added here as a precaution. If a browser that cannot understand VBScript is involved, the script section will be ignored. Without the comment tags, the code text may be displayed as it is written.

The code inside the script section closely resembles Visual Basic's Code window. Once you are inside this section, Visual Basic conventions apply. For example, if you want to add a comment, you need to use Rem or an apostrophe ('). When you enter code in this section, you are on your own. Many of the nice features available in Visual Basic's IDE—such as automatic spacing, indentation, case conversion, and syntax checking—are absent and you must do these by yourself.

You can use **JavaScript** just as easily as VBScript. Consider the following replacement for the above script. It will show an alert box as the previous example.

```
<SCRIPT LANGUAGE=JavaScript>
<!--
    alert("Hello, world.")
-->
</SCRIPT>
```

JavaScript mostly follows the C++/Java syntax. If you are familiar with C, C++, or Java, you can quickly learn to master JavaScript. This chapter concentrates on VBScript.

Comparing Visual Basic and VBScript

Between Visual Basic and VBScript there substantial similarities, as well as annoying minor differences. Your perfectly working Visual Basic code may not work in VBScript. You may spend hours catching minor bugs—until you discover that a simple Visual Basic feature is not supported by VBScript. This language is a work in progress. The latest version, the one that comes with Internet Explorer 4, is substantially different from the previous one. More Visual Basic features are incorporated; it also comes with more new features of its own.

NOTE   The scripts shown here are all tested in Internet Explorer 4. A few places may cause errors in Internet Explorer 3. Netscape will ignore scripts written in VBScript unless an appropriate plug-in is installed on your system.

If you are familiar with Visual Basic, you already know that you can manipulate objects (such as forms and command buttons) and their events (such as Load and Click) and methods (such as Move and SetFocus). Objects also have parent-child relationships such as a form is the parent of a command button inside the form. By the same token, the **Internet Explorer Object Model** (also called Scripting Object Model) supplies a series of objects and corresponding events and methods. This model is Microsoft's implementation of **Document Object Model (DOM)**, which is defined by W3C.

The top-level object is **Window**. It has **OnLoad** and **OnUnload** events. These are like a Visual Basic form's Load and Unload events. The Window object has a series of child objects. The most important is **Document**. It has one important method, namely **Write**. (**WriteLn** is also legal. It inserts a carriage return when an output text line is located inside the <PRE>-</PRE> or <XMP>-</XMP> pair; otherwise, it behaves the same as Write.) It's comparable to the Print method of the form object in Visual Basic.

In Visual Basic when a form is loaded, form-level code (such as form-level variables) is processed and a series of events, such as Form_Load, automatically occur. In VBScript, any code outside of a sub or function procedure is automatically executed during the parsing of the Web page. The **Window_OnLoad** event occurs only after the page has been processed. Before a page is unloaded, the OnUnload event is also triggered, just as closing a Visual Basic form at run time will trigger the Form_Unload event.

The Write method can output plain text and HTML tags to the current page. The browser will parse those tags and act on them. When writing VBScript code, you can use a format like this:

```
Window.Document.Write "Test line<P>"
Window.Document.Write "Test line<BR>"
```

Both will output a text string to the current page. The first will insert a paragraph break, and the second a line break.

NOTE   If you invoke the Write method after a page has been parsed and displayed, a new page will open up to display the new output. You can then use the Back or Forward button in the menu bar to navigate between the two windows.

Here we are writing a text string to the Document object which is the child of the Window object. That's comparable to this Visual Basic line:

```
Form1.Print "Test line"
```

You can omit the top-level object (Window) because that's the default, the same way as you can take out the Form1 object in the above Visual Basic example.

You can do many things, such as writing a text string or embedding an intrinsic control, both inside and outside a script section. Do them in a script if processing (such as adding two numbers or concatenating two strings) is needed and labor can be saved (such as using a loop to embed multiple intrinsic controls).

In Visual Basic, recognized words are automatically converted to the default case no matter how you type them. In VBScript, you can use any case you want as long as you are comfortable with it. To mimic Visual Basic, the code examples here use the same conventions.

NOTE   The names you supply can be in any case. As long as two names match in spelling, they will be treated as identical by VBScript. For example, a variable named MyVar will match Myvar or myVar. This rule does not apply to JavaScript, which requires identical names to match not only in spelling but also in case.

Variant is the only data type allowed in VBScript. A Variant variable can hold any type of data. You can use the **VarType** function to return a value which can tell you what type of data a variable is holding at a particular time.

A variable used inside a procedure is local in scope. It comes alive when the procedure is executed, and it ceases to exist when execution leaves that procedure. The **Static** keyword is not allowed, so you cannot keep a local variable's value between calls. To keep a variable's assigned value, you must declare that variable outside of a procedure.

A variable declared outside a procedure is a script-level variable. This is comparable to a global variable in Visual Basic. A script-level variable is visible and alive throughout the entire Web page. They cease to exist when the page is unloaded.

A variable doesn't have to be declared. However, to impose discipline and avoid unforeseen errors, you should adopt the habit of declaring a variable before using it. Enter **Option Explicit** at the script level (not inside a procedure). After that, a variable must be declared or an error will occur.

There are other differences as well. We'll point them out as they are encountered in the following sections.

Functions and Procedures

You can use many (but not all) of Visual Basic's intrinsic functions, such as MsgBox demonstrated earlier and InputBox shown below. In Internet Explorer 4, these functions also support many intrinsic constants available in Visual Basic.

You can also divide your script into sub and function procedures and make them call one another. With some exceptions, the same Visual Basic rules apply here as well.

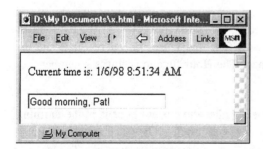

Figure 4.5   **Showing current time and time-based greeting**

The following script illustrates the use of sub procedures and some intrinsic functions. It will produce Figure 4.5.

```
<HTML>          <!-- Listing 1; Greet.html -->
<BODY>
<SCRIPT LANGUAGE=VBScript>
<!--
Option Explicit
Document.Write "Current time is: " & Now
Document.Write "<P>"
Document.Write "<INPUT TYPE=TEXT NAME=txtName SIZE=30>"

Sub Window_OnLoad
    Dim Name
    Name=InputBox ("What's your first name?")
    Call ShowMsg (Name)    'call and pass argument
End Sub

Sub ShowMsg (Name)
    Dim Msg
    Dim CurrHour
    CurrHour=Hour(Now)
    If CurrHour < 12 Then
        Msg="morning"
    ElseIf CurrHour < 18 Then
        Msg="afternoon"
    Else
        Msg="evening"
    End If
    txtName.Value="Good " & Msg & ", " & Name & "!"
    'show output in text box
End Sub
-->
</SCRIPT>
</BODY>
</HTML>
```

Notice that we use some date/time functions (**Now and Hour**). Most of these Visual Basic functions are available in VBScript. The Now function returns the current date and time string as shown at the beginning of the page. The Hour function returns a number indicating the hour of the day.

We use an If control structure to determine whether the current hour is in the morning, afternoon, or evening. It would seem logical to use a Select Case structure here. But it doesn't work, at least not elegantly. You can't use common operators like To, Is, >, or = in such a control structure; they will all lead to some sort of errors. That severely limits the usefulness of this ordinarily versatile tool.

Our sub procedure can be changed to a function procedure. Another section below demonstrates how to do it.

Event Handling

Most of the intrinsic controls discussed earlier can respond to events. The most common event is click, so you need to write code to respond to the control being clicked by the user. A command button (BUTTON, RESET, and SUBMIT), radio button, or check box has the **OnClick** event, just as their Visual Basic counterparts having the Click event. So writing an OnClick event procedure is a common task.

Figure 4.6   Demonstrating the OnClick event

How do you write an OnClick event procedure? Consider the following example. It will produce the display shown in Figure 4.6.

```
<HTML>
<BODY>
<INPUT TYPE=BUTTON NAME=cmdTest VALUE="Click Me">
<SCRIPT LANGUAGE=VBScript>
<!--
    Sub cmdTest_OnClick
        MsgBox "You clicked me."
    End Sub
-->
</SCRIPT>
</BODY>
</HTML>
```

The <INPUT> tag creates a button named cmdTest with the Click Me caption. When the cmdTest button is clicked, its OnClick event (cmdTest_OnClick) is triggered. The sub procedure then leads to the display of a message box.

The two Sub references can be changed to Function. The button will behave the same way.

You can specify an attribute for OnClick inside an <INPUT> tag. In that case, the sub or function procedure no longer needs the OnClick moniker. In this situation, you don't even need a name to identify the button, unless a name is needed for other purposes. The following version will behave the same way as before:

```
<HTML>
<BODY>
<INPUT TYPE=BUTTON VALUE="Click Me" OnClick=Test()>
<SCRIPT LANGUAGE=VBScript>
<!--
    Sub Test()
        MsgBox "You clicked me."
    End Sub
-->
</SCRIPT>
</BODY>
</HTML>
```

The OnClick attribute in the <INPUT> tag specifies what to do when this nameless button is clicked. Here we specify calling the Test( ) procedure. The parentheses here are required; their absence will lead to an error. The pair in the sub procedure, however, is optional.

This new arrangement even allows us to pass an argument to the procedure. In the following example, the attribute for OnClick contains a procedure call accompanied by an argument. The result is the same as before.

```
<HTML>
<BODY>
<INPUT TYPE=BUTTON VALUE="Click Me"
OnClick="Test('You clicked me.')">
<SCRIPT LANGUAGE=VBScript>
<!--
    Sub Test(Msg)
        MsgBox Msg
    End Sub
-->
</SCRIPT>
</BODY>
</HTML>
```

Notice the use of single and double quotes. The outer double quotes tell the browser the beginning and end of the entire attribute for OnClick. The inner single quotes enclose a text string as an argument to be passed.

Calculator Script

The script discussed in this section produces a two-number calculator as shown in Figure 4.7. It also demonstrates the use the **line continuation character** (_), a space followed by an underscore character placed at the end of a physical line to signify the line below as belonging to the same logical line.

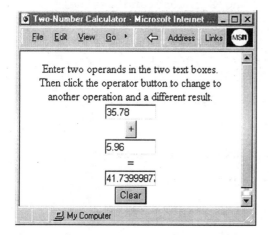

Figure 4.7   **A two-number calculator**

The following code produces the result shown in Figure 4.7.

```
<HTML>          <!-- Calc1-1.html -->
<HEAD>
<TITLE>Two-Number Calculator</TITLE>
</HEAD>
<BODY>
<CENTER>
Enter two operands in the two text boxes.<BR>
Then click the operator button to change to<BR>
another operation and a different result.<BR>
<FORM NAME=X>
<INPUT TYPE=TEXT NAME=txtOperand1 SIZE=10><BR>
<INPUT TYPE=BUTTON NAME=cmdOperator VALUE="Click"><BR>
<INPUT TYPE=TEXT NAME=txtOperand2 SIZE=10><BR>
<B>=</B><BR>
<INPUT TYPE=TEXT NAME=txtOutput SIZE=10><BR>
<INPUT TYPE=RESET VALUE="Clear" SIZE=15>
</CENTER>
```

```
</FORM>
<SCRIPT LANGUAGE=VBScript>
<!--
   Option Explicit
   Dim Operator     'make data persistent
   Sub cmdOperator_OnClick
       Operator = Operator Mod 4
       'rotate among four operators
       Select Case Operator
       Case 0
           X.txtOutput.Value = CSng(X.txtOperand1.Value) _
           + CSng(X.txtOperand2.Value)
           'convert at least one text entry to numeric
           'otherwise, concatenation, not addition
           'Val will cause a number of errors
           X.cmdOperator.Value = "+"
       Case 1
           X.txtOutput.Value = X.txtOperand1.Value - _
           X.txtOperand2.Value
           X.cmdOperator.Value = "-"
       Case 2
           X.txtOutput.Value = X.txtOperand1.Value * _
           X.txtOperand2.Value
           X.cmdOperator.Value = "*"
       Case 3
           X.txtOutput.Value = X.txtOperand1.Value / _
           X.txtOperand2.Value
           X.cmdOperator.Value = "/"
       End Select
       Operator = Operator + 1   'advance to next operator
   End Sub
-->
</SCRIPT>
</BODY>
</HTML>
```

We use the **CSng** function to covert one entry to the Single value. If no conversion is made, the two text box entries will be concatenated, not added up. So 12 + 34 will return 1234, not 46. (In Visual Basic you can use the **Val** function to convert a text entry to a numeric. But this function is not available in VBScript. So using it here will lead to a number of errors instead.) You can also use **Fix** or **Int** functions. But any decimal portion will be lost.

The **Format** function is also not available. If you want to format a value, use **FormatNumber, FormatCurrency, FormatDateTime, FormatPercent** or **Round**. The following statement, for example, will output 2.33. The second argument specifies the number of decimal places. The default is 2, so this number can be omitted in our example.

```
Document.Write FormatNumber(7/3, 2)
```

Notice that we use the <FORM>-</FORM> tags to enclose all the controls. This form has a name (X). In such an arrangement, every control must be referenced with this name; otherwise, the browser won't recognize them by their names alone. You can also use the Document.FormName.ControlName format to manipulate a control (this format is required in JavaScript).

The <FORM> tag is necessary if you want to submit the input data to the Web server for processing or if you want to use the Reset button to clear user entries. In our situation, the Reset button won't work unless it's inside <FORM> and </FORM>. (In Internet Explorer 3, the Reset button works without being inside a form.) If you want your script to reference a control inside a form (other than the RESET button), the form must have a name, and referencing must be done as described above.

We can use a **function procedure** to process data. Data can be passed to it, and the function will return the processed result. The following example will produce the same result as our previous example. Here we have added a function procedure. The chores we did in the OnClick procedure is done in the GetResult function. In this arrangement, the function can be called repeatedly, thus shortening the code.

```
<SCRIPT LANGUAGE=VBScript>        <!-- Calc1-2.html -->
<!--
    Option Explicit
    Dim Operator
    Sub cmdOperator_OnClick
        Operator = Operator Mod 4
        'rotate among four operators
        X.txtOutput.Value = GetResult (Operator)
        'call function, pass value, show result
        Operator = Operator + 1 'advance to next operator
    End Sub

    Function GetResult (Optr)
     Select Case Optr
      Case 0
         GetResult = CSng(X.txtOperand1.Value) + _
        X.txtOperand2.Value
         X.cmdOperator.Value = "+"
      Case 1
         GetResult = X.txtOperand1.Value - X.txtOperand2.Value
         X.cmdOperator.Value = "-"
      Case 2
         GetResult = X.txtOperand1.Value * X.txtOperand2.Value
         X.cmdOperator.Value = "*"
      Case 3
```

```
        GetResult = X.txtOperand1.Value / X.txtOperand2.Value
        X.cmdOperator.Value = "/"
    End Select
  End Function
-->
</SCRIPT>
```

Error Handling

Writing VBScript can be a frustrating experience. All the Visual Basic debugging tools are unavailable. For example, you cannot single-step through your code to see what variables are doing what. A tip posted in the Microsoft site advised programmers to use the Visual Basic IDE to debug code and then move it to a Web page. That is not an ideal solution because your HTML tags may cause problem in the Visual Basic IDE.

When a script is run, Internet Explorer may find an error and display a message. Typically, it tells you what line and what position causes the error. If your text editor (such as Notepad) doesn't have line or position numbering system, you'll have to manually locate the position. Furthermore, the resulting error message may not be particularly helpful, although Internet Explorer 4 is an improvement over Internet Explorer 3.

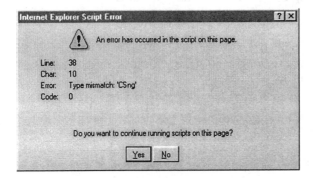

Figure 4.8   A run-time error

Figure 4.8 shows a sample error message. It appears if we click the middle button without supplying a value in the second text box. This *Type mismatch* error occurs when we ask the CSng function to convert an empty string to a Single value. If you now choose No (or click the X button), the script is disabled. If you click Yes instead, the script may or may not run, depending on what you put in the script. To start the page anew, you can press F5 to refresh the page or go to another page and then return.

In the above scenario, an ordinary user is not likely to understand the cryptic error message. To avoid this particular situation, Add the following to the beginning of the Sub cmdOperator_OnClick procedure. In this case, if either text box is empty, a message box appears and the procedure is not executed.

```
If txtOperand1.Value="" Or txtOperand2.Value="" Then
    MsgBox "You must supply numbers."
    Exit Sub
End If
```

Run-time errors can be trapped with the following statement:

```
On Error Resume Next
```

This is the only way you can trap an error. You cannot use GoTo to direct execution to another line number or line label.

After an error occurs, the **Err** object provides unique **Number** and **Description** properties related to that particular error. The numbers and descriptions are the same as those in Visual Basic, except that Visual Basic has more and that VBScript has a few of its own. Your code can then determine what to do in response.

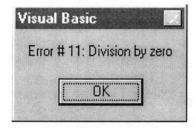

Figure 4.9   Generating a division by zero error

The script below generates the classic division by zero error. Running it will lead to Figure 4.9.

```
<HTML>
<BODY>
<SCRIPT LANGUAGE=VBScript>
<!--
```

```
    On Error Resume Next
    Dim Num
    Num=100/0        'error line
    If Err <> 0 Then
        MsgBox "Error # " & Err & ": " & Err.Description
    End If
    Document.Write "The output is: " & Num
-->
</SCRIPT>
</BODY>
</HTML>
```

We place the On Error Resume Next line at the beginning, before where an error is expected. That enables us to handle error when it occurs. If no error occurs, Err (the same as Err.Number since Number is the default property of the Err object) has a zero value. In that case, the If structure is ignored and the last line prints the output.

If an error occurs, as in our case, the Err.Number property has a nonzero value and the Err.Description is given a short descriptive string. The If structure is entered. So our message box shows these property values. Since we specify Resume Next when an error occurs, the last line is printed, but the variable (Num) has no value.

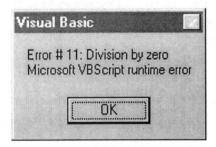

Figure 4.10   An error message produced by a sub procedure

Instead of inline error-handling code as in our preceding example, we can direct execution to a sub procedure. Consider our modification below. It will produce the result shown in Figure 4.10.

```
<HTML>
<BODY>
<SCRIPT LANGUAGE=VBScript>
<!--
    On Error Resume Next
    Dim Num
```

```
    Num=100/0          'error line
    If Err <> 0 Then CheckErr
    'run CheckErr if Err.Number is nonzero
    Document.Write "The output is: " & Num

    Sub CheckErr
        Dim Msg
        Msg="Error # " & Err & ": " & Err.Description
        MsgBox Msg & vbCr & Err.Source
        'using vbCr constant and Err.Source property
    End Sub
-->
</SCRIPT>
</BODY>
</HTML>
```

This arrangement is comparable to the On Error GoTo model which is commonly used in Visual Basic but not allowed in VBScript. This arrangement is more readable and manageable.

Notice the **Source** property. It always carries the string shown in the second line of Figure 4.10. You are free to assign a new value to it. For example, you can use it to tell the user where (in what procedure) the error occurred.

The Err object, based on my experience, is not reliable. It doesn't always register when errors occur. For example, on some occasions when an error occurs, Err.Number still has the 0 value. Using it to trap errors is a hit-and-miss proposition.

Handling Arrays

You can use arrays to store values. However, you must use the 0-based indexing mechanism. You cannot use the To keyword to specify an array's index range; doing so will lead to an error.

The following example is a slight variation of the Calculator script shown in a previous section. Here we use the Nums array to store the values in the two text boxes. Since the array is declared outside procedures, the elements are visible in both procedures. So when the first procedure calls the second, there is no need to pass the array.

```
<SCRIPT LANGUAGE=VBScript>      <!-- Calc1-3.html -->
<!--                            '-- Listing 2 --
    Dim Operator
    Dim Nums(1)    '0-based, 2 elements
    Sub cmdOperator_OnClick
```

```
        Operator = Operator Mod 4
        'rotate among four operators
        Nums(0) = CSng(X.txtOperand1.Value)
        Nums(1) = CSng(X.txtOperand2.Value)
        X.txtOutput.Value = GetResult (Operator)
        'call function, pass value, show result
        Operator = Operator + 1  'advance to next operator
     End Sub

     Function GetResult (Optr)
        Select Case Optr
        Case 0
          GetResult = Nums(0) + Nums(1)
          X.cmdOperator.Value = "+"
        Case 1
          GetResult = Nums(0) - Nums(1)
          X.cmdOperator.Value = "-"
        Case 2
          GetResult = Nums(0) * Nums(1)
          X.cmdOperator.Value = "*"
        Case 3
          GetResult = Nums(0) / Nums(1)
          X.cmdOperator.Value = "/"
        End Select
     End Function
-->
</SCRIPT>
```

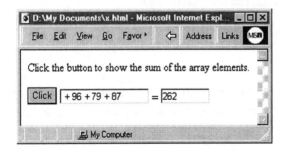

Figure 4.11   Using the Array function

You can use the **Array** function in Internet Explorer 4 (but not in version 3). You can use it to assign multiple values to a Variant variable, which in turn becomes an array. Below is an example. It will produce the result shown in Figure 4.11.

```
<HTML>
<BODY>
```

```
Click the button to show the sum of the array elements.
<P>
<INPUT TYPE=BUTTON NAME=cmdCalculate VALUE="Click">
<INPUT TYPE=TEXT NAME=txtArray SIZE=20> =
<INPUT TYPE=TEXT NAME=txtSum SIZE=10>
<BR>
<SCRIPT LANGUAGE=VBScript>
<!--
    Option Explicit
    Sub cmdCalculate_OnClick
     Dim Arr, I, Sum
     Arr = Array(96, 79, 87)
     'assign elements to a Variant
     For I = 0 To UBound(Arr)
         txtArray.Value = txtArray.Value & " + " & Arr(I)
         Sum = Sum + Arr(I)
     Next 'I not allowed here

     txtSum.Value = Sum
    End Sub
-->
</SCRIPT>
</BODY>
</HTML>
```

We use the **UBound** function to determine the array's highest index value. We also use **For-Next** to loop through all the array elements. Notice that no variable appears after Next. Adding a control variable here will cause an error.

Since we are handling an array, we can also use the **For Each-Next** command to loop through all the elements. The following changes will produce the same result as before:

```
For Each I In Arr
    txtArray.Value = txtArray.Value & " + " & I
    Sum = Sum + I
Next
```

Calculating Mortgage Payment

All financial functions available in Visual Basic are removed from VBScript. If you want to calculate financial transactions, you'll need to come up with your own formulas. In the following script, we use a formula that will produce the same result as the **Pmt** function (available in Visual Basic but not in VBScript). Figure 4.12 shows the monthly payment based on the figures supplied by the user.

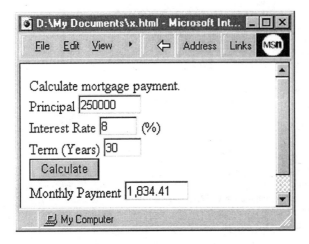

Figure 4.12   Calculating mortgage payment

```
<HTML>        <!-- Mortgage.html -->
<BODY>
Calculate mortgage payment.
<BR>
Principal
<INPUT TYPE=TEXT NAME=txtPrincipal SIZE=10>
<BR>
Interest Rate
<INPUT TYPE=TEXT NAME=txtRate SIZE=5>
(%)
<BR>
Term (Years) <INPUT TYPE=TEXT NAME=txtTerm SIZE=5>
<BR>
<INPUT TYPE=BUTTON NAME=cmdCalculate VALUE="Calculate">
<BR>
Monthly Payment
<INPUT TYPE=TEXT NAME=txtPayment SIZE=10 MAXLENGTH=2>
<BR>
<SCRIPT LANGUAGE=VBScript>
<!--
    Option Explicit
    Sub cmdCalculate_OnClick
      Dim R, T, P
      R = txtRate.Value / 100 / 12
      'convert to monthly output
      T = txtTerm.Value * 12
      P = txtPrincipal.Value
      txtPayment.Value = _
      FormatNumber(P*(R/(1-(R+1)^-T)), 2)
```

```
        'Pmt & Format functions not supported
      End Sub
-->
</SCRIPT>
</BODY>
</HTML>
```

Point-and-Click Calculator

The script in this section creates a point-and-click calculator (Figure 4.13). Here you click the displayed buttons as you would press the keys on an electronic calculator. After you enter a value by typing or clicking, click an operator button (the previous number will disappear from the text box), enter the second value, and finally click the = button. The result will appear in the text box (Figure 4.13 shows the result of 12.34 * 5.6). This number can then be treated as the first value. If you now click a number or decimal point, it will be added after that. If you click an operator, the number will disappear and you can enter the second operand.

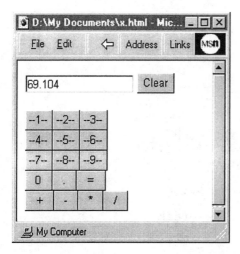

Figure 4.13   A point-and-click calculator

In Visual Basic, such a project can be implemented with a **control array**. Since control arrays are not available in VBScript, we are forced to create each button separately.

Fortunately, we can use string concatenation tricks to simplify the task of supplying the NAME and VALUE attributes of each button.

In a Visual Basic control array, when a button in that array is clicked, we can use the Index property to tell which button is involved. Here we are forced to set up an OnClick procedure to get the button's identification. (The number of procedures can be reduced if we use argument passing. A practice question will let you solve that problem.)

In the script below, we add extra hyphens and spaces inside button tags. Without these extra items, buttons will look very small. Internet Explorer 4 shrinks a button to fit its caption; Internet Explorer 3 doesn't do that.

Notice that we use single quotes inside double quotes. That's the simplest way to let the browser know that an extra quotation mark is needed.

```
<HTML>          <!-- PnCCalc.html -->
<BODY>
<INPUT TYPE=TEXT NAME=txtNum SIZE=20>
<INPUT TYPE=RESET NAME=cmdClear VALUE=Clear><P>
<SCRIPT LANGUAGE=VBScript>
<!--
   Option Explicit
   Dim I, Str, Op1, Op2, Optr
   On Error Resume Next
   If Err.Number <> 0 Then
     MsgBox Err.Description
   End If

   For I = 1 To 9
     Str = "<INPUT TYPE=BUTTON NAME=Btn" _
     & I & " VALUE=" & "--" & I & "--" & ">"
     'add padding to enlarge buttons
     Document.Write Str
     'create button based on above string
     If I Mod 3 = 0 Then
     Document.Write "<BR>"     'line break
     End If
   Next

   Document.Write "<INPUT TYPE=BUTTON NAME=Btn0" _
   & " VALUE='  0  '>"
   Document.Write "<INPUT TYPE=BUTTON NAME=BtnDot" _
   & " VALUE='  .  '>"
   Document.Write "<INPUT TYPE=BUTTON NAME=BtnEq" _
   & " VALUE='  =  '>"
   Document.Write "<BR>"
   Document.Write "<INPUT TYPE=BUTTON NAME=BtnP" _
   & " VALUE='  +  '>"
```

```
Document.Write "<INPUT TYPE=BUTTON NAME=BtnM" _
& " VALUE='  -   '>"
Document.Write "<INPUT TYPE=BUTTON NAME=BtnX" _
& " VALUE='  *   '>"
Document.Write "<INPUT TYPE=BUTTON NAME=BtnD" _
& " VALUE='  /   '>"

Sub Btn1_OnClick
  txtNum.Value = txtNum.Value & 1
End Sub

Sub Btn2_OnClick
  txtNum.Value = txtNum.Value & 2
End Sub

Sub Btn3_OnClick
  txtNum.Value = txtNum.Value & 3
End Sub

Sub Btn4_OnClick
  txtNum.Value = txtNum.Value & 4
End Sub

Sub Btn5_OnClick
  txtNum.Value = txtNum.Value & 5
End Sub

Sub Btn6_OnClick
  txtNum.Value = txtNum.Value & 6
End Sub

Sub Btn7_OnClick
  txtNum.Value = txtNum.Value & 7
End Sub

Sub Btn8_OnClick
  txtNum.Value = txtNum.Value & 8
End Sub

Sub Btn9_OnClick
  txtNum.Value = txtNum.Value & 9
End Sub

Sub Btn0_OnClick
  txtNum.Value = txtNum.Value & 0
End Sub

Sub BtnDot_OnClick
  txtNum.Value = txtNum.Value & "."
End Sub
```

```
Sub BtnP_OnClick
   Op1 = CSng(txtNum.Value)
   Optr = "+"
   txtNum.Value = ""
End Sub

Sub BtnM_OnClick
   Op1 = CSng(txtNum.Value)
   Optr = "-"
   txtNum.Value = ""
End Sub

Sub BtnX_OnClick
   Op1 = CSng(txtNum.Value)
   Optr = "*"
   txtNum.Value = ""
End Sub

Sub BtnD_OnClick
   Op1 = CSng(txtNum.Value)
   Optr = "/"
   txtNum.Value = ""
End Sub

Sub BtnEq_OnClick      '= clicked
   Op2 = CSng(txtNum.Value)
   Calc    'call Calc to show result
End Sub

Sub cmdClear_OnClick
   txtNum.Value = ""
   'clears text entry
   'Reset not work in IE4 unless a form is used
End Sub

Sub Calc
   Select Case Optr
      Case "+"
      txtNum.Value = Op1 + Op2
      Case "-"
      txtNum.Value = Op1 - Op2
      Case "*"
      txtNum.Value = Op1 * Op2
      Case "/"
      txtNum.Value = Op1 / Op2
   End Select
End Sub
-->
</SCRIPT>
</BODY>
</HTML>
```

Form Elements

When you use code to maneuver a large number of controls, you might consider using form elements. In HTML speak, an **element** is a tag. A tag placed inside a form becomes a **form element**, which can then be manipulated by a script.

According to the Document Object Model, a form is a child object of Document. The controls in a form are the form's child objects. These controls belong in the **Elements** collection. So Document.FormName.Elements(0) refers to the first control in the form; here Document can be omitted because it's the default.

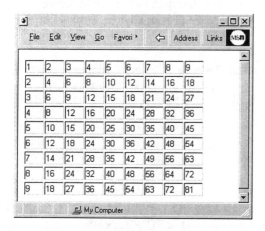

Figure 4.14   Using form elements

The following code will produce the multiplication table shown in Figure 4.14.

```
<HTML>           <!-- Element.html -->
<BODY>
<FORM NAME=Form1>
<SCRIPT LANGUAGE=VBScript>
<!--
    Option Explicit
    Dim I, J, K
    K=0      'control each element's index number
    For I=1 To 9
        For J=1 To 9
            Document.Write "<INPUT TYPE=TEXT SIZE=3>"
            Form1.Elements(K).Value=I*J   'text box number
            K=K+1 'next control's index number
```

```
        Next
        Document.Write "<BR>" 'new line
    Next
-->
</SCRIPT>
</FORM>
</BODY>
</HTML>
```

Our script is enclosed inside a form, which has the name of Form1. This enclosure is necessary. Inside this form, our script creates 81 text boxes, each of which is identified by an index number starting from 0. Instead of referencing a control by its own unique name, here we do it by using Elements and an index number. In our example, we can also replace TEXT with BUTTON to create 91 buttons. Using the technique discussed in this section, you can reduce the number of repetitive and substantially similar procedures in the previous section.

You can use the **Length** (instead of the typical Count as in Visual Basic) property to tell you how many elements there are in a form. So in our example, Form1.Elements.Length will return 81.

Tables

Tables are useful to present organized data. You use the < TABLE > tag to create a table. Then use < TH > for headings, < TR > for rows, and < TD > for cells. You can then embellish the table with colors, border width (or borderless), and so on.

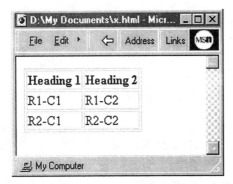

Figure 4.15   A 2 x 2 table with headings

The following code creates the table shown in Figure 4.15.

```
<HTML>
<BODY>
<TABLE BORDER=1>  <!-- pixels for borders -->
<TR>
    <TH>Heading 1</TH>
    <TH>Heading 2</TH>
</TR>
<TR>
    <TD>R1-C1</TD>
    <TD>R1-C2</TD>
</TR>
<TR>
    <TD>R2-C1</TD>
    <TD>R2-C2</TD>
</TR>
</TABLE>
</BODY>
</HTML>
```

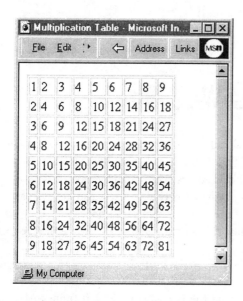

Figure 4.16   A 9 x 9 table multiplication table

Creating a table is a repetitive job, so it's best done with a script. The following script will create a multiplication table (Figure 4.16) and fill each cell with a number.

```
<HTML>          <!-- Table.html -->
<HEAD>
<TITLE>
Multiplication Table
</TITLE>
</HEAD>
<BODY>
<TABLE BORDER=1>
<SCRIPT LANGUAGE=VBScript>
<!--
    Dim I, J, Str
    For I = 1 To 9
        Document.Write "<TR BORDER=1>"      '9 rows
        For J = 1 To 9
           Str = "<TD>" & I * J & "</TD>"
           '9 columns for each row
           'create col and fill in number
        Document.Write Str
        Next
    Next
-->
</SCRIPT>
</TABLE>
</BODY>
</HTML>
```

Frames and This Book's Web Site

Many Web sites use **frames** to keep all the related pages together. Figure 4.17 shows an example. There are two frames (columns). The left frame shows all the available pages, each of which is a hyperlink. When a link is clicked, its corresponding page will be brought to the right frame. The left frame is always displayed so users can always use it to navigate to any of the available pages. Each frame has its own scroll boxes, so scrolling one side does not affect the other. The dividing line in the middle can also be dragged to one side to widen the other side.

To create such a site, you need at least three files. The first file provides the basic framework to control the two frames. The second file is loaded to the left frame. And the third file is initially loaded to the right frame. When the user clicks a link shown in the left frame, the pertinent file will be loaded to the right frame, replacing the existing one.

Our first file, listed below, is named Vbscript.html. It uses the <BASE> tag and the TARGET attribute to specify the name of the frame to load future files.

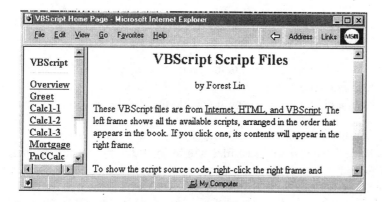

Figure 4.17   **A window with two frames**

```
<HTML>      <!-- Vbscript.html -->
<HEAD>
<TITLE>VBScript Home Page</TITLE>
<BASE TARGET=Main>
</HEAD>
<FRAMESET COLS="100,*">
<FRAME NAME=Content SRC="content.html">
<FRAME NAME=Main SRC="overview.html">
</FRAMESET>
<NOFRAMES>
Sorry, your browser doesn't support frames.
</NOFRAMES>
</HTML>
```

In the <FRAMESET> tag we specify COLS attribute of "100,*". That means 100 pixels
in the left frame and the remaining space for the right frame. So if the window's size is
changed, only the right frame will change in size. If you wish, you can use a percentage.
For example, "10%,*" will mean 10% for the left frame, whose actual size will then
depend of the size of the window. You can use the same system with the ROWS attribute
to create horizontal frames.

Notice that there is no <BODY> tag. It's replaced by <FRAMESET>. Their joint
presence may lead to an error.

Some older browsers may not recognize frames. You may want to use the
<NOFRAMES>-</NOFRAMES> pair to accommodate them (these tags are ignored
by frame-enabled browsers). Place an explanation here telling the visitor that the frames

are not displayed due to the browser. If you want to be even more accommodating, place a link here to another page that uses no frame.

We use the <FRAME> tag's NAME attribute to specify the left frame as Content and the SCR attribute to load the initial file. Here the file is to be loaded from the current directory. If it's stored in a different place, you'll need to provide the path specification.

So our left frame is named Content and the right frame is called Main. When this Vbscript.html file is loaded, the two specified files will be loaded to the specific frames. Since the TARGET name is Main, loading a page in the future will go to the Main frame.

The Content.html file, listed below, displays a list of links shown in the left frame of Figure 4.17. In each <A> tag we use the TARGET attribute to specify that if a hyperlink is clicked, the relevant file is to be loaded to the Main frame.

```
<HTML>      <!-- Content.html -->
<BODY BGCOLOR=#FFEECC>
<B>
VBScript<BR>
<HR>
<A HREF="overview.html" TARGET=Main>Overview</A><BR>
<A HREF="greet.html" TARGET=Main>Greet</A><BR>
<A HREF="calc1-1.html" TARGET=Main>Calc1-1</A><BR>
<A HREF="calc1-2.html" TARGET=Main>Calc1-2</A><BR>
<A HREF="calc1-3.html" TARGET=Main>Calc1-3</A><BR>
<A HREF="mortgage.html" TARGET=Main>Mortgage</A><BR>
<A HREF="pnccalc.html" TARGET=Main>PnCCalc</A><BR>
<A HREF="element.html" TARGET=Main>Element</A><BR>
<A HREF="table.html" TARGET=Main>Table</A><BR>
<A HREF="greet2.html" TARGET=Main>Greet2</A><BR>
<A HREF="calc1-4.html" TARGET=Main>Calc1-4</A><BR>
<A HREF="pnccalc2.html" TARGET=Main>PnCCalc2</A><BR>
<A HREF="tutor.html" TARGET=Main>Tutorial</A><BR>
</B>
</BODY>
</HTML>
```

This was my original framework for the Web site I planned to open for this book. Unfortunately, the server does not allow this kind of arrangement. So I was forced to give it up. Instead, when you go to this site, the initial page shows only the list of available files. Clicking one will show it, replacing the previous page. You'll then have to use the browser's Back button to return to the home page before you can branch to others. The Overview page provides more details. Here is the URL:

http://www.geocities.com/SiliconValley/Lab/7590/

CAI Tutorial

The last available page in the above list shows Tutorial. This is an interactive tutorial written in VBScript. It drives the Drill questions shown at the end of this chapter. It shows one question at a time and prompts you to supply an answer. If a wrong answer is given, you'll get a feedback instruction. The answers for these questions are available in this chapter. But if you want an explanation why another answer is wrong, you'll need to play with this tutorial.

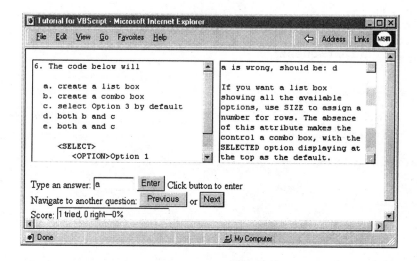

Figure 4.18   The CAI tutorial in this book's Web site

The Tutorial file is shown below. The top part creates the interface shown in Figure 4.18. The bottom portion shows the script to control the interactive mechanism. The questions/ answers portion in the middle shows only one example. This is what controls the display in Figure 4.18. This part is lengthy and involves string concatenation tricks to make the text appear neatly. If you want more details, visit the Web site.

```
<HTML>        <!-- Tutor.html -->
<TITLE>
Tutorial for VBScript
</TITLE>
<BODY BGCOLOR=#FFEECC>
<TEXTAREA COLS=33 ROWS=10 NAME=txtQues></TEXTAREA>
<TEXTAREA COLS=25 ROWS=10 NAME=txtFB></TEXTAREA>
```

```
<P>
Type an answer:
<INPUT NAME=txtAns SIZE=8>
<INPUT TYPE=BUTTON NAME=cmdAns VALUE=Enter>
Click button to enter<BR>
Navigate to another question:
<INPUT TYPE=BUTTON NAME=cmdPrev VALUE=Previous>
or
<INPUT TYPE=BUTTON NAME=cmdNext VALUE=Next width=100%>
<BR>
Score: <INPUT NAME=txtScore SIZE=25>

<SCRIPT LANGUAGE=VBScript>
<!--
Option Explicit
Dim Ques(19), Keys(19), Ans(19), FB(19), UFB(19)
     'array declarations, 20 items each
Dim I 'num of current question
Dim Score
Dim Tried
Dim CR        'carriage return

CR=Chr(13) & Chr(10)
Score=0       'initial score

'clear previous entries
txtAns.Value=""
txtFB.Value=""
txtScore.Value=""
'--------------------
'questions/answers here
Ques(5)="6. The code below will" _
& CR & CR _
& "   a. create a list box" & CR _
& "   b. create a combo box" & CR _
& "   c. select Option 3 by default" & CR _
& "   d. both b and c" & CR _
& "   e. both a and c" & CR _
& CR _
& "      <SELECT>" & CR _
& "         <OPTION>Option 1" & CR _
& "         <OPTION>Option 2" & CR _
& "         <OPTION SELECTED>Option 3" & CR _
& "      </SELECT>"
Keys(5)="d"
FB(5)="If you want a list box showing all the available
options, use SIZE to assign a number for rows. The absence of
this attribute makes the control a combo box, with the SELECTED
option displaying at the top as the default."
'--------------------
txtQues.Value=Ques(0)
```

```
        'show 1st question, ready for action

Sub cmdAns_OnClick     'when answer button is clicked
    If txtAns.Value="" Then
        Alert "You must type an answer."
        Exit Sub
    End If

    If Ans(I)<>"" Then
        Exit Sub     'not yet answered
    End If

    Tried=Tried+1   'tracked tried number
    Ans(I)=txtAns.Value 'user ans

    If UCase(Keys(I))=UCase(txtAns.Value) Then
        txtFB.Value=Ans(I) & " is right. Great!!!"
        Score=Score+1
    Else
        txtFB.Value=Ans(I) & " is wrong, should be: " & _
        Keys(I) & CR & CR & FB(I)
    End If

    UFB(I)=txtFB.Value   'user FB for later redisplay

    txtScore.Value=Tried & " tried, " & Score & " right---" _
    & FormatNumber(Score/Tried*100,0) & "%"
End Sub

Sub cmdNext_OnClick     'won't move beyond last
    If I>=19 Then
        Exit Sub
    End If

    I=I+1
    ShowQues
End Sub

Sub cmdPrev_OnClick
    If I<=0 Then     'won't move before 1st
        Exit Sub
    End If

    I=I-1
    ShowQues
End Sub

Sub ShowQues
    txtAns.Value=Ans(I)
    txtQues.Value=Ques(I)
    txtFB.Value=UFB(I)
```

```
End Sub
-->
</SCRIPT>
</BODY>
</HTML>
```

GETTING MORE HELP

There are many graphical Web tools that allow you to create Web pages without requiring you to know or manually enter HTML tags. By using drag and drop methods, you can quickly create fancy-looking Web pages. The most popular offerings by Microsoft are briefly discussed here.

Microsoft **Word 97** has become an easy-to-use Web-authoring tool. After you have created a document with fonts, colors, pictures, sounds, videos, anchors, controls, bookmarks, spreadsheets, database tables, etc., just save it as an HTML file. A browser can read such a file with most of the markups intact. If you look under the hood (so to speak), you'll find HTML tags there. Since this is an ASCII file, you can load it to Notepad if you wish to manually tinker with some tags.

Another popular offering by Microsoft is **FrontPage**. The latest version (98) came out in late 1997. A slimmed-down version called **FrontPage Express** is bundled with Internet Explorer 4. Both offer more Web tools than Word 97. Internet Explorer 4 can be downloaded (free of charge) from the Microsoft site. It's also included with new PCs.

A Web page can include one or more **ActiveX controls**. Such controls can be those that come with various Microsoft products, downloaded free from the Microsoft site, or created by you using Visual Basic 5. To include such a control in a Web page, you can manually enter a great deal of required information. Such information tells a browser encountering the control how, when, and where to download the control to the user's desktop so that it can be run there.

Since specifying a great deal of technical information is difficult, Microsoft has developed a tool for such an occasion. It's called **ActiveX Control Pad**. It's also available for free downloading from the Microsoft site. You can use it to insert an ActiveX control into a Web page. All the required technical information will automatically be entered into the page. See Chapter 3 for details.

If you run ActiveX Control Pad, you can go to its Help | **HTML Reference** screen to get a comprehensive list of the supported tags, each with its own syntax and example. This is a very useful reference for HTML. Here you can also find the codes for all the unusual characters discussed earlier (look for **Character Set**).

Choosing Help | **VBScript Reference** (when you are in ActiveX Control Pad) takes you to this Microsoft site:

http://www.microsoft.com/vbscript/

This is a good place to begin if you want to know more about VBScript. Here you'll find lots of related information, including JScript (Microsoft's version of JavaScript). If you are serious, be prepared to spend a great deal of time here at the outset. In the future, you can log in here when you want to know something more specific.

If you find it inconvenient or expensive to stay in the above site, download from it a file named **vbsdoc.exe**. This is a self-extracting documentation on VBScript. It's a relatively short file (226KB), so it doesn't take long to download it. Once downloaded to your desktop, double-click it to install it on your system. By default it will be installed in the Programs\VBScript Documentation folder. After you click Start from the Windows taskbar and point to this folder, you can choose to run VBScript Language Reference or VBScript Tutorial. Both will lead to similar results.

This documentation (and the HTML Reference in ActiveX Control Pad) represents the new way of presenting application assistance. Software developers (including Microsoft's programmers, one might surmise) have complained that it's difficult and time-consuming to write the traditional Windows help files. So Microsoft is now using the Web to deliver user help. This documentation consists of a series of Web pages that are linked to one another. If you follow the default installation, you can go to the Program Files\VBSdocs directory to see what's there. In my case, more than 600 files each with the .htm extension are stored there. Double-clicking any such a file will start the browser and open the page. From there you can navigate to any linked pages as you do when you browse the Web.

If you want to download ActiveX Control Pad (the **Setuppad.exe** file is 2.7 MB long), try the following site:

http://www.microsoft.com/workshop/author/cpad/

If you want to follow the latest about Internet Explorer, this is the site to visit:

http://www.microsoft.com/ie/msie.htm/

To get ActiveX controls from Microsoft, try this site:

http://www.microsoft.com/activex/gallery

If you are interested in Netscape Navigator, this is the site to visit:

http://home.netscape.com/

From the following site, you can get plug-ins to enable Netscape to run ActiveX:

http://www.ncompasslabs.com/

As 1998 began, the Web is attracting ever more attention. HTML 4.0 is poised to replace version 3.2. **DHTML** (D is for Dynamic) and **XML** (Extensible Markup Language) are emerging. If you want to get more from the horse's mouth, try this site of the World Wide Web Consortium (W3C is the final arbiter of the Web):

http://www.w3c.org/

Drill

_____ 1.   The <BIG> tag displays text in the biggest possible size. True or false?

_____ 2.   The <H1> tag displays text one size smaller than the <H2> tag. True or false?

_____ 3.   The _____ tag inserts a line on the screen.

_____ 4.   This tag lets you establish a hyperlink to another page:
      a.   <A>
      b.   <B>
      c.   <LI>
      d.   <MENU>

_____ 5.   The following code will lead to two separate lines in the browser window. True of false?

```
<BODY>
line 1
line 2
</BODY>
```

_____ 6.   The code below will
     a.   create a list box
     b.   create a combo box
     c.   select Option 3 by default
     d.   both b and c
     e.   both a and c

```
<SELECT>
  <OPTION>Option 1
  <OPTION>Option 2
  <OPTION SELECTED>Option 3
</SELECT>
```

_____ 7.   The BACKGROUND attribute is used with the <BODY> tag to specify a background:
     a.   sound
     b.   color
     c.   picture
     d.   all of the above

In the questions below, choose an answer from the list on the right:

_____ 8.   #000000   a. white
_____ 9.   #FFFFFF   b. black
_____ 10.   #FFFF00   c. cyan, combining green and blue
_____ 11.   #00FFFF   d. magenta, combining red and blue
_____ 12.   #FF00FF   e. yellow, combining red and green

Choose one or more events or methods on the right to match an object listed in 13 - 18:

_____ 13.   Text box   a. OnFocus
_____ 14.   Command button   b. OnLoad
_____ 15.   Reset button   c. OnClick
_____ 16.   Radio button   d. OnSelect
_____ 17.   Document   e. Write
_____ 18.   Window

_____ 19.   You can use _____ function to format a number to a specific number of decimal places.

_____ 20.   You can use On Error _____ _____ to trap a run-time error.

Answers

1.F; 2.F; 3<HR>; 4.<A>; 5.F; 6.d; 7.c; 8.b; 9.a; 10.e; 11.c; 12.d; 13.a/d; 14.a/c; 15.a/c; 16.a/c; 17.e; 18.b; 19.FormatNumber or Round; 20.Resume Next.

Practice

◙   1.   Explain the difference between the <BR> and <P> tags.

◙   2.   Explain what the following tags do.

```
<BASEFONT SIZE=1>
<FONT SIZE=+2>
```

◙   3.   Explain what the following tags do.

```
You can see our
<A HREF="#report">
annual report
</A> for details.
```

◙   4.   Explain how the following two tags differ.

```
<BODY BACKGROUND="http://www.mysite.com/pic.gif">
<IMG SRC="http://www.mysite.com/pic.gif">
```

◙   5.   Create a page with a centered and unordered list as shown in Figure 4.19.

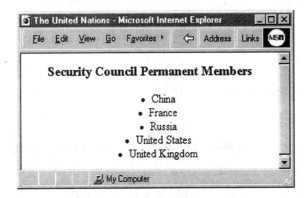

Figure 4.19   Centered and unordered list

◙   6.   Run the following script and report the result.

```
<HTML>
<BODY>
<SCRIPT LANGUAGE=VBScript>
<!--
    Sub Window_OnLoad
        MsgBox "Hi"
    End Sub

    Sub Window_OnUnload
        MsgBox "Bye"
    End Sub
-->
</SCRIPT>
</BODY>
</HTML>
```

◙   7.   Run the following script and report the result.

```
<HTML>
<BODY>
VBScript Demo<P>
<SCRIPT LANGUAGE=VBScript>
<!--
    Sub Window_OnLoad
        MsgBox "Hi"
    End Sub

    Sub Window_OnUnload
        MsgBox "Bye"
    End Sub

    Document.Write "<CENTER>"
    Document.Write "Welcome!"
    Document.Write "</CENTER>"
-->
</SCRIPT>
</BODY>
</HTML>
```

◙   8.   Explain what the following tag does.

```
<INPUT TYPE=BUTTON VALUE="Click Me"
OnClick=Test("Me")>
```

◙   9.   What does the following script do?

```
<SCRIPT LANGUAGE=VBScript>
<!--
   Document.WriteLn("<PRE>")
   Document.WriteLn("line 1")
   Document.WriteLn("line 2")
   Document.WriteLn("line 3")
   Document.WriteLn("</PRE>")
-->
</SCRIPT>
```

◙   10. Run the following script and report what happens.

```
<HTML>
<BODY>
<INPUT TYPE=TEXT NAME=Text1 OnFocus=Greet()>
<SCRIPT LANGUAGE=VBScript>
<!--
Sub Greet
    Text1.Value="Hi, there."
End Sub
-->
</SCRIPT>
</BODY>
</HTML>
```

◙   11. Modify the above so that when a blank area of the window is clicked the content
in the text box will disappear.

◙   12. Run the following script and report the result.

```
<HTML>
<BODY>
<INPUT TYPE=TEXT NAME=Text1 VALUE="no" OnChange=NoChange()>
<SCRIPT LANGUAGE=VBScript>
<!--
Sub NoChange
    MsgBox "You can't change this."
    Text1.Value=Text1.DefaultValue
End Sub
-->
</SCRIPT>
</BODY>
</HTML>
```

◙   13. Create a page that will do the following:

a.   Display four radio buttons as shown in Figure 4.20. The first button should be
selected by default.

b. When a button is clicked, a message box should respond by showing which button was clicked. The button number should appear in the message box. (Hint: In the <INPUT> tag, specify a procedure with an argument for OnClick; pass a number to the procedure.)

c. When a new button is clicked, only it should be selected and the others unselected. (Hint: Use the same name for all the buttons.)

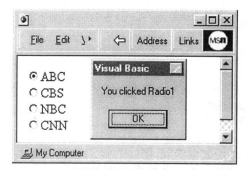

Figure 4.20   Demonstrating radio buttons and OnClick

14. Figure 4.21 shows a RESET button named Clear, a text box, and a combo box. The combo box has three options, each with a VALUE attribute. Write a script that will 1) show in the text box the value of the option selected (when an option is clicked) and 2) clear the text box entry when Clear is clicked.

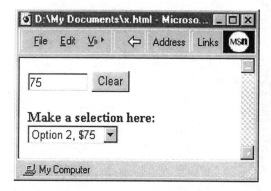

Figure 4.21   A combo box at run time

◙ 15. Create a page that will add up the values of the items based on the check boxes that are checked, as shown in Figure 4.22.

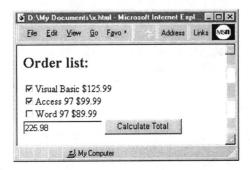

Figure 4.22   Demonstrating the Checked property

◙ 16. Alter the above by removing the command button. Each time a check box is clicked, the total should be calculated and entered in the text box.

◙ 17. Write a script to create a 5-row and 4-column table. Each cell in the table should be filled with a size-5 text box. Each text box should contain a text string indicating its column and row position in the table. The result should be similar to Figure 4.23.

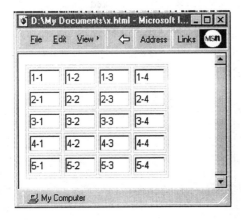

Figure 4.23   Text boxes inside table cells

◙ 18. Change the Sub ShowMsg procedure Listing 1 to a function procedure. This procedure should return a string, which the caller should then output to the text box as before.

◙ 19. In Listing 2, declare the Nums array in the Sub procedure and pass the array to the Function procedure.

◙ 20. In the Point-and-Click Calculator script, reduce the 11 OnClick procedures for the 10 digits and the decimal point to a single procedure. When a digit is clicked, the number should be passed to this procedure. Also reduce the four operator procedures to one procedure, to which the clicked operator should be passed.

Answers

1.
 inserts a line break and <P> adds a paragraph break, usually the equivalent of two line breaks. A browser ignores carriage returns in text and controls the flow of text with automatic word wrap and additional scroll bars. If you want to tell the browser to break up text, you need to use these tags.

2.   The first establishes the base font size as 1, the smallest. If this tag is not present, the default size is 3. The second tag increases the font size by 2, resulting in 3. So the text after the tag will be displayed in size-3 font.

3.   The text between <A> and </A>, "annual report" in this case, will be highlighted. Moving the pointer there will show a pointing hand. It is a hyperlink. Clicking it will show the area named "report." Before doing that, you need to use the <A NAME="report"> tag to bookmark the target area. Without a corresponding bookmark, clicking a link won't do anything.

4.   The first will load the GIF file from the specified site and use the picture as the background for the page. The second will load the picture file and display it at the location of the tag. In this case, you can specify the position of the picture (use ALIGN and specify TOP, BOTTOM, LEFT, RIGHT, or MIDDLE).

5.
```
<HTML>
<HEAD><TITLE>The United Nations</TITLE></HEAD>
<BODY>
<CENTER>
<H3>Security Council Permanent Members</H3>
<UL>
```

```
      <LI>China
      <LI>France
      <LI>Russia
      <LI>United States
      <LI>United Kingdom
</UL>
<CENTER>
</BODY>
</HTML>
```

6. When the page is loaded, a message box shows "Hi" and the OK button. When you unload the page (navigate to another page), the second message box appears. If you press F5 to refresh the screen after the page has been loaded, the "Bye" message will appear first because you are unloading the page. Then the "Hi" message appears.

7. The line before the <SCRIPT> tag will be printed first, followed by the centered "Welcome!" line. Only after that will the OnLoad procedure be executed.

8. It creates a button with Click Me as its caption. There is no name for this button. However, the OnClick attribute specifies that if this button is clicked, the sub or function procedure named Test will be called and that the string "Me" will be passed to the procedure.

9. Write three lines to the screen. Each line ends with a carriage return. Replacing <PRE>-</PRE> with <XMP>-</XMP> will do the same thing. Without these tags, the three lines will appear in one line.

10. When the text box is clicked (receives the focus), the Greet sub procedure will be executed. The string then enters the text box.

11.
Change the <INPUT> line as follows:

```
<INPUT TYPE=TEXT NAME=Text1 OnFocus=Greet() OnBlur=Clear()>
```

Then add this procedure:

```
Sub Clear
    Text1.Value=""
End Sub
```

12. The initial screen contains a text box with "no" inside. It cannot be changed. If you change it and then click the window, a message box shows a message. Then the

default value (the **DefaultValue** intrinsic constant contains the original value) is restored.

13.
```
<HTML>
<BODY>
<INPUT TYPE=RADIO NAME=Radio1 CHECKED OnClick=Test(1)>ABC<BR>
<INPUT TYPE=RADIO NAME=Radio1 OnClick=Test(2)>CBS<BR>
<INPUT TYPE=RADIO NAME=Radio1 OnClick=Test(3)>NBC<BR>
<INPUT TYPE=RADIO NAME=Radio1 OnClick=Test(4)>CNN<BR>
<SCRIPT LANGUAGE=VBScript>
<!--
Sub Test(Num)
    MsgBox "You clicked " & "Radio" & Num
End Sub
-->
</SCRIPT>
</BODY>
</HTML>
```

14.
```
<HTML>
<BODY>
<FORM NAME=X>
<INPUT TYPE=TEXT NAME=txtOutput SIZE=10>
<INPUT TYPE=RESET VALUE=Clear><BR>
<H4>Make a selection here:<BR>
<SELECT NAME=Options>
    <OPTION VALUE=50>Option 1, $50
    <OPTION VALUE=75>Option 2, $75
    <OPTION SELECTED VALUE=100>Option 3, $100
</SELECT>

<SCRIPT LANGUAGE=VBScript>
<!--
Sub Options_OnClick
    X.txtOutput.Value=X.Options.Value
End Sub
-->
</SCRIPT>
</BODY>
</HTML>
```

15.
```
<HTML>
<BODY>
<H3>Order list:</H3>
<INPUT TYPE=CHECKBOX NAME=CB1 VALUE=125.99>Visual Basic
$125.99<BR>
<INPUT TYPE=CHECKBOX NAME=CB2 VALUE=99.99>Access 97 $99.99<BR>
```

```
<INPUT TYPE=CHECKBOX NAME=CB3 VALUE=89.99>Word 97 $89.99<BR>
<INPUT TYPE=TEXT NAME=Total>
<INPUT TYPE=BUTTON NAME=Calc VALUE="Calculate Total">
<SCRIPT LANGUAGE=VBScript>
<!--
Sub Calc_OnClick
    Dim Sum
    If CB1.Checked Then Sum=Sum+125.99
    If CB2.Checked Then Sum=Sum+99.99
    If CB3.Checked Then Sum=Sum+89.99
    Total.Value=Sum
End Sub
-->
</BODY>
</SCRIPT>
</HTML>
```

16.
```
<HTML>
<BODY>
<H3>Order list:</H3>
<INPUT TYPE=CHECKBOX NAME=CB1 VALUE=125.99
OnClick=Calc()>Visual Basic $125.99<BR>
<INPUT TYPE=CHECKBOX NAME=CB2 VALUE=99.99 OnClick=Calc()>Access
97 $99.99<BR>
<INPUT TYPE=CHECKBOX NAME=CB3 VALUE=89.99 OnClick=Calc()>Word
97 $89.99<BR>
<INPUT TYPE=TEXT NAME=Total>
<SCRIPT LANGUAGE=VBScript>
<!--
Sub Calc()
    If CB1.Checked Then Sum=Sum+125.99
    If CB2.Checked Then Sum=Sum+99.99
    If CB3.Checked Then Sum=Sum+89.99
    Total.Value=Sum
End Sub
-->
</SCRIPT>
</BODY>
</HTML>
```

17.
```
<HTML>
<BODY>
<TABLE BORDER=1>
<SCRIPT LANGUAGE=VBScript>
<!--
    Dim I, J, Str
    For I = 1 To 5
      Document.Write "<TR>"      '5 rows
      For J = 1 To 4
```

```
               Str = "<TD>" & "<INPUT SIZE=5 VALUE=" & _
               I & "-" & J & ">" & "</TD>"
               '4 columns for each row
               'create col and add text box
       Document.Write Str
       Next
       Next
-->
</SCRIPT>
</TABLE>
</BODY>
</HTML>

18.
<HTML>          <!-- Greet2.html -->
<BODY>
<SCRIPT LANGUAGE=VBScript>
<!--
Option Explicit
Document.Write "Current time is: " & Now
Document.Write "<P>"
Document.Write "<INPUT TYPE=TEXT NAME=txtName SIZE=30>"

Sub Window_OnLoad
    Dim Name
    Dim RetMsg
    Name=InputBox ("What's your first name?")
    RetMsg=ShowMsg (Name)
    'call function, pass argument
    txtName.Value=RetMsg     'output to text box
End Sub

Function ShowMsg (Name)
    Dim Msg
    Dim CurrHour
    CurrHour=Hour(Now)
    If CurrHour < 12 Then
        Msg="morning"
    ElseIf CurrHour < 18 Then
        Msg="afternoon"
    Else
        Msg="evening"
    End If
    ShowMsg="Good " & Msg & ", " & Name & "!"
    'return result to caller
End Function
-->
</SCRIPT>
</BODY>
</HTML>
```

19.

```vbscript
<SCRIPT LANGUAGE=VBScript>       <!-- Calc1-4.html -->
<!--
    Dim Operator
    Sub cmdOperator_OnClick
     Operator = Operator Mod 4
     Dim Nums(1)    '0-based, 2 elements
     'rotate among four operators
     Nums(0) = CSng(X.txtOperand1.Value)
     Nums(1) = CSng(X.txtOperand2.Value)
     X.txtOutput.Value = GetResult (Operator, Nums)
     'call function, pass value, show result
     Operator = Operator + 1   'advance to next operator
    End Sub

    Function GetResult (Optr, Nums)
     Select Case Optr
     Case 0
         GetResult = Nums(0) + Nums(1)
         X.cmdOperator.Value = "+"
     Case 1
         GetResult = Nums(0) - Nums(1)
         X.cmdOperator.Value = "-"
     Case 2
         GetResult = Nums(0) * Nums(1)
         X.cmdOperator.Value = "*"
     Case 3
         GetResult = Nums(0) / Nums(1)
         X.cmdOperator.Value = "/"
     End Select
    End Function
-->
</SCRIPT>
```

20.

```vbscript
<SCRIPT LANGUAGE=VBScript>       <!-- PnCCalc2.html -->
<!--
    Option Explicit
    Dim I, Str, Op1, Op2, Optr

    On Error Resume Next
    If Err.Number <> 0 Then
        MsgBox Err.Description
    End If

    For I = 1 To 9
      Str = "<INPUT TYPE=BUTTON VALUE=--" & I & _
      "--" & " OnClick=AddNum('" & I & "')>"
      'add padding to enlarge buttons
      Document.Write Str
      'create button based on above string
```

```
   If I Mod 3 = 0 Then
   Document.Write "<BR>"      'line break
   End If
Next

Document.Write "<INPUT TYPE=BUTTON NAME=Btn0" _
& " VALUE='  0  ' OnClick=AddNum('0')>"
Document.Write "<INPUT TYPE=BUTTON NAME=BtnDot" _
& " VALUE='  .  ' OnClick=AddNum('.')>"
Document.Write "<INPUT TYPE=BUTTON NAME=BtnEq" _
& " VALUE='  =  '>"
Document.Write "<BR>"
Document.Write "<INPUT TYPE=BUTTON NAME=BtnP" _
& " VALUE='  +  ' OnClick=SetOp('+')>"
Document.Write "<INPUT TYPE=BUTTON NAME=BtnM" _
& " VALUE='  -  ' OnClick=SetOp('-')>"
Document.Write "<INPUT TYPE=BUTTON NAME=BtnX" _
& " VALUE='  *  ' OnClick=SetOp('*')>"
Document.Write "<INPUT TYPE=BUTTON NAME=BtnD" _
& " VALUE='  /  ' OnClick=SetOp('/')>"

Sub AddNum(Num) 'concatenate digits & decimal point
  txtNum.Value = txtNum.Value & Num
End Sub

Sub SetOp(Op)   'determine operator chosen
  Op1 = CSng(txtNum.Value)
  Optr = Op
  txtNum.Value = ""
End Sub

Sub BtnEq_OnClick      'when = clicked
  Op2 = CSng(txtNum.Value)
  Calc    'call Calc to show result
End Sub

Sub cmdClear_OnClick
  txtNum.Value = ""
  'clears text entry
  'Reset not work in IE4 unless a form is used
End Sub

Sub Calc
   Select Case Optr
      Case "+"
      txtNum.Value = Op1 + Op2
      Case "-"
      txtNum.Value = Op1 - Op2
      Case "*"
      txtNum.Value = Op1 * Op2
      Case "/"
```

```
            txtNum.Value = Op1 / Op2
        End Select
    End Sub
-->
</SCRIPT>
</BODY>
</HTML>
```

Appendix A
Component File Names

Visual Basic generates lots of files at authoring time, design time, and run time. Some are what you ordered, but others are automatically saved as companion files as a result of certain steps you've taken. These files could be either temporary or permanent. Each file type has a three-letter extension that tells you what it's for. If you see some unexpected files saved to your disk, use the following list to guide you.

bas	Basic (standard or code) module file
cls	Class module file
ctl	ActiveX control (UserControl) module file
ctx	Binary file for the above
dep	Dependency file created by Setup Wizard
dll	Dynamic Link Library; in-process ActiveX code component; the compiled version of a .cls file
dob	ActiveX document (UserDocument) module file
dox	Binary file for the above
exe	Compiled independent executable file or out-of-process ActiveX code component
frx	Binary file for the above
log	Log (ASCII) file containing loading error messages
oca	Control type library cache file
ocx	Compiled ActiveX control component file
pag	Property page module file
pgx	Binary file for the above
res	Resource file
vbg	Group project file
vbb	ActiveX document bootstrap file
vbd	ActiveX document, compiled or temporarily created (when a .dob file goes into run mode); treated as a Web page by Internet Explorer
vbl	Control licensing file
vbp	Project file
vbw	Workspace file
vbz	Wizard launch file

Index